THE EARLY TWENTIETH-CENTURY
DISPENSATIONALISM OF ARNO C. GAEBELEIN

THE EARLY TWENTIETH-CENTURY DISPENSATIONALISM OF ARNO C. GAEBELEIN

Michael D. Stallard

The Edwin Mellen Press
Lewiston•Queenston•Lampeter

Library of Congress Cataloging-in-Publication Data

Stallard, Michael D.
    The early twentieth-century dispensationalism of Arno C. Gaebelein / Michael D. Stallard.
      p. cm. --
    Includes bibliographical references and indexes.
    ISBN 0-7734-6924-9
    1. Gaebelein, Arno Clemens, 1861-1945. 2. Dispensationalism--History of
doctrines--20th century. I. Title.

BT157 .S73 2002
230'.0463'092--dc21

                         2002033798

hors série.

A CIP catalog record for this book is available from the British Library.

The Edwin Mellen Press
Box 450
Lewiston, New York
USA 14092-0450

The Edwin Mellen Press
Box 67
Queenston, Ontario
CANADA L0S 1L0

The Edwin Mellen Press, Ltd.
Lampeter, Ceredigion, Wales
UNITED KINGDOM SA48 8LT

Printed in the United States of America

DEDICATION

To my parents, Conley and Christine Stallard,
whose financial and emotional support made this project possible

CONTENTS

PREFACE

It is refreshing to see a scholarly work like this one, which seeks to enhance the significance of dispensationalism as a theological system by investigating the views of some of its earliest writers and the influences upon them. Heretofore no major work has been done on the enormous theological contribution of Arno C. Gaebelein and his theological method with regard to dispensationalism. Gaebelein was a prolific writer. He had close ties with C. I. Scofield and edited his Scofield Reference Bible. Without doubt, Gaebelein was a well-respected representative of dispensationalism and contributed much to its popularity in the early days of its formation.

Dr. Stallard examined most of Gaebelein's theological writings in his effort to devise his method of doing theology. There are three major divisions or parts to this valuable study. In the first part an overview of the man's life and ministry is given along with his embracing of premillennialism. His involvement with the Brethren movement and John Nelson Darby left an indelible impression upon Gaebelein.

In the second part, Stallard sets forth the basic rules Gaebelein used to argue for and support his theology. These two were the literal hermeneutic and dispensational integration. The basis of Gaebelein's distinction between God's program with Israel and his program with the church was the literal or normal interpretation of Scripture. It is very interesting to compare his strong defense for this distinction and contrast it with progressive dispensationalism which rejects the idea of distinct divine programs for Israel and the church.

Part three of this valuable study traces the themes in Gaebelein's writings to discover the core interpretive style by which he integrated his theology. That, Stallard argues, is the prophetic hope which centered in the Second Coming of Christ.

As he concludes this study, Stallard asks, "Is it possible that dispensationalism and covenant theology can move closer together?" His answer to that question is: "very few of the doctrinal and hermeneutical concerns cited earlier are negotiable without giving up the entire system." He suggests that "the final common ground of eschatology in evangelicalism may turn out to be a spirit of love in the heart when there is no agreement of mind."

Robert P. Lightner
Professor Emeritus of Systematic Theology
Dallas Theological Seminary

ACKNOWLEDGEMENTS

This present work provides an update to the author's doctoral dissertation on the theological method of Arno C. Gaebelein, which was finished in the summer of 1992 at Dallas Theological Seminary in Dallas, Texas. Minor modifications have been made in documentation to alert the reader to a few academic sources that have appeared in related discussions over the last decade since then. However, the documentation has not necessarily been updated for all referenced works, published or unpublished, which have been revised or put in print during that time. The most major modifications have been in the area of terminology for Gaebelein's method. In particular, *dispensational integration* has replaced *dispensational hermeneutic* to aid the reader in understanding the level of synthesis that is going on in the methodological discussion.

I owe an enormous debt to the readers of my dissertation at Dallas Seminary. Dr. John Hannah helped immensely in crafting historical argumentation and finding resources for historical backgrounds to Gaebelein's life. Dr. Lanier Burns provided encouragement and theological insight in the struggle to identify elements in Gaebelein's method. Perhaps my greatest gratitude is due Dr. Robert Lightner, the advisor for the work, who continually provided encouragement as issues were sorted through and as the process of doing such a work was undertaken. Dr. Lightner introduced me more fully to the thinking of Dr. Charles Ryrie, whose way of looking at dispensational issues has provided the basis for much of my thinking, even to this day. I also am grateful for interaction with other faculty members at Dallas Seminary who were not on my reading committee. Of special note among them would be Dr. Elliott Johnson, Dr. Craig Blaising, and Dr. Darrell Bock who provided fodder for discussion, pro and con, as the new movement of progressive dispensationalism was asserting a new methodology for dispensationalism. It is this debate that initially produced my interest in studying the theological method of a major figure in the history of dispensationalism.

In the reworking of my dissertation for publication, I owe much to interaction with colleagues at Baptist Bible Seminary where I have taught systematic theology the last eight years. Special kudos, however, go to my secretary Julie Wilson whose tireless efforts in typing (and retyping), formatting, indexing, and editing cannot go unmentioned.

Above all of the others, I must thank my wife Cindy and children, David, Philip, and Tiffany who many times unknowingly sacrificed time with Dad so that this project could become a reality. There must be great rewards in heaven for such people.

As is true for all such projects, any errors in argument, expression, or documentation are entirely the fault of this author and not those who have assisted along the way. It is my hope that many will profit from the discussions and that advancement in dispensational studies can take place.

Michael Stallard
July 2002

1

CHAPTER 1
INTRODUCTION

The Need for the Study

As one reads the literature concerning eschatology, particularly the debate between dispensationalists and nondispensationalists, a prominent notion seems to be that dispensationalism is in the midst of an identity crisis. As a whole, the evangelical community is seeking for some common ground in eschatology, certainly a worthwhile effort. Along these lines, discussions about the essence or core of dispensationalism have emerged. Surprisingly, the very term has been brought into question by some within the dispensational wing of evangelicalism.[1]

Such a state of affairs, while somewhat alarming to dispensationalists like the present writer, yields an opportunity to clarify what dispensationalism in historical context is all about. Floyd Elmore noted that before some new synthesis replaces the old understanding of dispensationalism, basic comprehension of the major tenet of the Israel-church distinction as it appears in the writings of John Nelson Darby, the father of modern dispensationalism, would be necessary.[2] Such correct thinking should be expanded to include many pertinent areas of theology and as broad a spectrum of dispensational writers as possible.

---

[1] Minutes of the Dispensational Theology Pre-Meeting of the Annual Meeting of the Evangelical Theological Society, 20 November 1986, Atlanta, GA, 2.

[2] Floyd S. Elmore, "A Critical Examination of the Doctrine of the Two Peoples of God in John Nelson Darby" (Th.D. diss., Dallas Theological Seminary, 1990), 7.

Such studies have only recently begun to emerge. Elmore is joined by Crutchfield who pursued a more general approach to the content of Darby in *The Origins of Dispensationalism*.[3] Carl Sanders has done admirable research on James H. Brooks.[4] Also, an analysis of the eschatology of the dispensationalist Lewis Sperry Chafer has recently been published.[5] The study of Arno C. Gaebelein provided in this work seeks to add to this collection of investigations of significant dispensational writers. The hope is that at a later time scholars can provide the new synthesis and perhaps confirm a *sine qua non* for what is known as dispensationalism.[6]

The dearth of past studies in the history of dispensational interpretation is not surprising in view of the deficiency of such work in the broader movement of American fundamentalism.[7] So one would not expect to find major work done on

---

[3] Larry V. Crutchfield, *The Origins of Dispensationalism*, with a Foreword by John A. Witmer (Lanham, MD: University Press of America, 1992).

[4] Carl E. Sanders, III, *Premillennial Faith of James Brooks: Reexamining the Roots of American Fundamentalism* (Lanham, MD: University Press of America, 2001).

[5] Jeffrey J. Richards, *The Promise of Dawn: The Eschatology of Lewis Sperry Chafer* (Lanham, MD: University Press of America, 1991). See also Jeffrey J. Richards, *Contemporary Christian Options of the World's End: The Eschatology of Lewis Sperry Chafer* (Lewiston, NY: Edwin Mellen Press, 1994).

[6] In the last decade or so works that have contributed to discussions about the definition and methodology of dispensationalism are Craig A. Blaising and Darrell L. Bock, eds., *Dispensationalism, Israel and the Church* (Grand Rapids, MI: Zondervan, 1992); Craig A. Blaising and Darrell L. Bock, *Progressive Dispensationalism* (Wheaton, IL: Victor Books, 1993); Robert L. Saucy, *The Case for Progressive Dispensationalism: The Interface Between Dispensational and Non-Dispensational Theology* (Grand Rapids, MI: Zondervan, 1993); John R. Master and Wesley R. Willis, eds., *Issues in Dispensationalism* (Chicago: Moody Press, 1994); Charles Ryrie, *Dispensationalism* (Chicago: Moody Press, 1995); and Herbert W. Bateman, IV, gen. ed., *Three Central Issues in Contemporary Dispensationalism* (Grand Rapids, MI: Kregel, 1999). Ryrie's book is a revision and expansion of his earlier significant work *Dispensationalism Today* (Chicago: Moody Press, 1965). This present writer has also addressed in a minor way some of the same issues in various articles. See especially Mike Stallard, "Literal Interpretation, Theological Method, and the Essence of Dispensationalism," *The Journal of Ministry and Theology* 1 (Spring 1997): 5-36.

[7] Ernest F. Sandeen, "Towards a Historical Interpretation of the Origins of Fundamentalism," *Church History* 36 (March 1967): 66; George M. Marsden, "Defining Fundamentalism," *Christian Scholar's Review* 1 (Winter 1971): 141. Some progress has been made in this area since these articles were written. See George M. Marsden, *Fundamentalism and American Culture: The Shap-*

the life, ministry, and writings of the dispensationalist and fundamentalist Gaebelein.[8] The only major work on Gaebelein has been David Rausch's biographical study.[9] Gaebelein's theology has not been touched in any definitive fashion while snapshots of his approach to ministry and theology have bordered on misrepresentation.[10]

The paucity of material on Gaebelein is unfortunate in light of the prominent role he had in the rise of dispensationalism in the early years of the twentieth century. His ministry was nationwide. His teaching ministry as an itinerant Bible conference speaker was not isolated to one part of the country. The journal, *Our Hope*, which he edited from 1894 to 1945, had national circulation. He authored more than forty commentaries and theological works in addition to publishing the *Annotated Bible*, a commentary on the entire Bible much like Darby's *Synopsis*. Wilbur Smith conservatively estimated the number of pages written by Gaebelein during his lifetime to be twelve thousand.[11] This writer calculates the number closer to twenty thousand. In this way, the prolific Gaebelein rivals the output of Darby.[12] His association with Scofield in conferences and in the editing of the

---

ing of *Twentieth-Century Evangelicalism, 1870-1925* (New York: Oxford University Press, 1980). A helpful work in this respect which brings the historical discussion up to the present is Joel A. Carpenter, *Revive Us Again: The Reawakening of American Fundamentalism* (New York: Oxford University Press, 1997).

[8] The words *fundamentalism* and *fundamentalist* need clarification in the light of the varied ways in which they have been used. In this work, fundamentalism will be used as a synonym for *evangelical* or a kind of orthodox Protestantism. As the movement developed in the first quarter of the twentieth century, it took on the characteristic of militancy in opposition to liberalism. Gaebelein fits either emphasis. For further clarification see John D. Hannah, "The Social and Intellectual History of the Origins of the Evangelical Theological College," (Ph.D. diss., University of Texas at Dallas, May 1988), 2.

[9] David A. Rausch, *Arno C. Gaebelein 1861-1945: Irenic Fundamentalist and Scholar* (New York: Edwin Mellen Press, 1983).

[10] Marsden's over simplistic labeling of Gaebelein as a "thoroughgoing literalist" is an example (*Fundamentalism*, 143). So also is the caricature of Gaebelein as an anti-Semite (210).

[11] Wilbur M. Smith, *Arno C. Gaebelein: A Memoir* (New York: Our Hope Press, 1946), 3.

[12] Elmore, "A Critical Examination," 1.

Scofield Reference Bible also points to the significant place Gaebelein possessed in the development of the dispensational movement in America. Because of these factors, Gaebelein can be viewed as one of the most representative dispensational writers in early twentieth-century America. Thus, he should be studied to receive the full spectrum of what the movement had to offer.

The Purpose of the Study

This study is designed to examine the theological method of Gaebelein with a view to establishing a dispensational approach to hermeneutics and theology. From this, a definition of dispensationalism, rooted largely in hermeneutics and theological method, can be suggested. At a different level, the study is provided to fill a gap in fundamentalist and dispensational historiography concerning this major theological figure within the tradition of early twentieth-century American dispensationalism.

The Scope of the Study

This study is not limited to a specific doctrine traced through the writings of Gaebelein nor to analysis of one particular theological work. Neither is it a comparison of Gaebelein to other writers nor a defense of his teachings. The present work will touch upon all of the above in some significant way. Nonetheless, the scope of the study involves the entire collection of Gaebelein's writings in an attempt to give an analytical description of his theological method. It is, however, limited to theological method and should not be read as an attempt to explore all of his theological conclusions fully.

The Sources for the Study

It is clear that Gaebelein never gave a detailed discussion of theological method. Although he had a method, he only practiced his approach. He did not

talk about it. Personal letters are rare.[13] Letters to ministerial colleagues mostly
take on the form of business letters arranging for speaking engagements.[14] A
search of important archival material reveals virtually nothing helpful in terms of
getting inside the life of Gaebelein.[15] There is only limited information identifying
which writings impacted Gaebelein the most.[16]

In addition to these limitations, one is confronted with little biographical
information of Gaebelein. The definitive work by Rausch has already been mentioned.[17] An autobiography by Gaebelein is available entitled *Half a Century: The*

---

[13] This unfortunate state of affairs was confirmed in a phone conversation on 1 October 1990
with Gretchen Hull, the granddaughter of Gaebelein. She referred to herself as the family archivist
and noted that he did not even communicate often in written form with her father (Gaebelein's son
Frank).

[14] For example, the correspondence with Lewis Sperry Chafer, founding president of Dallas
Theological Seminary where Gaebelein taught as a visiting teacher each year for a month from
1924-1931, yields mostly business-like letters scheduling Gaebelein's stay in Dallas, Texas, each
year. At times the passion for dispensationalism is clear such as the strong defense of C. I.
Scofield that comes through. See Letter, Arno C. Gaebelein to Lewis Sperry Chafer, New York
City, New York, 21 September 1928, Arno C. Gaebelein Papers, Archives, Dallas Theological
Seminary, Dallas, Texas (hereafter cited as ADTS); Letter, Lewis Sperry Chafer to Arno C. Gaebelein, Dallas, Texas, 26 May 1934, Arno C. Gaebelein Papers, ADTS. However, hints of methodology do not abound.

[15] Archival material is extremely light on Gaebelein. Of special note would be Nyack College,
The Christian Missionary Alliance headquarters (located in Colorado Springs, Colorado), Moody
Bible Institute, and the Billy Graham Center at Wheaton College. For example at the Billy Graham Center, only general advertising brochures for evangelistic meetings exist with Gaebelein's
name on them along with other known speakers. Even Stony Brook School, founded in the midst
of Gaebelein's ministry by his son Frank, has nothing of value outside of the formal writings of
Gaebelein.

[16] Gretchen Hull has confirmed in a personal phone call on 1 October 1990 that Arno C. Gaebelein's personal library was merged with Frank Gaebelein's library upon his death. With the
death of Frank in 1983 the books were distributed within the family. No attempt was made to
delineate at any time which books belonged to the elderly Gaebelein. We are left to statements he
made in his autobiography and elsewhere concerning the influences of other writings upon his
thinking. One exception to this is that Gaebelein's collection of books on Luther was sold to the
Concordia Theological Seminary in St. Louis (Rausch, *Irenic Fundamentalist*, 220).

[17] Up to this time, Rausch has probably done more research in the life of Gaebelein than anyone else.

6

Autobiography of a Servant.[18] It is useful but was written before the days of World War II and the Holocaust thus preventing one from getting autobiographical information during a critical time period. Furthermore, the account he gives of his ministry at times follows the same tenor as his business-like letters to colleagues as he recounts various places where he has spoken. While giving perhaps the only information available on the pre-1890 time period, it yields little in the way of gathering information about his thinking concerning theology. Influences made upon his life can be seen but are given in cursory fashion.

Fortunately, the sheer volume of Gaebelein's writings in *Our Hope* and in the forty-plus books reviewed in this study will allow an inductive analysis of how he argues theology and develops theological themes. If the historical background to Gaebelein's life and ministry turns out sketchy, his theological assertions will usually be seen in bold relief.

The Method of the Study

The approach which this study takes centers around three parts. First, the presuppositional framework of Gaebelein is examined. A review of his life and ministry (chapter two) will surface the conclusion that his conversion to premillennialism occurred as the result of contact with orthodox Jews and by reading the writing of Émile Guers, a Genevan pastor associated with the Brethren movement. His full adoption of Darbyite dispensationalism will be seen as the result of the direct influence of Brethren men involved with the Niagara Bible Conference

---

[18] Arno C. Gaebelein, *Half a Century: The Autobiography of a Servant*, New York: Publication Office "Our Hope," 1930.

movement.[19] This chapter will also include a defense of Gaebelein against the charge of anti-Semitism.[20]

Special influences related to these theological developments of Gaebelein will then be examined more closely (chapter three). Specifically, the methodology of Émile Guers, the Zionist movement, and specific factions from the Niagara Conference will be explored in more detail to find historical connections to Gaebelein's thinking in theology.[21] It will be observed that Guers' attention to methodology and premillennial theology has definite historical roots in Darby. Also, the primary influence of the Niagara Conference on Gaebelein will be identified as its general environment and the direct influence of Plymouth Brethren rather than the impact of James H. Brookes, C. I. Scofield, or Ernst Stroeter. Zionism, with its emphasis on a future home in Palestine for the Jews, will be shown to add to this Darbyite premillennialism by confirming the overall theological package through current events.

---

[19] The Niagara Bible Conference will variously be designated as Niagara, Niagara Conference, and Bible conference movement. Throughout this work, these designations refer to the same movement which will be discussed in chapters two and three.

[20] Much attention is given to this subject because of its importance as a matter of pre-understanding. Racism of any kind could deeply mark interpretation before the text is even approached. In addition, the limited defense of Gaebelein in these matters in the light of continuing misunderstanding of the complexity of his relationship to the Jews requires a corrective.

[21] The detail of the two chapters on historical backgrounds is designed to help fill in the relational gaps of a developing dispensationalism. This emphasis on presuppositional framework or historic milieu should not be construed as an overt acceptance of the philosophical hermeneutics of Hans-Georg Gadamer (*Philosophical Hermeneutics*, ed. and trans. David E. Linge [Los Angeles, CA: University of California Press, 1976] and *Truth and Method*, 2nd ed., trans. Joel Weinsheimer and Donald G. Marshall [New York: Crossroad Publishing Co., 1989]). The primary way that a person can understand the theological method of Gaebelein is found in the text of his writings. Gadamer moves interpretation of the Bible or any document to the realm of subjectivity. This writer's approach in this matter more closely follows that of E. D. Hirsch (*Validity in Interpretation* [London: Yale University Press, 1967] and *The Aims of Interpretation* [Chicago: University of Chicago Press, 1976]). For a discussion of the interaction of the two positions, see Elliott E. Johnson, *Expository Hermeneutics: An Introduction* (Grand Rapids, MI: Zondervan Publishing House, 1990), 225-29. For a more recent critique of the subjectivism of Gadamer see Paul R. Noble, *The Canonical Approach: A Critical Reconstruction of the Hermeneutics of Brevard S. Childs* (New York: E. J. Brill, 1995), 235-89.

8

The second part of the work consists of an analytical identification of two basic rules which Gaebelein used to argue theological points, the literal hermeneutic (chapter four) and dispensational integration (chapter five).[22] It will be shown that the primary use of the literal hermeneutic is to establish the absolute distinction between Israel and the church. The existence of dispensational integration in Gaebelein's approach demonstrates that the literal hermeneutic is not the only, or even the most used, method in his system.

Three aspects of dispensational integration will be uncovered: 1) the dispensational-theological aspect which usually speaks of Gaebelein's use of the already recognized distinction between Israel and the church to decide the meaning of a passage, 2) the dispensational-typological aspect which allows a secondary application of a passage through the use of typology, and 3) the dispensational-applicatory aspect which allows a secondary application of a passage without the use of typology. In all three of these aspects, the importance of distinctions, as seen in God's purposes through the scheme of dispensations in the light of progressive revelation, will be presented. That Gaebelein's dispensational integration involves a particular application of the analogy of faith will also be demonstrated.

The third part of this work is the tracing of themes in the writings of Gaebelein to determine the central interpretive motif which integrates his theological

---

[22] In the original dissertation form of this work, the term *dispensational hermeneutic* was used to describe the second interpretive approach of Gaebelein. It has been changed from *hermeneutic* to *integration* in this present work to help the reader understand that there is something going on that transcends basic exegetical concerns. In other words, Gaebelein's two approaches do not sit at the same level. The literal hermeneutic functions at the level of analysis, exegesis, and biblical theology. His dispensational integration renders a theological interpretation as other truths from elsewhere in the Bible are brought to bear on the passages in question to yield a theological, typological, or applicatory synthesis or integration. In other words, the dispensational integration of Gaebelein involves integration, synthesis, and systematic theology. Although the term *hermeneutic* is broad enough in it usage within the current state of biblical studies to cover Gaebelein's second approach, it is probably best to use different terminology such as *integration* to assist the reader in understanding this significant methodological distinction. It must be noted also that the two approaches are not necessarily contradictory, but can be seen in complementary fashion.

system (chapter six). It will be shown that within the context of a strong evangelical theology, the central interpretive motif is prophetic hope centered in the personal Second Coming of Jesus Christ. This hope in the premillennial coming of Christ is expressed by the realistic, yet negative, understanding of the hopelessness of the present age and the future realizations of the rapture of the church, the national restoration of Israel, the conversion of the nations, and the renewal of creation.

A final chapter will highlight the general significance of Gaebelein for the history of fundamentalism and dispensationalism (chapter seven). However, the contribution of this work will be seen in the fullest sense, when it is observed that Gaebelein's theological method provides a context for discussing the definition of dispensationalism. This definition will be given in terms of doctrinal and methodological concerns with an emphasis on the latter. Added to this definition will be a few suggestions for further study and final remarks about the relationship between dispensationalism and covenant theology.

CHAPTER 2
LIFE AND MINISTRY

Arno Clemens Gaebelein was born in Germany in 1861 and lived until
1945. At the age of twelve he accepted Christ as Savior. However, the event that
marked the beginning of Gaebelein's autobiography and overshadowed his physical and spiritual births was his surrender to the call of service. On 31 October
1879 in Lawrence, Massachusetts the future fundamentalist teacher at the age of
eighteen committed himself to a life of Christian service. He viewed his presence
in America as a fulfillment of earlier thoughts about being a Christian missionary.

According to his 1930 autobiography, Gaebelein viewed his life in three
distinct phases. First, his call to the ministry and the beginning phases of his work
for Christ constituted a type of preparatory time (1879-88).[1] It was near the end of
this time that Gaebelein converted to premillennialism in eschatology. Gaebelein
labeled the second phase of his life "The Testimony to Israel" (1888-98).[2] Outreach to the Jewish people of the New York City area and the beginning of the
Our Hope publications highlighted these pivotal years of Gaebelein's life. En-

---

[1] See Arno C. Gaebelein, *Half a Century: The Autobiography of a Servant* (New York: Publication Office "Our Hope," 1930), 1-21. The approximate years marking the beginning and end of
the respective phrases are given by this present writer and not explicitly by Gaebelein himself.
Gaebelein viewed these phases as somewhat overlapping.

[2] Ibid., 25-72.

12

trenchment in premillennialism marked Gaebelein's theological development at this time.

The third phase of his life's outline was his "New Commission" (1899-1930).[3] Gaebelein in 1899 embarked upon an independent, nondenominational ministry of Bible teaching. It was during this time that he rose to prominence in fundamentalist premillennial circles. At the beginning of this phase Gaebelein separated from the Methodist Episcopal Church due to the advance of higher criticism. In addition, and perhaps related to this decision, he came to an understanding of Messianic Judaism which deepened his recognition of the distinction between Israel and the church.[4] A lengthy and final chapter of his autobiography is entitled "Coast to Coast."[5] In survey fashion he described his travels as a Bible teacher mostly in this third phase of ministry.

David Rausch provided highlights of major areas of Gaebelein's career beyond the time of Gaebelein's autobiography. The post-1930 era (for which Gaebelein never updated his autobiography) is discussed under a section entitled "The Holocaust Years" in which Rausch ably showed the predictive insight Gaebelein seemed to possess as the rise of anti-Semitism reached its pinnacle during the Hitler era in Germany.[6] Rausch's discussion of the earlier periods of Gaebelein's life generally mirror Gaebelein's own assessments.[7]

---

[3] Ibid., 75-98.

[4] More will be said later concerning the change Gaebelein underwent in his feelings about Messianic Judaism.

[5] Gaebelein, *Autobiography*, 101-243.

[6] David Rausch, *Arno C. Gaebelein 1861-1945: Irenic Fundamentalist and Scholar*, (New York: Edwin Mellen Press, 1983), 161-89.

[7] Rausch's chapter titles of "The Formative Years," "Our Hope," and "Fundamentalist Statesman" correspond to the three major areas of preparation, Jewish outreach, and nondenominational Bible teaching which are highlighted by Gaebelein himself. Although the outlining schemes are not identical, they are close enough for the sake of comparison.

Gaebelein's Early Years

Gaebelein's first contact with an organized church appeared to be with a group of German Methodists in Lawrence, Massachusetts in 1879. In this group he met a young twenty year-old preacher named Augustus Wallon whom Gaebelein described as "the son of a godly Methodist preacher of Huguenot stock."[8] This contact proved to be extremely significant for further direction of Gaebelein's life. The father of this young man was a presiding elder named Louis Wallon. Several developments in Gaebelein's early ministry took place through this man.

First, Louis introduced Gaebelein to his first academic study of his theological convictions. This was done by recommending certain textbooks in church history, systematic theology, and apologetics.[9] Second, Gaebelein's decision to avoid any formal seminary training was based upon the advice of the elder Wallon. Gaebelein had quickly become a lay minister in the Methodist work in Lawrence and had begun studies on his own in Latin and Greek among other subjects. Apparently, Gaebelein never regretted by-passing the seminaries.[10] The scope of his ministry was unaffected by it and should not be denigrated because of it.[11]

---

[8] Gaebelein, *Autobiography*, 3.

[9] Ibid., 4. Unfortunately, Gaebelein did not mention the names of the textbooks involved.

[10] Gaebelein did take some courses in Semitic languages at John Hopkins University while in Baltimore (1881-82). He recounts an experience of demonstrating his knowledge of Arabic in a class taught by Professor Paul Haupt. However, Gaebelein never received an earned degree. See Gaebelein, *Autobiography*, 11. Wheaton Collage awarded him an honorary Doctor of Divinity degree in 1922; see *Who Was Who in America: A Companion Biographical Reference Work to Who's Who in America* (Chicago: A. N. Marquis Company, 1950), 2:201. That year Gaebelein gave the baccalaureate sermon at commencement for the college (Arno C. Gaebelein, "Editorial Notes," *Our Hope* 28 [May 1922]: 663).

[11] The Israeli scholar Yaakov S. Ariel spoke of Gaebelein's scholarship in glowing terms: "Gaebelein acquired an outstanding knowledge of Judaism which provided him with excellent tools to carry out his missionary work to the Jews. He did not graduate from a university or a theological seminary. His higher education consisted of only one year at Johns Hopkins University while he worked as a minister in Baltimore. The scope of his knowledge and the quality of his intellectual abilities were, however, like those of an academic scholar," Yaakov S. Ariel, *On Be-*

Rausch commented concerning Gaebelein's later itinerant ministry as a Bible teacher and author:

> As a speaker, Arno C. Gaebelein was viewed as a novel and detailed thinker; an excellent and lucid Bible teacher, the main impetus for this stimulation was his continued research and writing. He coupled the devotional with the commentary.[12]

The reason for a positive response to Gaebelein's teaching nationwide was couched in these terms by Rausch:

> Gaebelein's popularity increased not only because of his scholarly proficiency on the Bible, but also because of his knowledge of the Jewish people and Jewish customs. At conferences he added a dimension that appeared to be unique to those with little knowledge of Jewish tradition and culture. In spite of his broad knowledge of the Bible, many associated him with prophetic teaching and Jewish studies.[13]

The above statements by Rausch reinforce the truth that Gaebelein was always a student. Coupled with his later tenure as a seriatim Bible teacher at Evangelical Theological College (a graduate level seminary later to become Dallas Theological Seminary), it is easy to see that his scholarship was respected at least in fundamentalist circles.[14] Gaebelein in 1930 could say with confidence that Louis "spoke rightly" when he advised him to bypass seminary education.[15]

Third, Louis Wallon introduced the young Gaebelein to "Father Wallon," Augustus' grandfather and Louis' father. The eldest Wallon was a strong premillennialist and had given Gaebelein a book which the latter refers to as *La Future*

---

half of Israel: American Fundamentalist Attitudes Toward Jews, Judaism, and Zionism, 1865-1945, with a Preface by Martin E. Marty, Chicago Studies in the History of American Religion, no. 1 (Brooklyn, NY: Carlson Publishing, 1991), 98.

[12] Rausch, *Irenic Fundamentalist*, 62.

[13] Ibid., 63.

[14] Crutchfield noted that Gaebelein is "regarded by many as the best scholar among the early dispensational teachers" (*The Origins of Dispensationalism: The Darby Factor* [Lanham, MD: University Press of America, 1992], 13).

[15] Gaebelein, *Autobiography*, 4.

D'Israël.[16] This book, read by Gaebelein in 1881 and written by a Genevan pastor named Émile Guers, is significant because it was the first piece of premillennial literature that Gaebelein read.[17]

A final way that Louis Wallon influenced Gaebelein's life was to introduce him to the world of German Methodism in New York City. In 1881 Gaebelein became an assistant and apprentice under Louis' ministry as pastor of a church in New York. The resulting group of contacts colored Gaebelein's ministry for the rest of his life. Although Gaebelein left the area for a short pastorate in Baltimore, the New York City area became the home for virtually all other ministry for the rest of Gaebelein's life. The significance of this fact lies in the contacts he would make in the Jewish community. As later sections will show in more detail, his evangelical outreach to the Jews deepened his faith in the premillennial view of eschatology and opened up contacts with the men of the Bible conference movement which in turn provided opportunities for his nationwide ministry of Bible teaching.

Besides the overall impact of the Wallon family upon various facets of Gaebelein's life, other factors emerged as well during the early years of his ministry. Gaebelein was drawn to an intense study of Semitic languages during a short pastorate (1882-84) in Baltimore.[18] Gaebelein stated explicitly that his motivation to be a future missionary provided the impetus for such studies.[19] Three experi-

---

[16] Ibid., 5. The book which Gaebelein referred to is actually Émile Guers, *Israël aux Derniers Jours De L'Économie Actuelle ou Essai Sur La Restauration Prochaine De Ce Peuple, Suivi D'Un Fragment Sur Le Millénarisme*, (Genève: Émile Beroud, 1856). Throughout the remainder of this chapter, Gaebelein's shortened reference to *La Future D'Israël* will be used.

[17] A later chapter will deal with this influence on Gaebelein which leads one in the direction of John Nelson Darby and his brand of dispensational premillennialism.

[18] Gaebelein, *Autobiography*, 10-11. Besides Hebrew, Gaebelein studied Aramaic, Arabic, Syriac, and Persian. One cannot assume that his goal was to be a better exegete of the Hebrew Old Testament. Although Aramaic, Arabic, and Syriac were helpful, Persian appeared to be peripheral. In addition, Gaebelein's later experiences and statements indicated a different motivation.

[19] Ibid., 16.

ences during these early years of Gaebelein's ministry confirmed this desire in Gaebelein and finally led to his involvement in Jewish outreach in New York City.

The first experience began with an assignment in Harlem, New York, which Gaebelein took in 1884 upon leaving his church in Baltimore. While staying at the home of a presiding elder, one C. F. Grimm, Gaebelein fell in love with Grimm's daughter, Emma, and married her a year later. Throughout his autobiography Gaebelein spoke in glowing terms of his life-long partner referring to her as his "priceless gift."[20] In 1886 the young couple faced one of the greatest tragedies they would ever endure. Their first child was a little girl who passed away at only five months old. One finds it strange that Gaebelein never gave the name of his little girl in the autobiography while he did mention the names for his other children. He only noted that he called her "my little pilgrim" and had assurance that she was with Jesus.[21] This even stirred Gaebelein's heart concerning his call to the mission field:

> I began to be greatly troubled. Did the Lord permit this sudden home-call to remind me of my desire, if not call, to go to some foreign land or foreign people to preach the Gospel? This desire has always been before me. The study of different oriental languages, which I still kept up, was done with this in view. My wife knew all about it. At that time a small volume was put into my hand, *The Crisis of Missions*, by Dr. Arthur T. Pierson. I devoured it, and little did I think that eighteen years later I should number Dr. Pierson among my best friends and labor with him in different parts of the country and in Bible Conferences. I told him later how his excellent book fired my soul afresh to go to the regions beyond and to preach the

---

[20] Ibid., 14-15. Gaebelein's love for Emma remained a lifetime commitment. Although Gaebelein's personal letters to colleagues at times appear stern and demanding, one cannot fail to see the tender side of the man on occasion. One example is the exchange with Lewis Sperry Chafer when the latter's wife was ill (Letter, Arno C. Gaebelein to Lewis Sperry Chafer, New York City, New York, 9 November 1943, Arno C. Gaebelein Papers, Archives, Dallas Theological Seminary, Dallas, Texas [hereafter cited as ADTS]; Letter, Lewis Sperry Chafer to Arno C. Gaebelein, Dallas, Texas, 29 November 1943, Arno C. Gaebelein Papers, ADTS).

[21] Gaebelein, *Autobiography*, 15-16.

Gospel where Christ's name was not mentioned. I prayed earnestly and waited for providential leadings, which never seemed to come.[22]

This self-revelation by Gaebelein is significant on two counts. First, once again the missionary call was emphasized in his life with respect to the Orient. Ultimately, this is fulfilled in his ministry in New York to the Jews. Second, Gaebelein mentioned for the first time Arthur T. Pierson, who was associated with the Bible conference movement. These two threads, the Jewish outreach and the Bible conference movement, served as major influences in Gaebelein's ministry as a "missionary" and also impacted his development as a premillennialist.

The second experience with respect to the missionary call was the proposal made to Gaebelein by James M. Thoburn, a prominent Methodist missionary to India and eastern Asia. Openings in the Far East were available in Singapore and Java. Disagreements over this opportunity among the older men in the conference were encountered but in the final analysis it was the poor health of his wife, Emma, that caused Gaebelein finally to reject the proposals. Through these discussions, Gaebelein noted that "my old enthusiasm came back."[23]

Prior to the offers, the Methodist Episcopal Church had transferred Gaebelein to a new and larger congregation in Hoboken, New Jersey, just across the Hudson River (1887). The third experience impacting Gaebelein's missionary call involved a converted Hebrew named Samuel Goldstein who was a member of that congregation. Gaebelein remembered a particularly noteworthy encounter with Goldstein in this way:

> A short time after (discussions with Dr. Thoburn), something of great importance happened which ultimately led to the work in which the Lord has so graciously and greatly blessed me. In the congregation I served was a converted Hebrew, Samuel Goldstein, who acted as an interpreter in connection with the immigration office in New York. One day, being in my library, he looked over my books, and when he saw books in Hebrew and

---

[22] Ibid., 16.

[23] Ibid., 17-18.

18

other Semitic languages, he asked if I understood Hebrew. When I took down a Hebrew Bible and read to him, he burst out saying, "it is a shame that you do not make use of your knowledge. You should do a greater work than preaching to a German congregation." I told him that my studies since 1882 had been in Semitic and Oriental languages, because I felt called to go to the Orient to preach the Gospel there. He answered, "There is an Orient and there are thousands of foreigners right over here in New York; Jews are coming in by the thousands from every European and several Oriental countries. You should go and preach the Gospel to the Jews. I believe the Lord made you take up these studies because He wants you to go to my brethren, the Jews."[24]

While slightly resisting the idea, Gaebelein did consent to a trial ministry of preaching at the Hebrew Christian Mission on St. Marks Place, led by Jacob Freshman. This initial attempt to preach to the Jewish people continued for about one year with good attendance on Saturday afternoons.[25] It is during this time that Gaebelein saw the first stages of the fulfillment of his missionary call.[26]

However, Gaebelein's contact with the mostly orthodox Jews in the New York City area during this first year also impacted his theological thinking. The year of his ministry at the Hebrew Christian Mission (1887) marked Gaebelein's conversion to a premillennial view of eschatology. It had been six years since Grandfather Wallon had shown him a copy of Émile Guers' *La Future D'Israël*. Gaebelein recalled Wallon's influence, "However, I believe the old saint must have prayed earnestly for me, for six years later the light on unfulfilled prophecy came to me, and one of the first things I did was to order that French book (by Guers) for home study."[27]

Gaebelein, in the above statement, did not say how the light of unfulfilled prophecy came to him, but his later comments were clear and forceful:

[24] Ibid., 18-19.

[25] Ibid., 20.

[26] Ibid., 21.

[27] Ibid., 5-6.

This initial attempt to bring the Gospel to the Jews led me deeper into the Old Testament Scriptures. I began to study prophecy. Up to this time I had followed in the interpretation of Old Testament prophecy the so-called "spiritualization method." Israel, that method teaches, is no longer the Israel of old, but it means the Church now. For the natural Israel no hope of a future restoration is left. All their glorious and unfulfilled promises find now their fulfillment in the Church of Jesus Christ. But as I came in closer touch with this remarkable people, those who are still orthodox, I soon had to face their never-dying hope. As I began to read their *Machsorim,* their rituals and prayers, I found the expressions of hope and longing for Messiah's coming. Do they not say each time *Pesach* is celebrated, commemorating their supernatural deliverance out of Egypt's slavery, "This year here, next year in Jerusalem"? Many an old, long-bearded, orthodox Hebrew assured me that the Messiah, the Son of David, the Bethlehemite, will surely come to claim David's throne. In the beginning it sounded foreign to me, but as I turned to the Bible I soon discovered the real hope of Israel and the truth of the promised return of our Lord, and the earthly glories connected with that future event were brought through the Spirit of God to my heart. Then the study of the Bible became my most fascinating occupation, and as I continued in my search, I knew that the Lord wanted me to turn aside from the regular ministry and devote myself to work among God's ancient people. Now all seemed to become clear as to why the Lord prevented my going to the regions beyond.[28]

Several significant points come out of this declaration by Gaebelein. First, he asserts that his new found position is based upon a deeper study of the Scriptures under the leadership of the Holy Spirit. Gaebelein would reject the suggestion that he merely adopted the view of the Old Testament held by the orthodox Jews he was ministering to. However, the contact with them forced him to reexamine the prophecies in Scripture which in turn led to his premillennial convictions.

Gaebelein acknowledged a measure of dependence upon Jewish thinking about the restoration of Israel to the land of Palestine in his writings over the next several years. In August, 1895, in an article entitled "The Prayers of Orthodox Judaism" found in *Our Hope* magazine, Gaebelein said:

---

[28] Ibid., 20-21. This quotation may be the most remarkable and revealing single paragraph in Gaebelein's autobiography in terms of his theological thinking.

20

> Sometimes on a Friday night when the Jewish Sabbath commences, and in the many Hebrew homes around us the festive candles are lighted, I take the Hebrew prayer-book and read in the original some of their prayers, and more than once my eyes were dimmed with tears, and I called upon Him who is the Hope of Israel in the words of the inspired King, "Have mercy upon Zion, for the time to favor her, yea, the set time has come."[29]

These statements by Gaebelein demonstrate the spirit with which Gaebelein had entered into the Jewish world that he was trying to reach with the gospel. His use of Jewish insight into theological interpretations of Scripture, especially eschatological passages, can be seen in a series of articles in *Our Hope* published over a period of six months dealing with the topic of Jewish views of eschatology.[30] Gaebelein commented, referring to the teachings of traditional Judaism, that "there can be no doubt that the Spirit of God did enlighten many of the old Jewish writers, and they foretell the conditions correctly which will prevail when the King of Glory comes."[31] Showing breadth and depth of knowledge concerning rabbinical writings, he explained for his readers the traditional Jewish understanding that when Messiah returns to earth He will find "the world in a sad state and Israel in deep misery and ungodliness."[32] In another place, he justified the identification of the two witnesses in Revelation 11:3-12 as Moses and Elijah based upon Jewish predictions about the future comings of the two famous prophets.[33]

However, the most revealing words of Gaebelein in this series of articles showed the great delight he found and the large confidence he placed in much of the traditional literature of his Jewish friends:

---

[29] Arno C. Gaebelein, "The Prayers of Orthodox Judaism," *Our Hope* 2 (August 1895): 38.

[30] Arno C. Gaebelein, "Jewish Eschatology," *Our Hope* 5 (July 1898): 9-13; (August & September 1898): 48-51; (October 1898): 108-12; (November 1898): 149-52; (December 1898): 188-91.

[31] Gaebelein, "Jewish Eschatology," *Our Hope* 5 (August & September 1898): 50.

[32] Gaebelein, "Jewish Eschatology," *Our Hope* 5 (July 1898): 12.

[33] Ibid., 13.

Old Testament prophecy has been much better understood by the old synagogue than by most Christian commentators. Many a Christian Doctor of Divinity has with a few sentences dismissed the "carnal" expectations of the Jews and the literal interpretations of the Rabbis, and erected his own phantom, but nevertheless, the Jew with his "carnal" expectations and literal interpretations holds the truth. Yonder old orthodox Jew faithfully keeping the law and daily expecting his Messiah, the Redeemer of Israel, waiting for Him and His kingdom, believing in all the prophets said concerning the restoration of all things and Israel's glory, is a far more inspiring sight to us than many a professing Christian, who has very little knowledge of the Word, and none at all of God's purposes, and who moves in a little, narrow circle . . . There are many orthodox Jews who wait as eagerly for the Messiah as the true and orthodox Christian waits for God's Son from heaven. The Jew has in his many and ancient writings a wonderful treasure, which a Christian never dreams of. The Targumim, Medrashim and the Talmudic literature is filled with valuable suggestions, read and understood by not many Gentiles. The Jew has in these writings a wonderful eschatology or teachings on the last things, the end of this present age, and the world to come, which will no doubt astonish many of our Christian friends.[34]

Consequently, the impact of the orthodox Jews who had become part of Gaebelein's life can be easily established. However, the recent convert to premillennialism would still insist that these people simply forced him to take a longer and deeper look at the Bible.

Second, the main target for Gaebelein's renewed study is given as Old Testament prophecy. In particular, it was the promise of a restoration of natural Israel that caught his eye. This had been the precise focus of Guers in *La Future D'Israël* that Gaebelein was reviewing at the time. In addition, it may be possible to see, in beginning stages, Gaebelein's understanding of the centrality of the Old Testament text for defining dispensational premillennialism.[35] George Ladd, a

---

[34] Ibid., 10-11.

[35] Gaebelein in this section refrains from referring to *dispensationalism* and *premillennialism*. This could be his way of showing that his early comprehension of these truths was limited. More likely, however, one sees his preference for substance over labels.

nondispensational premillennialist, in more recent times has concurred with this understanding of dispensationalism:

> Here then is the basic watershed between a dispensational and a nondispensational theology. Dispensationalism forms its eschatology by a literal interpretation of the Old Testament and then fits the New Testament into it. A nondispensational eschatology forms its theology from the explicit teaching of the New Testament. It confesses that it cannot be sure how the Old Testament prophecies of the end are to be fulfilled, for (a) the first coming of Christ was accomplished in terms not foreseen by a literal interpretation of the Old Testament, and (b) there are unavoidable indications that the Old Testament promises to Israel are fulfilled in the Christian church.[36]

Third, Gaebelein reveals that he viewed his conversion to premillennialism as a change in methodology. Again, this is consistent with his reading of Guers who dealt at length with theological method.[37] Gaebelein labeled his once-held view "spiritualizing." Gaebelein probably referred to postmillennialism in this quotation, a view that Christ would return after the millennium and one filled with optimism about the progress of mankind.[38] His old view had little use for "natural" Israel or any earthly glories connected with the coming of the Lord. Apparently, by "natural" Gaebelein meant a political, earthly, and ethnic nation of Israel. His references to the hopes of the orthodox Jews in light of the Old

---

[36] George Eldon Ladd, "Historic Premillennialism," in *The Meaning of the Millennium: Four Views*, ed. Robert G. Clouse, (Downers Grove, IL: InterVarsity Press, 1977), 27.

[37] See especially Guers, *La Future D'Israël*, 1-61.

[38] Gaebelein made no distinctions between postmillennialism and amillennialism concerning this spiritualizing idea. That his former position was most likely a form of postmillennialism can reasonably be deduced from two facts: (1) it was the most widely held view of eschatology among theologians of that day, and (2) his early writings spend much time attacking postmillennialism by name; for example, see Arno C. Gaebelein, "Notes on Prophecy and the Jews," *Our Hope* 8 (October 1901): 242. If his former position had been amillennialism, it probably would have shown up in his discussions more often in those early years. At any rate, he appears to have had little interest in prophecy until the year of his conversion to premillennialism. Common comparisons by premillennial writers in the late nineteenth century spoke of judgment versus progress. See Robert Cameron, *The Doctrine of the Ages*, (New York: Fleming H. Revell Co., 1896), 102-9 for an example.

Testament prophecies highlighted his new methodology as one of "literal" fulfillment.[39]

The Decade of Jewish Outreach

Gaebelein's first tentative steps into Jewish missions had occurred in 1887. He continued in this evangelistic outreach by holding Saturday meetings at the Hebrew Christian Mission while he pastored in Hoboken, NewJersey. However, when that appointment was over in 1891, he lobbied to be sent to full time work among the Jews in New York. Approval being granted, Gaebelein continued his speaking at the Hebrew Christian Mission for a short time. However, he soon found himself in the facilities of the large and famous Allen Street Memorial Methodist Episcopal Church located on Rivington Street on Saturday afternoons (and eventually mornings) preaching mostly to Jewish immigrants. As Gaebelein experienced numerical success in this ministry, several developments took place.

First, Gaebelein created a Yiddish monthly magazine in 1893 entitled *Tiqweth Israel* (*The Hope of Israel Monthly*). Thousands of copies were distributed to the immigrant Jews in New York City. The scope of influence for the magazine, however, was international. Gaebelein recalled with pride the time he was greeted in Kiev, Russia, by men who possessed his little magazine.[40] The larger significance of this paper may have been the groundwork it laid for a future magazine named *Our Hope*.

Before *Our Hope* is discussed, another development must be mentioned. The Methodist Church, in response to the rising prominence of Gaebelein's ministry to the Jews in New York City, transferred him to the New York East Confer-

---

[39] Compare Guers, *La Future D'Israël*, 22-28, in which literalism is a major topic. A later chapter will include a discussion of Gaebelein's understanding and practice of literal interpretation.

[40] Gaebelein, *Autobiography*, 33.

24

ence and placed the ministry under the auspices of the New York City Church Extension and Missionary Society.[41]

Despite this expanded effort, the progress of the work soon took on dimensions that required interdenominational cooperation. Although Gaebelein did not specify exactly why, it was clear that full financial support for his specialized ministry would not be forthcoming from Methodist sources. Development of the ministry along broad lines which would include non-Methodist participation was allowed and encouraged. In accordance with that broad support a lessening of denominational narrowness in the ministry followed.[42] The name used for this new expanded ministry was *The Hope of Israel Movement*. The expansion with respect to the many religious denominations foreshadowed Gaebelein's decision a few years later to become independent and maintain a nondenominational profile. The motif of "hope" became for him the center piece for his entire ministry and highlighted his whole theological system.[43]

Gaebelein began another publication the next year with the help of Ernst F. Stroeter, a professor from Denver Seminary in Denver, Colorado, who moved to New York to help in the outreach to the Jews. An English monthly magazine initiated in July 1894, *Our Hope*, was designed to do two things. It targeted Christian people to acquaint them with the ongoing ministry to the Jews. In addition, *Our Hope* provided an emphasis on the teachings of the prophetic portions of Scripture.[44] This magazine, without commercial advertising, continued for the

---

[41] Ibid., 34.

[42] Ibid., 36-38, 68. Gaebelein preferred the word *undenominational* rather than *interdenominational*. The year when monthly support for Gaebelein became interdenominational was 1897.

[43] A later chapter will be devoted to the central interpretive motif of Gaebelein.

[44] Gaebelein, *Autobiography*, 44. Sandeen carefully noted that one of the purposes of Gaebelein was to "alert Gentiles to the remarkable Zionist awakening among the Jewish population." See Ernest R. Sandeen, *The Roots of Fundamentalism: British and American Millenarianism 1800-1930*, (Chicago: University of Chicago Press, 1970), 215. The references to Zionism in the

length of Gaebelein's ministry and became one of the strongest outlets of the dispensational fundamentalist viewpoint in the United States.[45]

David Rausch accurately described the three emphases of the magazine at its inception: 1) the restoration of the Jewish people to Palestine, 2) the castigation of the Christian Church for belittling the Jewish people, and 3) the need for a Jewish convert to Christianity to continue observation of the Mosaic legislation in the Old Testament.[46] The first two were consistently maintained throughout the ministry of Gaebelein. The third emphasis changed within a few years as will be seen below. This change marked a major step in Gaebelein's ministry and theological thinking.

The most influential development of this period of Gaebelein's life was the beginning of his association with the men of the Niagara Bible Conferences. As *Our Hope* began to gain circulation across the country, invitations requesting either Stroeter or Gaebelein to come and hold meetings increased. Usually such speaking engagements were held in churches. Gaebelein remarked concerning one such conference (the date is unknown, but it is within this period):

> In Harrisburg, Pa. a few days Bible Conference had been arranged by George C. Needham, the well-known Evangelist. Some of the Niagara Conference brethren were there, and I addressed a large audience in one of the Lutheran churches.[47]

Here Gaebelein's encounters with the men of the Niagara Conferences are clearly seen. Sandeen mistakenly claimed that Gaebelein probably never spoke at any of

---

magazine appear to be used by Gaebelein to bolster the theological viewpoint that was being expressed about the restoration of Israel to the land of Palestine.

[45] In 1958, *Our Hope* merged with *Eternity* magazine. See Rausch, *Irenic Fundamentalist*, 19.

[46] Ibid., 19-20.

[47] Gaebelein, *Autobiography*, 47. Gaebelein recorded a sermon a few days later entitled "The Future of the Jewish People in the Light of the Bible." In light of his specialized, missionary ministry at the time, this probably represented the emphasis of many of his sermons during these kinds of conferences during that phase of his life.

the Niagara conferences but was in attendance.[48] Gaebelein recalled his growing involvement in various conferences with these words:

> In May, 1898 our first prophetic conference was held in Berkeley Temple, Boston, Mass. The speakers besides me were: W. J. Erdman, J. M. Gray, Frank Weston and Professor Chapell. This was followed by a conference in Brockton, Mass. During this summer I was one of the speakers at the Niagara Bible Conference, which was held at Point Chautauqua, Lake Chautauqua, N.Y. The speakers were: Professor W. G. Morehead, Major Whittle, C. I. Scofield, J. B. Parsons, Elmore Harris, L. W. Munhall and myself. I delivered three addresses on "The Song of Moses," "The Parables of Balaam," and "The Ode of Habakkuk." Dear Dr. Brookes was much missed. But here I met for the first time a beloved brother and his good wife, Mr. and Mrs. Francis Emory Fitch, who became later such a help in my ministry.[49]

In this statement Gaebelein spoke in familiar terms about James Brookes whom he had met for the first time in late 1893. He also mentioned C. I. Scofield who was rapidly becoming one of his closest allies in the ministry. His first encounter with Francis Fitch, a printer in New York City and a layman associated with the Plymouth Brethren, was also significant as a way of introduction to the Brethren Movement.[50]

In addition, it can be said with certainty that the men of the Niagara Conference found Gaebelein more than he found them. Apparently after hearing of Gaebelein's work Stroeter traveled all the way to New York in 1893 to attend one of Gaebelein's Saturday meetings and to discuss joining with Gaebelein in that

---

[48] Sandeen, *Roots of Fundamentalism*, 215.

[49] Gaebelein, *Autobiography*, 71. Sandeen noted how the word *Niagara* had become the customary designation for these conferences even though the history of the conferences saw the location change at least nine times (*Roots of Fundamentalism*, 134). In 1922, Gaebelein remembered that "the Editor (of *Our Hope*) attended but two of the old Niagara Bible Conferences, giving four addresses in one of these" (Editorial Notes," *Our Hope* 29 [July 1922]: 22). That would mean that he missed either the 1899 conference at Point Chautauqua, New York, or the one in 1900 at Asbury Park, New Jersey. In light of his rising leadership at that very moment in the Bible Conference movement, one is tempted to believe that his memory on this particular point was faulty.

[50] The influence of each of these men upon Gaebelein's life and ministry will be explored in more detail in a later chapter.

particular outreach to the Jews. A year later the two were working together on *Our Hope.*[51]

Gaebelein described the general interest his ministry was generating:

> The Friends of Israel were beginning to take notice of the work which was being done among God's ancient people. Among those who became very much interested were the noble witnesses of the Niagara Bible Conference movement. Under the leadership of that stalwart champion of the Truth of God, a giant in Bible knowledge and Bible teaching, Dr. James H. Brookes, Pastor of the Washington Avenue Presbyterian Church, St. Louis, Missouri, summer Bible Conferences had been held for about twelve years. His associates were Drs. Nathaneal West, W. J. Erdman, and his brother Albert, Professor Morehead, A. J. Gordon, George C. Needham, J. M. Stifler, Arthur T. Pierson, Dr. Parsons, C. I. Scofield and others. All these beloved brethren, who are no longer here, showed a lively interest in my work.[52]

Gaebelein specially notes his first meeting with Brookes in late 1893.[53] Shortly after this meeting, Brookes willingly gave some free advertising to the young Gaebelein's ministry:

> In this country several periodicals have taken up the cause of the hated and homeless people (the Jews), and quite a number of missions have been established in their behalf. They are found in New York, Philadelphia, Chicago, and elsewhere, under the care of Rev. Jacob Freshman and Warsaviak in the first of the cities named, W. E. Blackstone in Chicago, and others in various places. Perhaps the most promising of these missions is in charge of Prof. A. C. Gaebelein, 91 Rivington St., New York City. He is a German, a Gentile, and accomplished scholar, who feels called of God to devote his life to the work of preaching the gospel to the Jews; and already the Lord has set His seal of approval upon the ministry of His dear servant.[54]

---

[51] Gaebelein noted that he had met Stroeter before, but did not give the substance of their first meeting (Gaebelein, *Autobiography*, 44).

[52] Gaebelein, *Autobiography*, 39.

[53] Ibid., 39-40.

[54] James H. Brookes, "Work Among the Jews," *The Truth*, 20 (January 1894): 15.

28

This interest on the part of Brookes predates the magazine *Our Hope* by six months and shows the national status of Gaebelein's work before any real effort on Gaebelein's part is made to make it so.

The contact between Gaebelein and the Niagara group was initiated in the 1893-94 time frame. It was motivated mostly by the interest on the part of the conference men in outreach to the Jewish people.[55] By 1898 Gaebelein was speaking at prophetic conferences across the country, representing his Jewish outreach ministry. In addition, he was sharing the platform with men from the Niagara Bible Conference movement as one of them.

The Emergence of a National Ministry

The year 1899 was a pivotal one in the life of Arno C. Gaebelein. It marked the transition from the Jewish outreach in New York City and the constant need for travel and support of the local ministry to a truly national ministry where the declaration of the message was the major thrust. According to Rausch, Gaebelein was, at this point, taking on the mantle of the Fundamentalist Statesman.[56] Gaebelein himself labeled this turn his "new commission" or the "renewed commission."[57] The turn was actually made in 1899 but the currents that swept him to these new heights were already in motion throughout the years of outreach to the Jews in New York City.

Two critical changes in Gaebelein's ministry and thinking took place in 1899, both related to Gaebelein's understanding of and relationship to the church. First, Gaebelein severed his relationship to the Methodist Episcopal Church. Second, he abandoned his beliefs concerning Messianic Judaism. Both of these de-

---

[55] Notice the interest already displayed in Freshman and Blackstone in Brookes' quotation above.

[56] Rausch, *Irenic Fundamentalist*, 53-62.

[57] Gaebelein, *Autobiography*, 79.

velopments revealed the change of his convictions concerning the nature of the church, including its distinction from the nation of Israel.

Gaebelein's Withdrawal from the Methodist Church

The advance of higher criticism sparked Gaebelein's withdrawal from his own denomination. Gaebelein vigorously complained about a weekly meeting of ministers in which the speaker promoted higher criticism over against the integrity of the Bible:

> The meeting mentioned was the weekly Methodist preacher's meeting held in the Methodist Book Concern. I was present and listened to the address given by the now nationally famous radio speaker, Dr. S. P. Cadman. He was at that time pastor of the Central Methodist Church. In that address the Mosaic authorship of the Pentateuch was denied. The historicity of the Book of Jonah and other Scriptures was attacked. Yet here were several hundred Methodist preachers applauding the remarks which were but a faint echo of German rationalism. When I protested and suggested that charges should be brought against a man who uttered such unwarranted attacks upon the Book of books, I was told by high officials not to be hasty about this, "for," as one said, "sooner or later we must fall in line with these results of scholarly Bible Criticism." When I heard this, I decided at once to sever my fellowship with the denomination, and though different inducements were offered me, if I would change my mind, the Lord gave courage to carry out my decision and I withdrew to follow, as a servant, Him who has promised the open door to those who keep His Word and who do not deny His Name.[58]

This withdrawal occurred in the Spring of 1899. However, one would be hasty to conclude that this event in isolation generated enough emotion in Gaebelein to cause such a stern response.

In his autobiography, he noted that it was during that time period that he had been going though "deep soul exercise."[59] The issue with which he was strug-

---

[58] Ibid., 81-82

[59] Ibid., 77-78. One cannot help but make the comparison to John Nelson Darby's personal struggle in the area of ecclesiology. See Floyd S. Elmore, "A Critical Examination of the Doctrine of the Two Peoples of God in John Nelson Darby," (Th.D. diss., Dallas Theological Seminary, 1990), 15-43.

30

gling was the nature of the church. Specifically, Gaebelein referred to the prayer of unity by Jesus in John 17, the baptism of believers into the body of Christ taught in 1 Corinthians 12:13, and the book of Ephesians as portions of Scripture which forced him to rethink his position and give practical expression in his life.[60] One result was his desire to be unaffiliated in his ministry:

> We are exhorted to give all diligence to keep the unity of the Spirit in the bond of peace (Ephes. iv:3), but denominational is a practical denial of that unity. The sad divisions as they exist in Protestantism appeared to me not as the work of the Spirit, but as the work of the flesh, even as the New Testament teaches. Then I meditated much on the ministry in that body... Then it gradually came to me that my future ministry whether to Jews or Gentiles, believers in Christ, must be exercised according to this truth. The new commission came to me in the early part of 1899 to go forth denominationally unaffiliated, to minister to the body of Christ, wherever it is found and wherever my Lord would open the door.[61]

Thus, the encounter with higher criticism in his denomination only served as the proverbial straw that broke the camel's back. Gaebelein was already headed in that direction and such a conflict only hastened the inevitable.

Gaebelein's Rejection of Messianic Judaism

Later in 1899 Gaebelein for similar reasons abandoned his views on Messianic Judaism. It is interesting that in his autobiography, his presentation of this change came before his discussion of his withdrawal from the Methodist Church. In fact, the entire chapter covering this strategic year in his theological life blurred the rejection of Messianic Judaism, his rejection of his own denomination, and his new awareness of what he believed to be superior ecclesiology.[62]

---

[60] Ibid., 78.

[61] Ibid., 78-79

[62] Ibid., 75-85.

Messianic Judaism involves a belief that a Jew who converts to Christianity should not be gentilized.[63] Under the heading of Christian Judaism, the first edition of *Our Hope* in July, 1894, explained the idea in these terms:

> For the Jew, then, to believe in Jesus as the promised Messiah does not mean the adoption of a new religion entirely, it means simply the acceptance of the divinely appointed, covenanted Israelism, as it will be restored or re-established under Messiah, the King, Jesus, the son of David. The Jew does not, like the heathen, have to turn from idols ... The Jew who accepts Jesus of Nazareth as his personal and his nation's true Messiah and Lord, is in the "true apostolic succession." There is absolutely no necessity of his doing or becoming anything else.[64]

A later issue of *Our Hope* clarified these principles in terms of ecclesiastical connections:

> The Jew had no need whatever of the organizations or institutions of historical (i.e., Gentile and denominational) Christianity. All he needs is personal, saving faith in his own Jewish Messiah, the Christ of God, nothing more. And all that was Divinely given him through Moses he has full liberty to retain and uphold as far as possible when he becomes a believer in Jesus Christ.[65]

Ernst Stroeter in a passionate article entitled "Does the Jew, In Christ, Cease to be a Jew?" answered his own question with an emphatic "No!" His discussion also

---

[63] Rausch provided a caution regarding use of the term: "Today, this same emphasis is found in the modern Messianic Jewish congregation movement. One must differentiate this modern movement from fundamentalism's Jews for Jesus and other such Hebrew Christian enterprises. Furthermore, one is impressed with the fact that pure Messianic Judaism goes back to a much earlier period than scholars had suspected. The term is used in the nineteenth century; the concept is considerably older: (Rausch, *Irenic Fundamentalist*, 35). See also David Raush, *Messianic Judaism: Its History, Theology and Polity* (New York: Edwin Mellen Press, 1982). For a Jewish perspective on Gaebelein's early Jewish outreach and his abandonment of Messianic Judaism see Yaakov S. Ariel, *On Behalf of Israel*, 243-56.

[64] "Christian Judaism," *Our Hope* 1 (July 1894): 8. It is not clear whether Stroeter or Gaebelein wrote this section, but one can safely assume that both had input.

[65] "The Principles of the Hope of Israel Movement," *Our Hope* 3 (November-December 1896): 149-50. Again, it is not clear who wrote this article. Since Stroeter was the official editor of the magazine at this time, it was probably his actual work. However, Gaebelein, no doubt, helped to formulate the principles.

tied the entire question together with the overall issue of premillennialism.[66] Not surprisingly then, Gaebelein went through a time of genuine soul-searching concerning his convictions in this matter.

Gaebelein's break with Stroeter and Messianic Judaism was announced in *Our Hope* in September 1899:

> The principles which teach that a Jew who has believed in Christ and is therefore a member of His body, the church, should or may continue as under the law, practice circumcision, keep the seventh day (Saturday), eat only clean food as commanded by Moses and keep the different feasts, the writer does no longer believe to be scriptural. The great revelations of the Lord in the Church Epistles concerning His body are entirely ignored in these principles.[67]

At this point Stroeter and Gaebelein parted on friendly terms, yet decidedly in disagreement. The change on Gaebelein's part may have been necessary for his future national ministry to develop along the lines that it did.[68]

Gaebelein claimed that Scripture passages in the New Testament, especially the Pauline doctrine of the church as a body, had forced him to reevaluate his ecclesiology in theory and in practice. He noted that it was the prophetic portions of the Old Testament that had caused his shift to premillennialism twelve years earlier. Apparently, now an adjustment within premillennialism was occur-

---

[66] Ernst F. Stroeter, "Does the Jew, In Christ, Cease to be a Jew?" *Our Hope* 2 (January 1896): 148-54.

[67] Arno C. Gaebelein, "A Short Review of Our Mission and the Principles of the Hope of Israel Movement," *Our Hope* 6 (September 1899): 69. Gaebelein then cited several New Testament passages concerning the doctrine of the church to substantiate the change (e.g., Eph. 2:14-18, Col. 2:11-18). That Gaebelein quoted at length and verbatim in his autobiography concerning this decision shows he was clearly aware of the ramifications of such a choice (*Autobiography*, 76-77). See also, Ariel, *On Behalf of Israel*, 255.

[68] Rausch noted: "It is debatable whether or not Arno Gaebelein would ever have become the fundamentalist leader that he did if he had not changed his view on Messianic Judaism. The cry that Messianic Jews were 'rebuilding the wall of partition' would echo throughout the fundamentalist-evangelical movement during the twentieth century. Fundamentalism would join liberal Protestantism and most of the Jewish community in combating the Messianic Jewish 'heresy,'" Rausch, *Irenic Fundamentalist*, 59.

ring as he saw the church as a body of all believers in the present age whether Jew or Gentile. This concept forced a sharper distinction between Israel as a nation and the Church as the body of Christ.

Gaebelein's First Exposure to the Plymouth Brethren

What factors caused Gaebelein's concentration on the passages in question? Rausch in his analysis focused on the Bible conference movement in general terms:

> As he became intricately involved with the fundamentalist Bible conference circuit, Arno Gaebelein was pressured to wrestle with the fundamentalist teaching that a converted Jew becomes part of the true Christian church and therefore is no longer a Jew. A change of view on this topic was bound to have radical implications for the Hope of Israel Movement, because it was alien to the founding principles which Gaebelein had written himself. Nevertheless, he came to believe that the fundamentalist conference circuit interpretation was the correct biblical teaching, and he gave up his former interpretation.[69]

However, one can argue that the immediate influence on Gaebelein's thinking at this time was one group within the Niagara company, namely, the Plymouth Brethren.

Gaebelein in the same chapter of his autobiography (in which he rejected the Methodist Church and Messianic Judaism) gave strong clues of the chief influence without clearly stating the cause and effect relationship. In 1898, he met Francis Fitch at the Niagara Bible Conference where Gaebelein spoke. Fitch, a dedicated layman, became the printer for *Our Hope* using his own printing business in New York City.[70] Gaebelein fondly remembered those days:

> I had turned over to him the printing of *Our Hope*, and as he was a beloved brother in the Lord I had confided in him as to my vision of ministry

---

[69] Ibid., 56-57.

[70] Fitch was already publishing the Bible Correspondence Course being written by C. I. Scofield. See Arno C. Gaebelein, *The History of the Scofield Reference Bible* (New York: Our Hope Publications, 1943), 37.

and about my separation from denominationalism. He felt very happy about it, for he was one of the "Brethren," commonly called "Plymouth Brethren," of whose existence I knew nothing till I met Mr. Fitch. Knowing my struggles, he was very generous in his fellowship and helped in many ways.[71]

Thus, major support for the life-changing decisions Gaebelein made at the time came from his first contact among the Plymouth Brethren. However, it would be a mistake to believe that the Brethren influence stood alone in those meetings. Ernst Stroeter had been part of the conference movement years longer than Gaebelein.[72] Yet he did not take the same road as Gaebelein.

Nonetheless, among the Niagara men, it was Gaebelein's ties to the Brethren that deepened. Gaebelein's association with Fitch led to his leadership in daily and weekly Bible studies involving other Brethren men as well. Gaebelein mentioned John T. Pirie, Frederick K. Day, Hugh R. Monro, and Alwyn Ball as new friends among the Brethren. One result of his fellowship with these men was clear in Gaebelein's mind thirty years later:

> Through these brethren beloved I had become acquainted with the works of those able and godly men who were used in the great spiritual movement of the Brethren in the early part of the nineteenth century, John Nelson Darby and others. I found in his writings, and in the works of William Kelly, McIntosh, F. W. Grant, Bellett and others the soul food I needed. I esteem these men next to the Apostles in their sound and spiritual teaching.[73]

Here the influence of Darbyism on Gaebelein is admitted.

---

[71] Gaebelein, *Autobiography*, 83.

[72] For example, Stroeter appeared at the International Prophetic Conference held in Chicago in November 1886. He spoke on the premillennial coming of Christ. For a reprint of the message see Ernst F. Stroeter, "Christ's Second Coming Premillennial," in *The Prophecy Conference Movement*, ed. Donald W. Dayton (New York: Garland Publishing Co., 1988), 14-20.

[73] Gaebelein, *Autobiography*, 84-85.

However, it is also clear that Gaebelein had no knowledge of the Brethren and of Darby until 1898.[74] His conversion to premillenialism in 1887 was only indirectly influenced by Darby through Guers. Nonetheless, at this juncture one can safely argue that Gaebelein became, due to Brethren influence, more entrenched in premillennialism with a firmer distinction in his mind between Israel and the Church. Gaebelein clearly grouped together in his thinking the rejection of his Methodist denomination, the abandonment of Messianic Judaism, and his first exposure to the Plymouth Brethren. In this light, there can be no doubt that the contact with the Brethren played a major contributing role to the formulation of Gaebelein's ideas.

However, one must not look at this shift in Gaebelein's theology as a wholesale surrender to Brethren thinking.[75] Gaebelein cautiously added a twist from his own deliberation as he wrapped up the chapter discussing these dramatic changes in 1899:

> But as for an actual affiliation with any of the numerous parties of Brethrenism I could not consent to this, for I found that the party-spirit among these different divisions was even more sectarian than the sectarianism of the larger denominations. Nor did I feel that it was my commission to denounce denominations, as is so often done. Denominationalism exists, and there is nothing that will change it. But my commission was to go and minister the Truth wherever the Lord would open a door for His servant.[76]

Gaebelein told of a later encounter with what he called the "exclusive party of the Open Brethren." His response to one particular individual of that group was that "I include in my love and fellowship all the saints of God irrespective of name, or

---

[74] This may mean that Gaebelein had not yet met C. I. Scofield until this time. Fitch may have been the one who introduced the younger Gaebelein to the noted Bible teacher. However, an earlier meeting cannot be ruled out because of the growing fellowship of Gaebelein with the Niagara circle going back to 1893.

[75] Sandeen made this mistake when he referred to Gaebelein as a "virtual convert" to Brethren theology (*Roots of Fundamentalism*, 215).

[76] Gaebelein, *Autobiography*, 85.

sect, or party; that all whom the Lord has received, I receive."[77] Gaebelein apparently felt that the Brethren had not put into practice the principles that they were teaching. His own personal application was to remain independent for the rest of his life and ministry.[78]

The Controversy Over the Timing of the Rapture

Shortly after his conversion to the "new commission," Gaebelein had an opportunity to demonstrate his commitment to the newfound emphasis on the unique nature of the church. The premillennial camp of evangelicalism was embroiled in a controversy over the imminency of Christ's return. Would Christ return before the Tribulation to rapture the church or would the church be forced to endure that time of testing on the earth before the coming of the Lord? Another way of wording the question was to inquire if there was a distinction between Christ coming *for* the saints and Christ coming *with* the saints.[79] Sandeen pointed out that this debate was the American repeat of the Darby-Newton conflict in England in the 1840s concerning the secret rapture.[80] It also marked the breakup of the Niagara Bible Conferences when the contention came to a head in 1901.[81] Sandeen may again have overstated the case when he suggested that the split in

---

[77] Ibid., 192-93.

[78] This may mean that Gaebelein was unwilling to divorce himself from the mainstream of American dispensationalism which accepted the Darby approach to prophetic topics, but refused to take separation as seriously as Darby had done. Gaebelein's hesitancy to preach against denominationalism points in this direction. On the other hand, it could also mean that Gaebelein took the Darby doctrine to its logical conclusion of withdrawal from institutionalism of any kind since he involved all groups in his decision including the Brethren. See George M. Marsden, *Fundamentalism and American Culture: The Shaping of Twentieth-Century Evangelicalism, 1870-1925*, (New York: Oxford University Press, 1980), 70. The combination certainly made Gaebelein a unique figure in premillennial fundamentalism at that time.

[79] Gaebelein worded the controversy this way (*History of the Scofield Reference Bible*, 40-41).

[80] Sandeen, *Roots of Fundamentalism*, 219.

[81] Ibid., 212-13. See also Marsden, *Fundamentalism*, 93. Following Sandeen's lead, Marsden added that the international prophetic conferences were not held from 1901 until 1914 because of the controversy.

the dispensational fundamentalist camp prevented a victory over the rise of criti-cal views in the American churches.[82] However, the issue was not minor, although Gaebelein curiously toned down this dispute in his autobiography.[83]

On one side was the major instigator of the discussions, Robert Cameron, a Baptist pastor in Boston, who came to believe strongly that the church would go through the Tribulation. He was joined by Nathaniel West and William J. Erdman. The latter served as an editor with Gaebelein and Stroeter of *Our Hope* and contributed several articles in the early years of the magazine. Gaebelein and C. I. Scofield formed the major duo on the pretribulation side.

Although initial salvos were couched in friendly terms, the journals were soon filled with intensely negative retorts.[84] Gaebelein in February of 1901 writes in the pages of *Our Hope*:

---

[82] Sandeen, *Roots of Fundamentalism*, 208. Members from both sides continued to fellowship in some way as evidenced by the appearance of William J. Erdman's name among the associate editors of the *Scofield Reference Bible* in spite of his acceptance of posttribulationism. In addition, cooperation between premillennialists and other conservatives was demonstrated by Gaebelein's contribution to *The Fundamentals*. It is questionable whether a united front on this issue would have prevented the advance of liberalism in the churches.

[83] Gaebelein commented in a later section of his autobiography: "In 1901 and 1902 *Our Hope* almost doubled its subscription list. It came about in a strange way. A certain magazine, which no longer exists and whose Editor is also gone home, so that I do not care to mention either, attacked my testimony on prophetic lines. Everything was done to belittle my efforts. A whole issue was devoted to discredit me in every way. I kept silent and did a lot of praying those days and at the same time I continued to teach the truth through my pages. Then letters came from everywhere. They wanted sample copies of that paper they had read about. Others admired the Christian spirit in not answering back. One brother wrote that he subscribed for the other magazine not alone for himself, but for thirty other friends, and he transferred the whole list to me. About two thousand new subscribers came to me in this way." See Gaebelein, *Autobiography*, 161. However, Gae-belein made the topic a major item of discussion shortly before his own death when he recited the history of the Scofield Reference Bible. See Gaebelein, *History of the Scofield Reference Bible*, 37-50. Consequently, one can assume that Gaebelein did not discuss fully all items of major sig-nificance in his memoirs which were written in 1930.

[84] See William J. Erdman, "The Oral Teachings of St. Paul at Thessalonica," *Our Hope* 5 (July 1898):17-19. Gaebelein's response to Erdman was given in *Our Hope* four months later, Arno C. Gaebelein, "Our Blessed Hope," *Our Hope* 5 (November 1898): 156-62. What is interesting about this response by Gaebelein is that it comes only a few months after his first meeting with Fitch and the other Plymouth Brethren. The quickness with which Gaebelein took up the cause may suggest their increased influence although it is possible that the general teaching of the Bible conferences gained more weight as he participated in them.

38

The post-tribulation teaching, that the church, the one body, will pass through the great tribulation or a part of it, is a theory which seems to have unsettled not a few. It is a theory which cannot be proven from the scriptures; all scriptural proofs which are advanced to sustain this theory are insufficient, and Jewish events relating to the future remnant of Israel and the church, what she is and her high calling, are not distinguished. The scriptures are all on the other side, namely, that the church will *not* pass through the tribulation but the whole church, that saints who have fallen asleep in Jesus and *all* living believers, will be taken up *before* that time of trouble and distress comes. Some of our readers have written us about this new theory. Others were disturbed by it, but have been delivered from its influence. We have noticed in a number of cases that whenever those who believed in the imminency of the coming of the Lord had, through the teaching of some one, accepted the post-tribulation theory, there seemed to be a sad relapse, and soon the blessed Hope was no longer mentioned. No one can continue to give out a true, scriptural, *edifying* testimony of the coming of the Lord who believes that certain events must come to pass before the Lord comes or that the church will pass through the tribulation.[85]

To Gaebelein the evidence was overwhelming. The post-tribulation view was unsettling, totally unscriptural, destructive of the overall doctrine of premillennialism, and not conducive for the edifying of the saints. Perhaps most important, however, was its blurring of the distinction between the nation of Israel and the church as they are made to share the same Tribulation. This last point, more than the others, reveals that Gaebelein had become firmly established in Darby's view of this matter.[86]

The next month Cameron responded angrily with his own exegesis in *Watchword and Truth*:

---

[85] Arno C. Gaebelein, "The Post-Tribulation Theory," *Our Hope* 7 (February 1901): 261-62. Sandeen caustically remarked that with this statement "Gaebelein had, in effect, excommunicated the postribulationists and had begun to treat them as defectors from the grand old party" (*Roots of Fundamentalism*, 216).

[86] There is evidence that Scofield was speaking through Gaebelein in *Our Hope*. An article in *Our Hope* was published without the author's name in February, 1902. It was not until 1943 that Gaebelein revealed that it was Scofield's pen addressing the issue of the any-moment rapture. See Gaebelein, *Scofield Reference Bible*, 43-44. It is not unlikely that Scofield influenced Gaebelein's own articles as well. Between 1900 and 1902 the pair met frequently (39-40).

Now, if Peter and James and John and Paul gave "a true, scriptural, *edify-ing* testimony of the coming of the Lord," while believing "that certain events must come to pass before the Lord comes," then we, too, can "Give out a true, scriptural, *edifying* testimony of the coming of the Lord," while expecting events to transpire. If these men had the right attitude of heart towards the return of the Lord,-- and no one can have any doubt on that point,--then the expectation of events preceding the Lord's return did not destroy that right attitude of heart, for they did expect events to come first.[87]

In spite of Cameron's protests, the grand winners of the American debate were Gaebelein and Scofield.[88] Although both Cameron and Gaebelein continued as editors of their respective magazines, *Our Hope* became the national favorite while the converts to Cameron's side grew fewer in number.[89] Of course, the debate raged on down through the years. In a book review in September, 1912, Cameron criticized *The Coming One*, written by Albert B. Simpson, founder of the Christian Missionary Alliance. He ridiculed the book for its crass dependence upon "Edward Irving's theory of the secret Rapture before the Tribulation" which he felt was the source of the Darby doctrine.[90]

---

[87] Robert Cameron, "Confusion on the Lord's Coming," *Watchword and Truth* 23 (March 1901): 70-71.

[88] Unfortunately, Sandeen was probably correct when he remarked that the controversy centered around more than theology (*Roots of Fundamentalism*, 216-17). Cameron had essentially merged his magazine, *The Watchword*, with Brookes' periodical, *The Truth*, upon the death of the latter in 1897 to form *The Watchword and Truth*. The aggressive Gaebelein, as the relative newcomer to the premillennial conference movement, posed a threat to the leadership. At stake was the claim to be the rightful heir to James Brookes as the national spokesman. In this aspect of the debate, Cameron showed more sensitivity than Gaebelein, who had, at times, a tendency toward harshness. In later years Gaebelein would note that "there was a most satisfactory result of this controversy. It added to the mailing lists of *Our Hope* hundreds of new subscribers, many of whom had followed the controversy in connection with the Niagara Conference" (*Scofield Reference Bible*, 44). Yet in the same article, Gaebelein showed clearly that, for him, the issue was primarily theological and only secondarily political.

[89] Sandeen, *Roots of Fundamentalism*, 220.

[90] Robert Cameron, "Review of *The Coming One* by Albert B. Simpson," *Watchword and Truth* 34 (September 1912): 271.

40

Just before he died (ca. 1922), Cameron's last book was published entitled *Scriptural Truth About the Lord's Return*.[91] It contained less sensitivity than his earlier writings. He wrote at times almost bitterly as he attempted to show that his position was a majority view within the ranks of fundamentalism. His main goal was to prove that many great names such as George Muller and James Brookes changed their minds before they died and adopted post-tribulationalism.[92] Apparently, Cameron never recovered emotionally from the loss of the debate to Gaebelein. However, he also firmly held his convictions to the end.

The Extension of the Conference Ministry

With the emergence of Gaebelein as one of the leaders of the premillennial camp at the turn of the century, several consequences become readily apparent. First, Gaebelein's relationship with C. I. Scofield was solidified, a relationship that deserves more attention in a later section. For the first two decades of the twentieth century, Scofield and Gaebelein were perhaps the two most prominent names in the world of dispensational premillennialism on the American scene.

Second, Gaebelein and Scofield teamed up to attempt to do for the premillennial movement in the early twentieth century what James Brookes had done for the latter part of the nineteenth century. Their desire was to maintain a witness to the premillennial and pretribulational coming of Christ as had been done in the Niagara Conferences. Scofield suggested a conference in the Park Street Congregational Church in Boston which Gaebelein promptly orchestrated in February, 1901. At this conference there was a sense of urgency about formally establishing summer conferences, so that Niagara, in a new form, might be continued. Gaebelein wrote:

---

[91] Robert Cameron, *Scriptural Truth About the Lord's Return*, (New York: Fleming H. Revell, 1922).

[92] Ibid., 58, 146.

It was during the first conference, in 1901, that Dr. Scofield, F. E. Fitch, Alwyn Ball, Jr., and the writer conversed about perpetuating the testimony of the extinct Niagara Conference in a new summer Bible conference. We all agreed with Dr. Scofield that plans should be made at once. The list of subscribers to *The Truth*, many of whom supported the Niagara Conference, had been handed to the writer by Dr. Brookes before his home call, in order to help *Our Hope*, and Dr. Scofield thought that not a few of the attendants of Niagara could be interested in a new movement.[93]

As a result of these discussions, a summer Bible conference was announced to be held at Sea Cliff on Long Island, New York, on July 23-29 (1901).[94] An elaborate write-up advertising the conference appeared in the July issue of *Our Hope* announcing the need for securing lodging for those coming in expectation of a large crowd.[95] Gaebelein reported that his hope was realized the next month.[96] The September issue of *Our Hope* was a printing of the conference sermons.

Gaebelein gave every appearance that he virtually controlled the conference. In his opening address he expressed the sentiment of the moment for him:

> We gather in view of the approaching day. The blessed Hope of His Coming, the IMMINENCY of the coming of the Lord and all that which is connected with it for Israel, the nations and creation will be made very prominent in the studies here in Sea Cliff.[97]

Gaebelein placed the word *imminency* in bold letters for the readers of *Our Hope*. The any-moment rapture concept was going to be taught as a central truth of these conferences. In addition, Gaebelein's listing of Israel first (and the surprising ab-

---

[93] Gaebelein, *Scofield Reference Bible*, 40.

[94] One should understand that Gaebelein continued to speak at various locations as requests would come. The purpose of the Sea Cliff Conference was to maintain a national scope. Other conferences, regional and local, were ongoing. See Sandeen, *Roots of Fundamentalism*, 221-22.

[95] Arno C. Gaebelein, "Editorial Notes," *Our Hope* 8 (July 1901): 3-4.

[96] Arno C. Gaebelein, "Editorial Notes," *Our Hope* 8 (August 1901): 49-50.

[97] Arno C. Gaebelein, "Opening Address," *Our Hope* 8 (September 1901): 96.

42

sence of the word *church*) reminded one that this was the same man who used to speak to Jewish immigrants on Saturdays. He also hinted that the intention of the Sea Cliff Conference was a perpetual, annual fellowship to remember the coming of the Lord.

The Sea Cliff Conferences continued through the summer of 1911. Gradually, *Our Hope* gave smaller coverage of the conferences as regional conferences across the nation began to emerge. Promotion of one summer conference of national scope was replaced by the advertising of several summer conferences.[98] Whether this is to be taken as a weakening of the Bible Conference movement does not take away from Gaebelein's central involvement. His ministry truly became national, not only through the printed pages of *Our Hope*, but by virtue of his presence and sermonizing in Bible and prophecy conferences throughout the land. This national ministry continued for the duration of Gaebelein's life.[99]

Besides the conference ministry, Gaebelein began to publish commentaries on the Bible and prophetic themes to such an extent that he is one of the most prolific premillennial writers of all time.[100] He served as an associate editor of the Scofield Reference Bible, again a point to be discussed in further detail in a later section. He contributed one article in *The Fundamentals* dedicated to proving the inspiration of the Bible through its accurate prophecy.[101] In addition, the Evangeli-

---

[98] The last time that the Sea Cliff Conference was announced by itself was 1907. See Arno C. Gaebelein, "Editorial Notes," *Our Hope* 14 (July 1907): 17. In 1910 a Southern Bible Conference was announced to be held in Asheville, North Carolina along with a Rocky Mountain Conference in Denver, Colorado (Arno C. Gaebelein, "Editorial Notes," *Our Hope* 17 [July 1910]: 12). By the summer of 1912 the conference announcements had become a long list of meetings at various locations around the country. Sea Cliff had also been replaced by meetings at Stony Brook (Arno C. Gaebelein, "Editorial Notes," *Our Hope* 19 [July 1912]: 15).

[99] See Gaebelein, *Autobiography*, 116-18.

[100] The amount of material produced by Gaebelein probably exceeds that written by Brookes and Scofield combined.

[101] Arno C. Gaebelein, "Fulfilled Prophecy, a Potent Argument for the Bible," in *The Fundamentals: A Testimony to the Truth*, ed. Reuben A. Torrey (Chicago: Testimony Publishing Co., 1910), 11:55-86.

cal Theological College (now Dallas Theological Seminary), founded in 1924 in Dallas, Texas, became his home for one month a year from 1924 until 1931 while he served as a seriatim Bible teacher for President Lewis Sperry Chafer, an understudy of Scofield.[102] This breadth of ministry exhibited the attainments of a man of national influence in the premillennial realm, an influence exercised primarily through conferences and by the pages of *Our Hope*.

The Holocaust Years

During the last fifteen years of Gaebelein's life (1931-45), the conference ministry continued, but at times Gaebelein's age forced him to slow down.[103] He also continued to write books as well as edit formally (and informally after 1939) the magazine *Our Hope*.[104] No major controversy with respect to theology, such as the earlier rapture debate, occurred during this time of his life.

However, smaller theological controversies seemed to be a natural part of his ministry. In response to an apparent invitation from Lewis Sperry Chafer to teach at Evangelical Theological College in 1933, Gaebelein apologetically noted a personal penchant for controversy in theology: "But I confess the topics you mentioned, I believe the Books of Samuel, do not attract me. It is too tame – excuse the expression."[105] He preferred sacred prophecy or the person and work of the Holy Spirit. On another occasion in a request sent to Chafer, he asked for pub-

---

[102] John D. Hannah, "The Social and Intellectual History of the Origins of the Evangelical Theological College" (Ph.D. diss., University of Texas at Dallas, 1988), 265. See also Gaebelein, *Autobiography*, 193. Gaebelein also frequently spent a few weeks out of a year to teach at Moody Bible Institute in Chicago (115), the Bible Institute of Los Angeles (207-8), and Elim Chapel in Winnipeg (178-80).

[103] As early as March 1930, Lewis Sperry Chafer wrote to Gaebelein exhorting the aged teacher to watch his health and preserve his strength, lest some worse health problems come upon him (Letter, Lewis Sperry Chafer to Arno C. Gaebelein, 3 March 1930, Arno C. Gaebelein Papers, ADTS).

[104] Rausch, *Irenic Fundamentalist*, 172.

[105] Letter, Arno C. Gaebelein to Lewis Sperry Chafer, 3 January 1933, Arno C. Gaebelein Papers, ADTS.

44

lic prayer in chapel because, he noted, "I have a fight on with one of these 'heal-ers' who threatens me with everything."[106] Thus, the last decade and a half of Gaebelein's ministry was vibrant. Even a trip to Germany was possible for the aging Bible teacher.[107]

Two main points of interest during this period deserve special attention. The first involves his book entitled *The Conflict of the Ages, the Mystery of Law-lessness: Its Origin, Historic Development and Coming Defeat*, written in 1933, which fostered controversy over his attitude toward the Jews which lasts until this day. The second involves his documentation of and reaction to the rise of anti-Semitism in Europe. Gaebelein's handling of the latter issue in actuality almost makes the first issue a moot point, but continuing discussions will not let it die.

Gaebelein and The Protocols of the Elders of Zion

This writer considers it amazing that anyone can read the voluminous writings of Arno Gaebelein, whether in book form or on the pages of *Our Hope*, and come away with the idea that this man was anti-Semitic. Yet Gaebelein left himself open for the charge with some unfortunate words, especially in *Conflict of the Ages*, which, if read without reference to Gaebelein's overall life and message, could be taken for anti-Semitism.

The catalyst for the controversy was a bizarre document entitled *The Pro-tocols of the Elders of Zion*.[108] This text purported to be a Russian writing by one

---

[106] Letter, Arno C. Gaebelein to Lewis Sperry Chafer, 20 October 1931, Arno C. Gaebelein Papers, ADTS.

[107] Rausch, *Irenic Fundamentalist*, 167-68.

[108] This document was made popular in the early 1920s by Henry Ford who published a so-called investigation into the Jewish Question in "The Dearborn Independent," the official organ of the Ford Motor Company. It is doubtful that Ford did any of the actual writing himself. Weekly articles, which began on 22 May 1920 and ended on 14 January 1922, were quickly republished in four volumes with no byline. The first volume covered the articles from 22 May 1920 to 2 October, 1920. See *The International Jew: The World's Foremost Problem* (Dearborn, MI: Dearborn Independent, 1920). The second volume covered the articles from 9 October 1920 to 19 March 1921. See *Jewish Activities in the United States* (Dearborn, MI: Dearborn Independent, 1921). The

Serge Nilus around the turn of the twentieth century.[109] Rausch described the significance of *The Protocols* in this way:

> The *Protocols* are of Russian origin and are the alleged secret proceedings of a group of Jews plotting to destroy Christianity, challenge civil government and disrupt the international economy in an effort to control the world. This document added to the anti-Semitism prevalent in the world, and when Henry Ford's *Dearborn Independent* published excerpts of the *Protocols*, it gave anti-Semites in America another torch in their parade of anti-Jewish propaganda.[110]

Rausch added that Gaebelein did not immediately know how to take the document.[111] It is clear that *The Protocols* had caught Gaebelein's attention. *Our Hope* made reference to this document a total of four times in 1920 and 1921.[112] The first and longest reference emphasized that the goal advocated in *The Protocols* was world anarchy which was consistent with predictions made in the Bible and which had already begun to be carried out literally in the Soviet government.[113]

---

third volume covered the articles from 4 June 1921 to 16 July 1921. See *Jewish Influences in American Life* (Dearborn, MI: Dearborn Independent, 1921). The final volume covered the articles from 17 December 1921 to 14 January 1922. See *Aspects of Jewish Power in the United States* (Dearborn, MI: Dearborn Independent, 1922). The titles of the last three volumes were actually considered subtitles with the title of the first volume considered the title of a four volume single work. The writings are difficult to reference. Gerald L. K. Smith later edited an abridged edition with a byline for Henry Ford as publisher or editor. See Henry Ford, Sr., ed. *The International Jew, the World's Foremost Problem*, abridged by Gerald L. K. Smith, (Boston: Small, Maynard & Co., n.d.).

[109] The actual publishing date seems difficult to determine as sources conflict. Ariel said *The Protocols* was published in Russia in 1903, but probably originated in the 1890s (Yaakov S. Ariel, "American Premillenialism and its Attitudes Towards the Jewish People, Judaism and Zionism, 1875-1925," [Ph.D. diss., University of Chicago, 1986], 262). Note that these details were left out of the publication of Ariel's dissertation in the book form (*On Behalf of Israel*, 111). Timothy Weber dated the document's Russian origin as 1901 (*Living in the Shadow of the Second Coming: American Premillennialism 1875-1925* [New York: Oxford University Press, 1979], 185). Gaebelein himself dated *The Protocols of Zion* as 1905 ("Current Events and Signs of the Times," *Our Hope* 27 [November 1920]: 297).

[110] Rausch, *Irenic Fundamentalist*, 130-131.

[111] Ibid.

[112] Ibid., 131-34.

[113] Gaebelein, "Current Events," 297-98.

Our Hope considered the idea that *The Protocols* was a forged document in the second reference.[114] The third article lamented the anti-Zionistic Jews who then controlled Russia.[115] The fourth reference to *The Protocols* during this time showed the influence of Henry Ford's publishing of the document. Gaebelein remarked:

> The new volume issued by the "Dearborn Independent" contains a great deal of truth concerning the Jew, especially that part of Jewry which rejects the law and the testimony of their fathers. There is nothing so vile on earth as an apostate Jew, who denies God and His Word. All true Jews will be grateful for an expose like the one published by the Independent. The evidence is unimpeachable. It shows how Jews gained control over the American Liquor trust; it gives a history of the Gigantic Jewish Liquor trust; it shows the prominence of the Jewish element in the Bootlegging evil. There is no question that many of the bandits, highway robbers and other lawbreakers have Jewish names; the court records bear witness to it. The volume concludes with two excellent addresses to the Jews and another address to the Gentiles. This Jewish apostasy and immorality of the worse type which strikes at the very foundations of our government is also a sign of the times. It is predicted in the Word of God that a large part of the Jews will become apostate, along with the Gentile masses.
>
> But not all Jews are liquor fiends, apostates and immoral. There is another side to this question.[116]

It appears clear that Gaebelein saw some truth to *The Protocols*, even if he was not in full agreement with what they were about. In his controversial work, *The Conflict of the Ages* (1933), Gaebelein outlined a world conspiracy against

---

[114] Frederick C. Jennings, "Isaiah Chapter xix - - (Continued)," *Our Hope*, 27 (April 1921): 601. Jennings, a lay teacher among the Plymouth Brethren, wrote the article as part of an exposition of Isaiah which lasted for several months in *Our Hope*. Although in the April edition no author was cited, a comparison with the later published commentary by Jennings shows only minor editing. See Frederick C. Jennings, *Studies in Isaiah*, (New York: Loizeaux Brothers, Bible Truth Depot, 1930[?]), 231-36. Still, Gaebelein, as editor, approved the article. It is interesting to note that Jennings, in his commentary, opted to take out any specific reference to *The Protocols*. Instead, a general statement about Jewish involvement in revolutionary movements was substituted (231). Gaebelein's editorial influence on the original article may be suggested.

[115] Arno C. Gaebelein, "Current Events in the Light of the Bible," *Our Hope* 27 (June 1921): 734-35.

[116] Arno C. Gaebelein, "Current Events" *Our Hope* 29 (August 1922): 103.

Christian civilization headed by Satanic forces. He traced several historical movements such as the Illuminati and Bolshevism which, in his thinking, promoted world revolution. In this analysis, Gaebelein was highly critical of atheistic and communistic Jews who appeared to play a leading role. It is in this context that Gaebelein asserted:

> A painstaking and deeper study of the Protocols, compared with present day world conditions, must lead, and does lead, to the conviction, that the plan of the Protocols, whoever concocted it, is not a *crude forgery*. Behind it are hidden, unseen actors, powerful and cunning, who follow the plan still, bent on the overthrow of our civilization.[117]

Assessment of Gaebelein's true position has varied among historians. For example, a rather recent article by Mouly and Robertson, while generally well-balanced, leaves one with an overstatement about Gaebelein's relationship to *The Protocols*. While discussing the premillennial interest in current events surrounding the Middle East during World War I, they parenthetically add the statement, "It should be noted, however, that some premillennialists were taken with the fabricated *Protocols of the Elders of Zion*, Gaebelein later writing a book which spoke in clearly anti-Jewish terms."[118] This comment is disappointing for its lack of explanation while it gives the reader the impression that Gaebelein was anti-Semitic.

A book, *Apostles of Discord*, by Ralph Lord Roy was written within ten years of Gaebelein's death and associated the Bible teacher with the well-known, anti-Semitic Gerald Winrod.[119] Rausch in an interview with Frank Gaebelein documented how Arno's son was able to convince Roy to change his mind by

---

[117] Arno C. Gaebelein, *The Conflict of the Ages, the Mystery of Lawlessness: Its Origin, Historic Development and Coming Defeat*, (New York: Publication Office "Our Hope," 1933), 100.

[118] Ruth Mouly and Roland Robertson, "Zionism in American Premillenarian Fundamentalism," *American Journal of Theology and Philosophy* 4 (September 1983): 102.

[119] Ralph Lord Roy, *The Apostles of Discord*, (Boston: Beacon Press, 1953), 47. A chapter of the book also appeared as an article ("Religion and Race," *Christian Century* 70 [April 22, 1953]: 474-76).

showing him the evidence of the elder Gaebelein's love for the Jews throughout his ministry.[120]

George Marsden commented concerning what he considered to be extreme beliefs among the premillennialists of the 1930s:

> Arno C. Gaebelein in *The Conflict of the Ages* (1933) presented probably the most comprehensive catalog of interrelated conspiracies. Starting with the struggle between God and Satan in the Garden of Eden, Gaebelein compiled a classic list of conspiratorial threats that had faced America, including the Illuminati who promoted the infidelity of the French Revolution, secret societies, Roman Catholics, socialists, and the Jews. The Jews were condemned on the basis of the post-World-War-I publication of the factitious *Protocols of the Elders of Zion*. . . (W. B.) Riley, like Gaebelein and a few other fundamentalists of the 1930s, was convinced by the spurious *Protocols* of the Jewish aspect of the international threat. This anti-Jewish sentiment, while no means characteristic of fundamentalists generally, was remarkable in light of the strong pro-Zionist convictions of most premillennialists.[121]

Hence, Marsden spoke of Gaebelein's writings in this connection as anti-Jewish. The impression that remains is one of a tinge of anti-Semitism.

Reaction to Gaebelein's statements was not confined to later writers. The League of American Writers published a small booklet named *We Hold These Truths* in which Gaebelein was severely criticized.[122] The Our Hope Publication Office was accused of being a "pseudo-religious organization whose main purpose is to promulgate 'Aryan,' 'Gentile' and white supremacy." Gaebelein was accused of attacking all Jews as communist antichrists and of being vicious in attacks on Negroes. He was also seen as a collaborator with Gerald Winrod and a host of other people associated with anti-Semitism.

---

[120] Rausch, *Irenic Fundamentalist*, 269-80.

[121] Marsden, *Fundamentalism*, 210.

[122] *We Hold These Truths: Statements on Anti-Semitism by 54 Leading American Writers, Statesmen, Educators, Clergymen and Trade-Unionists* (New York: League of American Writers, 1939), 121. The criticism came in an annotated list of supposedly anti-Semitic publishers, organizations, and individuals in America (115-23).

Gaebelein's response was swift, emotional, and to the point. In a lengthy article in *Our Hope*, he accused the pamphlet of outright slander which could easily be proven in a court of law.[123] Rausch considered this response significant enough to quote the entire reply.[124] Gaebelein passionately pointed his slanderers to the pages of *Our Hope* (where he had consistently attacked Aryanism), to his early Jewish ministry, and to his ongoing ministry of preaching the future restoration of the land of Israel (i.e., his eschatological views). He also branded the accusations of association with known anti-Semites as exaggerations and downright fabrications. He closed on a note raising the question of the League's own association with communism. One notes a sense of surprise, as well as hurt, in Gaebelein's fiery words. Ariel correctly noted that Gaebelein simply did not look at himself as an anti-Semite.[125]

More sophisticated analyses of premillennial reaction to *The Protocols*, which included mention of Gaebelein, come from Ariel, Weber, Wilson, and Rausch.[126] Of these, only Rausch defended Gaebelein strongly. Wilson, whose main concern was the misuse, as he saw it, of current events involving Russia and Israel by premillennialists, argued that "Arno C. Gaebelein in his book, *The Conflict of the Ages: The Mystery of Lawlessness: Its Origin, Historic Development and Coming Defeat*, seemed to provide legitimacy for the Nazi attitude."[127] In a rather nasty exchange Weber and Rausch debated Weber's thesis that there was

---

[123] Arno C. Gaebelein, "Misrepresenting 'Our Hope,'" *Our Hope* 46 (December 1939): 379-82.

[124] Rausch, *Irenic Fundamentalist*, 150-53.

[125] Ariel, *On Behalf of Israel*, 113.

[126] Ibid., 111-17; Dwight Wilson, *Armageddon Now! The Premillennial Response to Russia and Israel Since 1917* (Grand Rapids, MI: Baker Book House, 1977): 86-106; Timothy Weber, *Living in the Shadow*, 143-57; Rausch, *Irenic Fundamentalist*, 128-53.

[127] Wilson, *Armageddon Now!*, 97.

an "ironic ambivalence in the premillennialist attitude toward Jews."[128] Weber saw
a tension between the pro-Zionist view consistently taught in premillennialism
and the usual acceptance of *The Protocols* on the part of premillennialists. Such
friction between the two poles was certainly evident on the surface. The theological Zionism of the premillennial fundamentalists seemed to conflict with the hostility toward perceived Jewish involvement in the rise of communism, a system
whose goal was world domination and whose existence provided a basis for prophetic discussions.

The most recent analysis of Gaebelein in this matter has been written by
Yaakov S. Ariel who took offense at Gaebelein's use of terms such as "apostate,"
"infidel," or "deformed" when speaking of unorthodox Jews.[129] While acknowledging the many positive statements made by Gaebelein toward the Jews and
against anti-Semitism, Ariel noted that "Gaebelein's attitudes towards the Jewish
people are, indeed complex and varied, and cannot be judged solely on the basis
of statements he made concerning the 'Protocols of the Elders of Zion.'"[130] In the
final analysis, however, Ariel still misjudged Gaebelein's thoughts and life.

---

[128] The statement came from Weber's book (*Living in the Shadow*, 154). The nasty salvos took
place in a series of articles: David A. Rausch, "Fundamentalism and the Jew: An Interpretive
Essay," *Journal of the Evangelical Theological Society* 23 (June 1980): 105-12; Timothy P. Weber, "A Reply to David Rausch's 'Fundamentalism and the Jew,'" *Journal of the Evangelical
Theological Society* 24 (March 1981): 67-71; David A. Rausch, "A Rejoinder to Timothy Weber's
Reply," *Journal of the Evangelical Theological Society* 24 (March 1981): 73-77; Timothy P. Weber, "A Surrejoinder to David Rausch's Rejoinder," *Journal of the Evangelical Theological Society* 24 (March 1981): 79-82. Much of the discussion dealt with semantics. Weber defended the
language of his presentation by noting that his negative statements about premillennialism in re-
gards to anti-Semitism did not constitute a claim that they were in fact anti-Semitic. Rausch was
irritated that the language left readers with the impression that men such as Gaebelein were anti-
Semitic. Both writers wanted to deny any indictments of anti-Semitism, but disagreed about the
significance of the negative language influenced by such things as *The Protocols*. Rausch wanted
to minimize such statements on the part of premillennialists in light of the larger context of their
lives and ministries. Weber was comfortable in allowing the tension to exist. With the overwhelming amount of pro-Jewish material, and some of it concurrent with *The Protocols*, Rausch's approach may deserve more attention.

[129] Ariel, *On Behalf of Israel*, 114.

[130] Ibid., 112.

First, he accused Gaebelein of inconsistency in his approach to the Jews:

> The origin of Gaebelein's suspicious attitude towards Jews, an attitude that might seem on the surface to deny his more positive words concerning that people, can be found in his differentiation between various groups of Jews. Gaebelein held a certain amount of appreciation for Orthodox Jews, who regarded the Bible as divinely inspired and without error, kept hoping for the arrival of the Messiah and prayed for the national restoration of Israel. . . Orthodox Judaism was, to a large degree, an exception for Gaebelein. It was the only religious manifestation aside from evangelical Protestantism for which he found any use and purpose. Although it was erroneous, it had a role in God's plan for humanity. Gaebelein not only rejected all religions except Christianity but he also expressed harsh criticism of all Christian groups that did not conform to his understanding of what true Christianity was. He rejected Roman Catholicism, Orthodox and Eastern Christianity and dissenting Protestant groups such as the Mormons, Seventh-Day Adventists and Christian Scientists.[131]

Ariel went on to lament Gaebelein's attitudes toward the secular and Reform Jew who was a vile apostate that would "neither convert to Christianity nor await the Messiah and participate in the Jewish national restoration."[132] Ariel agreed with the overall assessment of Gaebelein as someone who cannot be labeled an anti-Semite.[133] Yet his condemnatory tone reveals that he reluctantly does so.

What Ariel missed, in what was an otherwise correct understanding of Gaebelein's position, was that those points show that Gaebelein had no animosity towards the Jews simply because they were Jews. Several specifics can be noted. First, the basic motivation for Gaebelein was clearly theological, not racial.[134] It was one's attitude toward the Old Testament prophecies about the restoration of Israel that attracted his attention. Second, the fact that Gaebelein did not hesitate

---

[131] Ibid., 113-14.

[132] Ibid., 114.

[133] Ibid., 146 n. 50.

[134] Ariel appears to be aware of this, but simply did not give it the weight that it deserves in the discussion.

to criticize non-Jews along the same lines shows that he was not attacking any group of Jews because they were Jews. Third, he expressed positive appreciation for unorthodox Jews who were involved in the Zionist movement thereby showing that not all of his invectives were to be taken universally.[135] Finally, Gaebelein's stand against anti-Semitism in Europe during the Hitler era was not confined to a defense of orthodox Jews. In this, he viewed the Jews as a people without reference to their particular religious persuasion.[136]

The second accusation which Ariel leveled at Gaebelein in this matter involved a perceived change on Gaebelein's part:

> One should bear in mind that the tracts and articles that Gaebelein wrote in earlier periods of his life had been intended for distribution among Jews as part of the missionary efforts. These writings naturally emphasized the more favorable aspects of the dispensationalist attitudes towards the Jews. It might also be that when Gaebelein worked as an evangelist to the Jews, his attitude towards them was somewhat warmer and reflected a greater amount of good will and concern than when he wrote *The Conflict of the Ages*. By that time, he had no more contact with Jews.[137]

Though couched in tentative terms, these statements by Ariel lead one to wrong conclusions.

First, the indication that missionary work among the Jews in Gaebelein's early ministry naturally caused an outward favorable response meets head on with

---

[135] Ibid., 114-16. Ariel would not agree with this statement.

[136] Later sections will highlight Gaebelein's distaste for Nazism and the contrasting fondness he had for the Zionist movement. The spirit of Gaebelein's reception by Ariel is a good example of the mixed feelings displayed by the Jewish community toward evangelicals in general. In recent times, for example, the question concerning the relationship of Jerry Falwell, a prominent fundamentalist pastor and founder of the politically conservative Moral Majority (1979), with the Jews remarkably parallels that of Gaebelein. This is especially true when one notes how Falwell, like Gaebelein, has a deep concern for how the Jewish people fit into world events (including anti-Semitism) and the relationship Israel, as a nation, has to theological and evangelistic concerns for the Christian. See Merrill Simon, *Jerry Falwell and the Jews*, with a Forward by Emanuel Rackman (Middle Village, NY: Jonathan David Publishers, 1984), 15, 18-19, 25-47. Also helpful is David Rausch, *Building Bridges* (Chicago: Moody Press, 1988), 199-200, 205, 215-16.

[137] Ariel, *On Behalf of Israel*, 115.

some convictions held by Gaebelein even in those early years. For example, Gaebelein refused to follow the lead of disgraceful missionary efforts (which he believed existed) in which Jews were won over presumably to false conversions
with the promise of aid in education to become a doctor, dentist, or preacher.[138]
Gaebelein in 1930 angrily remembered that

> The accusation from the side of intelligent Hebrews, that the Jewish Mis-
> sions have encouraged such a miserable spirit and these mercenary mo-
> tives in order to make converts, is not wholly unfounded. Many of the
> converts of certain Missions conducted by Jewish converts are nothing but
> hirelings and a disgrace to both Judaism and Christianity.[139]

There is nothing in Gaebelein's attitude that would soft peddle the gospel or his
views of the Bible. It is not unreasonable to assume that the same characteristic
would be true of his entire theological system.

Second, Ariel contrasted this supposed friendliness toward Jews on the
part of Gaebelein (with missionary motives) to a later harshness toward them as
his life and ministry drifted farther away from contact with Jewish people. However, this also was a shallow suggestion. The same statement quoted above with
respect to Gaebelein's outreach to the Jews in New York City was written in his
autobiography in 1930 just three years before the controversial *The Conflict of the
Ages* was written. Furthermore, Gaebelein's interest in combating anti-Semitism
in Europe had not yet reached the heights it would attain just a few years later as
Hitler consolidated his power and expanded his treachery. It is also clear that
Gaebelein's interest in Zionism was consistent throughout his life.[140]

---

[138] Gaebelein, *Autobiography*, 29-30.

[139] Ibid., 30. See also Rausch, *Irenic Fundamentalist*, 7-8.

[140] Ariel understated Gaebelein's interest in Zionism (*On Behalf of Israel*, 114-16). He recognized Gaebelein's contribution to the awakening of the Christian public to the Holocaust as it was
in progress (116-17). Yet, Ariel downplayed these positive factors in Gaebelein's ministry and
refused to let the whole scope of Gaebelein's communications speak for themselves.

In summary, Gaebelein's language in the 1920s and 1930s concerning *The Protocols* should not be taken as inherently anti-Semitic. Rausch was right when he urged consideration of his overall life and ministry, including the numerous words of love aimed at Jewish people written in *Our Hope* and elsewhere. The apparent harshness at times toward Jews was not aimed at them because they were Jews, but, in most cases, because the Jews in question were communists who rejected God and His Word. That Gaebelein's aggressiveness in *The Conflict of the Ages* should not be turned into accusations of anti-Semitism can be highlighted by the fact that in 1939 he joined a host of other fundamentalist leaders in signing a document repudiating *The Protocols of the Elders of Zion*.[141]

Gaebelein's Opposition to Anti-Semitism

David Rausch has done an excellent service in documenting in detail Gaebelein's heroic stand against anti-Semitism given in *Our Hope* from the early 1930s until the latter days of World War II.[142] During this period of great unrest, he viewed the chaos developing in political and governmental institutions as alarming. In them he saw the potential world conditions leading up to the revealing of the personal Antichrist and the return of the Lord Jesus. However, the basic thrust of Gaebelein's ministry never changed while world conditions fomented. He still spoke at Bible conferences and continued as the editor of *Our Hope*.

The spirit of Gaebelein's global concerns was captured in *Our Hope* in January 1935:

> The greatest sign of the times is the spirit of lawlessness, centering in the demon possessed Soviets, working strenuously for a world revolution. The leaven is working and will work till the great dictator appears. France, falling in line with Russian diplomacy, making an alliance with Sovietism, is opening the road for the triumph of Communism. Hitlerism still domineers

---

[141] Roy, *Apostles of Discord*, 378-79. The document in question was the "Manifesto to the Jews."

[142] Rausch, *Irenic Fundamentalist*, 161-89.

in Germany! The Balkans are seething with the spirit of jealousy and re-
venge. The far East is coming to the front. The so-called "yellow peril" is
not an idle dream. The giant Asia is fully awake! And here are Jewish
conditions. Anti-Semitism is arising everywhere. The shadows of their
great tribulation lengthen and threatening and well deserved judgments for
that part of Jewry which has abandoned faith in God and lines up with
world-revolution will surely come.[143]

Gaebelein's perspective involved the whole world.[144] Yet he concentrated on two

historical realities: communism and anti-Semitism.

Often the concerns about the two overlapped. In defending his book *The

Conflict of the Ages*, Gaebelein alerted the readers of *Our Hope* in 1934 about a

"ruthless Jew" named Kaganovich and another Jew named Litvinoff who held

leadership positions in Soviet Russia:

This makes interesting reading in view of the fact that a well meaning
teacher charged the Editor with having committed a big error in his *Conflict of the Ages* in identifying the Jews with Communism. It also answers
over and over again a certain "Jewish Missionary" sheet which tried to
discredit our book. It also should teach another Jewish "convert" that he is
wrong when he claims that they have nothing to do with Communism.

We love true Jews. We never had, and never shall have any sympathy whatever with Anti-Semitism. Our sympathy is with them as a nation.
We gave ten of our best years to them, but we can never sympathize with
the atheistic, the communistic Jews. They are a menace to their own people as well as a disgrace, and why "Jewish Missionaries" should rise for
their defense is difficult to understand.[145]

Gaebelein sincerely believed that, in the days before the coming of Christ,

unbelieving Jews would rise up against believing Jews, the apostates against the

orthodox. Surprisingly, perhaps, Gaebelein expected this Jewish aspect of anti-

---

[143] Arno C. Gaebelein, "Editorial Notes," *Our Hope* 41 (January 1935): 390.

[144] Gaebelein did not limit his analysis of anti-Semitism to European practices. Quite often he
criticized the Arab abuse of the Jews in Palestine. See Arno C. Gaebelein, "Current Events in the
Light of the Bible," *Our Hope* 36 (October 1929): 230 and "Current Events in the Light of the
Bible," *Our Hope* 37 (July 1930): 56.

[145] Arno C. Gaebelein, "Current Events in the Light of the Bible," *Our Hope* 40 (May 1934):
672-73.

Semitism and was not ashamed to mention it for his readers. As early as 1932, he quoted a Russian source establishing the large number of Jews in the Soviet bureaucracy. His analysis of the situation was enlightening:

> All this is interesting and significant to the student of prophecy. Apostate Judaism plays an important part during the end of the age, and finally it will pass away through the judgment of the coming King. The same fate is in store for the Gentile Apostasy. But let us not forget that there are also Jews who are not atheists, who still hope in the promises of God, who continue to keep their feasts, though in unbelief. The day is not far away when God will call out of their number that remnant, which will oppose the apostate Jews and will suffer during the time of Jacob's trouble.[146]

As the above comment shows, Gaebelein did not single out Communist Jews as the only agents of anti-Semitism; he saw the involvement of Gentiles as well in a large overall attack upon the Jews engineered by Satan.[147]

Such a picture which Gaebelein painted for the future and correlated with current events was grounded in his view of biblical prophecy.[148] This writer is convinced that Gaebelein's dependence upon biblical prophecy was the decisive factor in his willingness to believe the incoming evidence about the holocaust when others were dismissing the reports. He believed the holocaust was occurring

---

[146] Arno C. Gaebelein, "Current Events in the Light of the Bible," *Our Hope* 39 (December 1932): 376-77. See also "Editorial Notes," *Our Hope* 41 (January 1935): 393-94.

[147] See also Arno C. Gaebelein, "Current Events in the Light of the Bible," *Our Hope* 40 (May 1934): 673.

[148] Gaebelein's *Conflict of the Ages* (1933) was his attempt to trace historically the current events leading up to the last days. Current events confirmed that existing conditions made it hopeful that the end was near. The next year (1934) Gaebelein published *World Prospects, How Is It All Going to End? A Study in Sacred Prophecy and Present Day World Conditions* (New York: Publication Office, "Our Hope"), 1934. Although touching upon current events occasionally, this second book actually concentrated on the scriptural or theological justification for Gaebelein's world view. However, again world events were used to confirm scriptural conclusions. In fact, the overall message of *World Prospects* paralleled much of what was in Guers' *La Future D'Israël*. Gaebelein noted that *World Prospects* was a companion volume to *Conflict of the Ages* so they should be read together; see Arno C. Gaebelein, "Editorial Notes," *Our Hope* 41 (September 1934): 144-45.

because he expected it to happen. He anticipated it, because, for him, the Bible predicted it would come to pass.

At times during this period of his ministry Gaebelein maintained an optimism which in hindsight was not warranted. For example, his early impressions of Mussolini were favorable.[149] In fairness to Gaebelein, even when events turned to show the imperial inclinations of the Italian dictator, such as the invasion of Ethiopia in the spring of 1936, it must be said that Gaebelein showed a balanced attitude in his application of prophecy to world events. In July of the same year Gaebelein combined excitement with caution:

> Such startling events, in full line with Bible Prophecy, God's waiting true Church has never seen before. It seems as if this man has prominent marks of that final great European dictator, the little horn of Daniel's vision (Dan. 7). But we dare not prophesy. Should the Church be called hence to meet the Lord in the air we can be sure that Mussolini would be the man. But who can fathom the wisdom, the ways and purposes of our God! He alone knows what the immediate future is going to bring.[150]

When one reads the pronouncements of Gaebelein about world events during this period, he must keep in mind this balanced thinking. At times Gaebelein showed his readers how current events could fit into the plan of biblical prophecy. He did not always categorically demonstrate how they would do so.

Concerning anti-Semitism in his childhood homeland of Germany, Gaebelein again showed signs of optimistic thinking. While fully deploring Hitler as another wicked Haman, he was glad that the dictator was strongly anti-

---

[149] Arno C. Gaebelein, "Current Events in the Light of the Bible," *Our Hope* 39 (March 1933): 548-49.

[150] Arno C. Gaebelein, "Editorial Notes," *Our Hope* 43 (July 1936): 9-10 and "Speculative Prophecy," *Our Hope* 51 (December 1944): 407-10. In addition, Gaebelein published a small book which made it clear that speculation would always be tempered by the fact that one can only come to some general conclusions concerning world events and that the identification of the Antichrist as either Hitler or Mussolini was another affair altogether. See *What Will Become of Europe?*, (New York: Our Hope Publications, 1940).

communist.[151] In addition, his sources told him that there was a growing evangelical awakening in Germany along with the rise of anti-Semitism and atheism.[152] Gaebelein wrote to his friend Lewis Sperry Chafer in the fall of 1933 that "God willing in January, February, and March I hope to be on the coast. There is a movement on foot to have me go after that to Germany to participate in the wonderful spiritual come-back in that country."[153] Gaebelein did not make that trip until 1937. However, his first-hand encounter with Hitler's Germany tremendously dampened his optimism for any spiritual revival.[154]

Consequently, the pages of *Our Hope* intensified in their warnings of the anti-Semitism of the horrible Nazi machine.[155] During World War II Gaebelein matter-of-factly accepted the reports of the Jewish magazine *Contemporary Jewish Record* which noted the details of atrocities against Jews in Europe.[156] Without reservation *Our Hope* recorded for its readers that at least two million Jews, and probably more, had been exterminated by Hitler.[157]

In evaluating these revelations of current events to Gaebelein's audience, one must remember the theological hope which stood behind his practical con-

---

[151] Arno C. Gaebelein, "Current Events in the Light of the Bible," *Our Hope* 39 (July 1932): 27-28 and "Current Events in the Light of the Bible," *Our Hope* 39 (September 1932): 159.

[152] Arno C. Gaebelein, "Current Events in the Light of the Bible," *Our Hope* 38 (March 1932): 557.

[153] Letter, Arno C. Gaebelein to Lewis Sperry Chafer, 10 October 1933, Arno C. Gaebelein Papers, ADTS.

[154] One of the problems Gaebelein saw first-hand was the development of a new German religion which was not only anti-Jewish, but anti-Christian ("Observations and Experiences," *Our Hope* 44 [January 1938]: 460-65).

[155] See Rausch, *Irenic Fundamentalist*, 167-83.

[156] Arno C. Gaebelein, "The New Great World Crisis," *Our Hope* 49 (June 1943): 815. See also Rausch, *Irenic Fundamentalist*, 176.

[157] Gaebelein, "The New Great World Crisis," 815.

cerns. Gaebelein was genuinely horrified by what was going on. In a passionate moment in September 1943 he noted:

> But what is all the destruction of material things in comparison with the wholesale destruction of human lives and human sufferings? We think of the sufferings of women and children. We think of the thousands, tens of thousands, hundreds of thousands who suffered an untimely death. We think of the terrible sufferings of the Jews throughout Europe. It is now a fact that more than two million Jews have been slaughtered in this four-year-old war. We say it again—all these sufferings and these terrible devastations it is our lot to hear about, move the Christian believer to deep sympathy, and millions of prayers are now made that our all-wise God, Whose oft mysterious ways are beyond our ken, may soon end it.[158]

But there was a theological hope that the events were harbingers of the coming of the Lord. In 1931 after mentioning Hitler as the "new political light" in Germany and predicting his failure because of his anti-Semitic tendencies, Gaebelein described the theological convictions that gripped him throughout the period:

> But as this age closes and the final end is almost upon us, new outbreaks of Antisemitism will be in order, till the great Anti-semite, the man of sin, the son of perdition appears. He will be Satan inspired. Satan knows that Israel will ultimately be triumphant; that their King, our Lord, will return. That His return will result in the salvation of the Jewish remnant, the establishment of Christ's kingdom on earth, and will bring about Satan's complete defeat. All through history Satan has been trying to frustrate God's purposes, and his final attempt will be aimed once more at the nation of destiny. He will war against them, and like Haman in the days of Esther, will try to exterminate them. But as Haman failed, even greater will be the final attempt against Israel.[159]

Perhaps Gaebelein's attitude of this time could be summed up from the title of a book he published in 1935. As he looked at world conditions and then at the Bible, he observed that things looked *Hopeless, Yet There is Hope*.[160]

---

[158] Arno C. Gaebelein, "The New Great World Crisis," *Our Hope* 50 (October 1943): 237.

[159] Arno C. Gaebelein, "Notes on Prophecy and the Jews," *Our Hope* 37 (January 1931): 427-28.

[160] Arno C. Gaebelein, *Hopeless, Yet There is Hope*, (New York: Publication Office "Our Hope"), 1935.

CHAPTER 3
SPECIAL INFLUENCES: ÉMILE GUERS, ZIONISM,
AND THE NIAGARA CONFERENCE

In the last chapter the flow of Gaebelein's life was presented with the ministerial and theological influences noticed along the way. The current chapter seeks to expand an understanding of Gaebelein's theological thinking by a detailed examination of three major areas of influence in his life and ministry: Émile Guers, Zionism, and the Niagara Bible Conference.

The Methodology of Émile Guers

One of the more interesting connections discovered during this writer's research into the theological influences upon Gaebelein is the first book on premillennialism that Gaebelein read. As mentioned before, in 1881 through the influences of the Wallon family, the young Gaebelein was introduced to Émile Guers' *La Future D'Israël*. He referred to the author as Pasteur Guers and noted that it was a book in French.[1] There can be no doubt that Émile Guers, a pastor in Geneva, is the author in question. But it is equally clear that Gaebelein was only giving a short paraphrase of the actual title.

---

[1] Arno C. Gaebelein, *Half a Century: The Autobiography of a Servant* (New York: Publication Office "Our Hope," 1930), 5.

62

The book in question is *Israël aux Derniers Jours De L'Économie Actuelle ou Essai Sur La Restauration Prochaine De Ce Peuple, Suivi D'Un Fragment Sur Le Millénarisme.* It was published in 1856 in Geneva and circulated among the Protestant churches, especially the independent churches, of that city and in England as well. A translation in English was provided in 1862.[2] No mention of the work as a major influence on premillennialism can be found anywhere in the historiography of the movement. Guers remains an obscure figure, yet the English version of the book had some circulation as late as the 1930s.[3] In light of Gaebelein's mention of the significance of this book and his study of it at a critical time as he developed his missionary outreach to the Jewish people in the 1880s, a study of the background and methodology of Guers would be expected to yield some light concerning the derivation of thinking on the part of Gaebelein.

The Background of Émile Guers

Émile Guers (1794-1882) was a product of the Genevan awakening[4] which took place in the early years of the nineteenth century.[5] The movement was rooted

---

[2] Émile Guers, *Israel in the Last Days of the Present Economy; or, An Essay on the Coming Restoration of this People. Also, a Fragment on Millenarianism,* trans. with a preface by Aubrey C. Price, (London: Wertheim, Macintosh, and Hunt, 1862). All references to this book will use Gaebelein's designation of *La Future D'Israël.*

[3] A copy of the book obtained from the Elkhart Library of the Associated Mennonite Biblical Seminaries showed evidence of a reader at least as late as 1936, a date rather late in the life of Gaebelein. A certain reader was free with handwritten comments in the margins of the book. Mussolini, Stalin, and Hitler all get mention with the former getting the greater number of remarks. In one example, when Guers gave comments on Daniel 11:43, the speculative reader penned the comment "Mussolini's War with Ethiopia, 1935 & 1936!" See Guers, *La Future D'Israël,* 96.

[4] The Genevan réveil or "awakening" was an expression used by Guers and his contemporaries to refer to a movement begun in the second decade of the nineteenth century in Geneva, Switzerland, composed of dissidents against existing ecclesiastical institutions. A pietistic approach to life, concern for biblical exposition, and, at times, separation from traditional ecclesiastical authorities were the main emphases. See Émile Guers, *Le Premier Réveil et la Première Église Indépendante a Genève* (Genève: Librairie Beroud & Kaufmann, 1871).

[5] Guers was a prolific writer and a multi-talented individual. In addition to his work as a pastor, he labored as a historian and, late in life, served as a military chaplain. There are at least twelve books by Guers known to this writer. Among his historical works are *Le Premier Réveil*

in Moravian pietistic tendencies along with the influence of British evangelical-ism.[6] A particular influence of this Genevan awakening was the Scottish Robert Haldane who visited Geneva in 1816 and started a Bible exposition ministry. He influenced some men such as Louis Gaussen and Merle d'Aubigne who remained within the State Church. A second group Haldane impacted centered around the strict Calvinist Cesar Malan and his followers. A third congregational group, and by far the most separatistic or dissident, was the Bourg-de-Four assembly for which Guers served as one of the pastors in a multiple pastor scheme.[7]

---

mentioned in a previous note; *Histoire Abrégée de l'Église de Jésus-Christ, Principalement Pendant Les Siècles du Moyen Âge, Rattachee Aux Grands Traits de la Prophétie*, (Genève: Madame Susan Guers, 1833); *Notice Historique sur l'Église Évangélique Libre de Genève*, (Genève: n.p., 1875); *Vie de Henri Pyt, Ministre de la Parole de Dieu*, (Toulouse: Delhorbe, 1850); *Les Droits de la Papauté et le Devoir Actuel de la France*, (Lyon: P.-N. Josserand, 1871); *Les Prisonniers Français en Allemagne*, (Lyon: J. Rossier, 1871). The last work was probably included in a larger work entitled *How French Soldiers Fared in German Prisons: Being the Reminiscences of a French Army Chaplain During and After the Franco-German War*, ed. Henry Hayward, (London: Dean and Son, 1890). Guers dabbled in biblical exposition as well: *Le Camp et le Tabernacle du Désert, ou, Le Christ dans le Cuite Lévitique*, (Genève: Chez Mmes Beroud, et Susan Guers, 1849); *Jonas Fils d'Amittai, ou, Méditations, Sur la Mission de ce Prophète*, (Paris: Delay, 1846). An interesting work by Guers, especially in light of the criticism of H. de Goltz in 1862 (see below), was his 1853 book comparing and criticizing the views of revelation in Irvingism and Mormonism, *L'Irvingisme et le Mormonisme Juges Par la Parole de Dieu*, (Genève: E. Beroud, 1853). This book was translated into English in 1854. It showed at once the detailed awareness of what was happening in a new movement in America (Mormonism) and the distance which Guers considered himself to be from Edward Irving's position concerning the "Pentecostal" experience. An excerpt from this book was also translated into German and published in pamphlet form. Of course, Guers' primary theological work is the one already referred to as *La Future D'Israël* which was also translated into German (*Israel's Zukunft*, [Leipzig: E. Bredt, 1860]). This German title, translated into French, yields the title used by Gaebelein.

[6] Timothy Stunt, "Geneva and British Evangelicals in the Early Nineteenth Century," *Journal of Ecclesiastical History* 32 (January 1981): 36. Studies are now emerging with respect to Geneva and its relationship to developing evangelicalism in Europe. See, for example, Olivier Fatio, "Quelle Réformation? Les Commémorations Gevevoises de la Réformation à Travers Les Siècles," *Revue de Théologie et de Philosophie* 118 (1986): 111-30; Olivier Fatio, ed., *Genève Protestante en 1831*, (Genève: Labor et Fides, 1983) and Olivier Fatio, "Commémoration: Gevève et le Refuge," *Bulletin de la Société de l'Histoire du Protestantisme Français* 133 (January-March 1987): 115-19. Older works yielding information and analysis about this movement exist: Francis Chaponniere, *Pasteurs et Laïques de L'Église de Genève au Dix-Neuvième Siècle*, (Genève: n.p., 1889); H. de Goltz, *Genève Religieuse au Dix-Neuvième Siècle*, (Genève: n.p., 1862) and Guers, *Le Premier Réveil*.

[7] Stunt, "Geneva," 36.

The relationship between these Genevan pastors and British evangelicals quickly developed into a strong bond. In 1821 Guers, along with an associate named J. G. Gonthier, was consecrated or ordained by a congregation in London for the work in Geneva. It appears that Guers may have joined other Genevans in traveling on deputation in Britain to raise funds for his work.[8] In a practical way the British evangelicals considered the Geneva pastors as national missionaries.

In the growing communication between the British evangelicals and the Genevan separatists, one encounters the question of the roots of the Plymouth Brethren movement. There is evidence that as early as 1824 Guers' congregation was classified with the Brethren.[9] Of special interest are comments given by Guers in *La Future D'Israël* in the preface dated 1855:

> Le présent écrit devait paraître beaucoup plus tot. La publication en a été retardée par des circonstances indépendantes de la volonté de l'auteur. Le sujet qu'il y expose s'est graduellement développé dans sa pensée des l'année 1831. Six ou sept ans plus tard, les traits les plus saillants de l'Essai qu'il publie aujourd'hui étainet complètement formes et arretes dans son esprit. Le principe d'interprétation prophétique auquel il se ratache est le littéralisme. Ce principe, au found, n'est pas nouveau. Il n'est d'ailleurs la propriété de personne. Une dénomination religieuse contemporaine l'a beaucoup exploité, mais elle ne l'a point crée. Avant qu'elle prit naissance plus d'un théologien l'avait adopté. Nous croyons, du reste, à la possibilité de concilier, dans une certaine mesure au moins, le littéralism avec le principe plus généralement suivi jusqu'a ce jour. En soumettant à nos frères le résultat de nos recherches, nous ne requerons de leur impartiallité qu'une seule chose, c'est qu'avant de juger notre travail, ils veuillent bien le lire d'un bout à l'autre en le comparant avec les Écritures, pour l'accepter ensuite dans tous les points où ils le trouveront

---

[8] Ibid., 43.

[9] Ibid., 42. The 1824 date may be surprising in light of the fact that 1826 has been cited as the official year of the origin of the Plymouth Brethren. However, Brethren historians acknowledge that the roots of the Brethren go back to the second decade of the nineteenth century. See Napoleon Noel, *The History of the Brethren* ed. William F. Knapp (Denver, CO: W. F. Knapp, 1936), 1:19-20.

d'accord avec cette règle infaillable, quoi qu'il puisse en coûter à leurs opinions personnelles.[10]

These words from Guers demonstrate a pilgrimage in eschatological and ecclesiological development that mirrors that of John Nelson Darby. Both clarified ecclesiastical notions that led to a separatist position with respect to the established church.[11]

The significance of the 1831 date which Guers gave coupled with Darby's own development reminds one of the Powerscourt Conferences which began in October of that year.[12] There is no evidence that Guers ever attended the conferences. However, there can be no doubt that he was aware of the debates. The main topic of the restoration of Israel, the many detailed analyses concerning the personal Antichrist, interpretations of the book of Daniel, and the Second Coming of Christ, which fill the pages of *La Future D'Israël*, matched the topics discussed at the conferences during the early 1830s. That Guers' assembly had contacts with that part of Ireland is proven by the fact that one of the pastors of the Bourg-de-Four assembly named Henri Pyt represented the work in Dublin and throughout northern Ireland a year before the conferences were first held.[13] In addition, Guers demonstrated Brethren associations with an acceptance of the Darbyite view of the coming of Christ in two stages.[14]

H. de Goltz, a contemporary of Guers writing critically of the separatist movement (including Guers' church, Darbyism, Irvingism, and others), demonstrated a clear connection between Darby, the Brethren, and Guers:

[10] Guers, *La Future D'Israël*, 5.

[11] See Floyd S. Elmore, "A Critical Examination of the Doctrine of the Two Peoples of God in John Nelson Darby," (Th.D. diss., Dallas Theological Seminary, 1990), 16-62.

[12] Ibid., 34.

[13] Guers, *Le Premier Réveil*, 278.

[14] Guers, *La Future D'Israël*, 239.

L'Église du Bourg-de-four entra, en 1835, dans des rapports intimes et fraternels avec les "frères de Plymouth," par l'intermédiaire de leur missionnaire *de Rodt*. Darby lui-même vint à Genève dan l'automne de 1837, et il y fut reçu à bras ouverts par l'Église, et de la façon la plus hospitalière par tous ses membres.[15]

Thus, the process of thinking about millennial questions and the future of Israel which Guers said began in 1831 and was finalized six or seven years later was apparently consummated at the time of Darby's visit to Geneva.

Guers also admitted a second influence involving the Brethren. Concerning the literalism which was stressed in the above statement from the preface to *La Future D'Israël*, he gave partial credit to Benjamin Wills Newton:

L'auteur le plus éminent de l'école littéraliste en Angleterre est M. Benjamin Newton. Il a publie sur la Prophétie, interréttée d'après le littéralisme, de nombreux et intéressants écrits qui nous ont été plus d'une fois utiles. Nous craignons seulement qu'il ne se soit exagéré le portée de ce principe, et que meme il ne l'ait quelquefois compromis par des applications qui nous semblent un peu hardies.[16]

Clearly Guers did not follow Newton uncritically. However, he recognized Newton's contribution to an understanding of a literal approach to biblical prophecy.

In light of all of these connections between Guers, Newton, and Darby, it is hard to escape the conclusion that Guers and his fellow compatriots in the ministry were associated with the growing Brethren movement and were much involved in the ongoing theological discussions surrounding millennial expectations. The significance for this study on Gaebelein's theological method is that he, although he had not yet heard of Darby and the Brethren, was indirectly influenced by them through Guers at the time of his conversion to premillenialism.

---

[15] H. de Goltz, *Genève Religieuse*, 452.

[16] Guers, *La Future D'Israël*, 5.

The Methodological Approach of Émile Guers

One of Guers' contributions in *La Future D'Israël* was the detailed presentation of what he considered to be proper methodology when studying prophetic portions of the Bible. After an introductory chapter yielding motives for being interested in prophecy related to Israel, Guers cited three general principles which should guide prophetic study: literalism, the diversity of classes and privileges in the entire body of the redeemed, and the literal value of the word *day* in prophecy. He also described the spirit and general plan of prophecy followed by five chapters discussing the major biblical prophecies about Israel's future restoration. He covered Daniel, Revelation, Joel, Obadiah, Isaiah, Ezekiel, Zechariah, Matthew 24, and 2 Thessalonians 2 while adding an overview of the nature of Israel's restoration.[17]

Guers also outlined a detailed and interesting chronology of the seven phases of Israel's restoration: 1) the partial return of the Jewish state to Palestine, 2) Jerusalem becomes the residence of the Antichrist and the principal seat of apostasy on the Roman earth, 3) the judgment of Jerusalem, 4) the deliverance of Jerusalem from Antichrist and the nations, 5) the general conversion of Israel by the appearing of Christ, 6) the general reestablishment of the nation of Israel, and 7) the establishment of the glory of the Holy City, and the Chosen Race in the age to come.[18] Guers concluded this particular discussion with a presentation of signs of the times including an interesting discussion about the possibility of the Sultan in Palestine letting Jews return to the land and how it would be possible for the reshaping of a political Israel in Palestine.[19]

A closing appendix to *La Future D'Israël* entitled "Fragment on Millenarianism" attempted to prove the premillennial coming of the Lord, the distinc-

---

[17] Ibid., 14-189.

[18] Ibid., 190-342.

[19] Ibid., 307.

tion between the resurrection of the righteous and the resurrection of the wicked, and finally, the personal reign of the Messiah on earth.[20] In all of these Guers maintained that prophetic study should follow clearly the principles which he had laid out at the beginning.

The Principle of Literalism

The three principles of prophetic study which Guers promoted begin with the already mentioned literalism.[21] Prophecy was to be interpreted just like all of the other passages of scripture. By observation three forms or modes of language in prophecy were seen: 1) the figurative or metaphorical in which images are taken from the order of ordinary or natural things, 2) the symbolic in which images are taken from the order of supernatural or superhuman things, 3) the literal or historical form.[22]

All of these were encompassed in Guers' overall understanding of literalism in interpretation. Yet it is the third case that simple, natural language should be taken at face value which was emphasized while rules for governing the other two cases were worked out. As it applied to the restoration of Israel, Guers maintained that a literal interpretation of Old Testament prophecies led automatically to an understanding that Israel would one day be restored to political viability as a nation in God's future economy.

The Principle of Diversity of Classes and Privileges in the Entire Body of the Redeemed

The second principle of prophetic interpretation which Guers insisted on was one which he believed was simply an application of the principle of literal-

---

[20] Ibid., 371-98.

[21] Ibid., 22-28. The next chapter will deal with literal interpretation as Gaebelein understood and used it. At that time it will be more evident how dependent Gaebelein was on Guers for his view. In light of the debate about literal or normal interpretation, it is interesting that Guers demonstrated an awareness of the nuances and subtleties of the discussion.

[22] Ibid., 23.

ism. Within the realm of the redeemed there were different classes of peoples with differing privileges. Guers commented:

> Diversité dans l'unité, tel est le cachet général des œuvres de Dieu. Il y a dans l'ensemble des Rachetes des catégories distinctes. Il ne faut pas confondre Israël avec l'Église. Il ne faut pas non plus confondre ce peuple avec les nations qui serviront dieu durant le millenium. Israël, en sa qualité de peuple, garde son individualité dans la prophétie, comme il la garde aussi dans l'histoire.[23]

In short, Guers stated a belief in two peoples of God, one the nation of Israel and one the Church. In prophetic interpretation these two were not to be confounded. The privileges were likewise different. Israel inherits eternal salvation and national restoration as provided in the Abrahamic Covenant.[24] The church shares in the glory of Christ, a kind of heavenly or spiritual inheritance which is not as concretely described, but which involves eternal salvation, a deeper bond with Christ, and a locus in heaven.[25]

What Guers has stated was apparently no different than the view of John Nelson Darby.[26] Guers and Darby had certainly discussed these things in person

---

[23] Ibid., 29.

[24] Ibid., 34-35.

[25] Ibid., 35-37.

[26] Some aspects of Guers' view are unclear. For example, concerning the destiny of the different classes of the redeemed he precisely described the church as a heavenly people located in heaven during the coming millennium and the nation of Israel as an earthly people located on earth at the same time. In addition, he articulated the existence of the redeemed Gentiles or nations who came out of the great tribulation which would share with Israel the millennial blessing on the earth. Within this outline of the redeemed people, rank persisted in the order of church, the nation Israel, and the redeemed nations other than Israel (389). This much is identical to Darby's formulations of the heavenly people and the earthly people. See Elmore, "A Critical Examination," 261-70. However, Guers did not clearly identify the destiny of the Old Testament saints who had died. Darby saw them resurrected at the same time as the rapture of the church and, therefore, being part of the heavenly people, although on a lower plane than the church. However, throughout Guers' discussions, the emphasis was upon the church as the heavenly people and Israel as the earthly people (29-47). The Gentile nations on the earth during the millennium, who comprise part of the redeemed, were almost an afterthought. For Guers, all distinctions within the general body of the redeemed will vanish when the millennium gives way to eternity (33). One can reasonably specu-

as early as 1837. It is possible that there was mutual influence, but Guers' testimony cited earlier indicates that Darby's presence in Geneva put the finishing touches on Guers' thinking and, therefore, on *La Future D'Israël*.

Another observation which can be made is the comparison to Charles Ryrie's *sine qua non* of dispensationalism given in 1965 over a century later. These first two principles given by Guers are identical to the first two elements which constitute the essence of dispensationalism as understood by Ryrie.[27] Dispensationalism is marked by a literal interpretation of prophetic portions of the Bible and an understanding that Israel is distinct from the church. Like Guers, Ryrie suggested that the latter flows as a natural consequence from the former.[28]

A final point concerning this second principle concerns Guers' understanding of what happens to the Jew in this present age who becomes a Christian. The Jew who becomes a Christian loses his identity as a Jew. He will not inherit the national promises through the Abrahamic Covenant, but will be part of the body of Christ, the church. As part of the church, he receives only the privileges assigned for those who are in Christ. Gaebelein, it may be recalled, rejected this idea until his split with Ernst Stroeter in 1899 over Messianic Judaism. Therefore, Gaebelein was a premillennialist for twelve years before coming to the same view as Guers concerning the nature of the distinction between Israel and the church in the specific case of a Jew who becomes a Christian. This demonstrates that Gaebelein, although appreciating Guers' work, did not read it uncritically.

---

late that Guers' view of the destiny of the Old Testament saints was substantially the same as Darby's.

[27] Charles C. Ryrie, *Dispensationalism Today*, (Chicago: Moody Press, 1965), 43-47. See also Charles C. Ryrie, *Dispensationalism*, (Chicago: Moody Press, 1995).

[28] Ibid., 45. The correlation between Guers-Darby and Ryrie demonstrates an amazing consistency for over a century. This is not to say that these views have never undergone any changes; see Craig A. Blaising, "Development of Dispensationalism by Contemporary Dispensationalists," *Bibliotheca Sacra* 145 (July-September 1988): 254-80. It does suggest, however, that there may be a clear doctrinal center which distinguishes Darbyite dispensationalism from all other interpretive schemes.

The Literal Value of the Word *Day* in Prophecy

The third principle which Guers enunciated is that the word *day* in prophecy should be taken naturally as a twenty-four hour period.[29] Guers here combated the view that one day in prophecy is to be taken symbolically as one year.[30] After discussing various passages in Daniel and Revelation for which it would be absurd to take one day to mean one year, Guers opted for the notion that one day should be taken as one twenty-four hour period. This conclusion he believed to be of great consequence.

> La notion que nous venons d'exposer est d'une haute portée; elle est à la base du futurisme, ou système qui soutient que la prophétie du quatrième empire (l'Apoc. du chap. IV au XIX) n'a pas encore obtenu son accomplissement. C'est le système vers lequel nous inclinons; mais, comme on le verra tout-à- l'heure, nous ne l'admettons pourtant pas dans toute sa rigueur.[31]

Guers admitted to possible exceptions, but saw the general rule of a single prophetic day taken to mean exactly twenty-four hours. The result was a futuristic approach to passages, especially in Daniel and Revelation.

Guers' Impact on Gaebelein

The seriousness with which Gaebelein examined Guers' book was indicated by his ordering of the book, six years after he first read it, to help him sort through prophecy as he began his work among Jews in New York City.[32] In this light, several points emerge concerning the influence Guers had on Gaebelein.

---

[29] Guers, *La Future D'Israël*, 47-49.

[30] This issue was one of the first prophetic issues taken up at the Powerscourt Conferences in 1831. See Ernest R. Sandeen, *The Roots of Fundamentalism: British and American Millenarianism 1800-1939*, (Chicago: University of Chicago Press, 1970), 35 and Elmore, "A Critical Examination," 38.

[31] Guers, *La Future D'Israël*, 49.

[32] Gaebelein, *Autobiography*, 6, 20-21.

First, Guers' book *La Future D'Israël* was a definite factor in leading Gaebelein into a premillennial faith. The Messianic expectations of the orthodox Jews Gaebelein ministered to dovetailed nicely with the prophetic picture painted by Guers. Premillennialism was a natural product of the two which Gaebelein readily embraced.

Second, the combination of Guers' writing and the Jewish expectations forced a look at Old Testament prophecy for itself. The Jewish Scriptures were looked upon without reference to the previous Christian, and for Gaebelein, post-millennial, interpretations of them, especially concerning the promises to God's redeemed.

Third, it is clear that the dispensationalism that Gaebelein was accepting as his own was first and foremost a way of looking at Scripture, not primarily a set of doctrines to be believed. Guers forced him to think about principles with which to approach the Old Testament prophecies. Methodology was to be at the center of the question. It is not surprising then to find Arno Gaebelein's son, Frank, writing in the foreword to Ryrie's *Dispensationalism Today* in 1965 his opinion that dispensationalism was primarily a methodological approach to the Bible.[33]

Finally, one is led to the conclusion that Gaebelein through Guers has been influenced for the first time by the dispensational system of John Nelson Darby. The influence at the time Gaebelein read Guers (1881, 1887) is indirect. Gaebelein claimed never to have been aware of Darby and the Brethren movement until 1898 when he met Francis Fitch at the summer Niagara Conference.[34] Nonetheless, to the extent that the connection between Guers and Darby has been established above, one can safely say that Gaebelein was a follower of Darby in

---

[33] Frank E. Gaebelein, Foreword to *Dispensationalism Today*, by Charles C. Ryrie (Chicago: Moody Press, 1965), 8.

[34] Gaebelein, *Autobiography*, 83.

some respect before he knew Darby's name. This may account for the rather quick embrace of the Brethren view of the church that appears to have taken place in 1898, the radical change in ministry that marked 1899, and, finally, Gaebelein's strong leadership with Scofield in the rapture debate beginning in the last year of the Niagara Bible Conference (1900).

The Hope of Zionism

Introduction

By reading the pages of *Our Hope* and other writings which the productive Gaebelein penned, especially the reports on current events in the world, one easily recognizes that the love for the Jewish people that began to be shaped in the late 1880s never dissipated as Gaebelein's ministry progressed.[35] One manifestation of that feeling for the Jewish people was Gaebelein's attraction to the political movement known as Zionism.[36]

Although Gaebelein kept an analytical eye on the happenings of the world scene, he was never more alert than when judging events touching the Jewish people. When writing for *The Fundamentals* Gaebelein singled out the Jewish nation for special treatment. In general terms, he noted:

> When Frederick the Great, King of Prussia, asked the court chaplain for an argument that the Bible is an inspired book, he answered, "Your majesty, the Jews." It was well said. The Scriptures are filled with predictions relating to Israel's history. Their unbelief, the rejection of the Messiah, the results of that rejection, their world-wide dispersion, the persecutions and

---

[35] Rausch's chapter on the Holocaust years is probably the best contribution that he makes in the coverage of Gaebelein's life. See Rausch, *Irenic Fundamentalist*, 161-89. The issue of anti-Semitism has already been taken up. This section on Zionism will reinforce the idea that Gaebelein had no personal animosity at all toward the Jews as a people.

[36] David Rausch notes that the term *Zionism* has been widely debated as to definition. See David A. Rausch, *Zionism Within Early American Fundamentalism: A Convergence of Two Traditions* (New York: Edwin Mellen Press, 1979), 59-65. When Zionism is discussed in this study with respect to Gaebelein, Rausch's simple notion of Zionism as "the philosophy of the Jewish people's restoration to Palestine" is meant. See also David A. Rausch, *Building Bridges* (Chicago: Moody Press, 1988), 155-58.

sorrows they were to suffer, their miraculous preservation as a nation, their future great tribulation, and final restoration—all these were repeatedly announced by their own prophets.[37]

Israel's role in history was prominent in Gaebelein's thinking because he saw that role exalted in the Bible.

A biblical passage which arrested Gaebelein's attention was Deuteronomy 28. In this chapter Gaebelein saw "pre-written the sad history" of Israel.[38] Moses had predicted the scattering of the nation, suffering, tribulation, and ultimately, a final restoration for the Jews, "the enigma of history."[39] This last point is pivotal for Gaebelein's view of things. He asserted strongly in his commentary on Deuteronomy 30 in *The Annotated Bible* that "the Old Testament is practically a sealed book to every person who does not believe in a literal restoration of Israel to their land."[40]

Thus, it is not surprising to see the Zionist movement, headed up by Theodor Herzl, become the focus of an intent gaze from the editor of *Our Hope*. From 1894 to 1897, the pages of *Our Hope* were given over to extensive reporting about the Jewish people and the Zionist efforts.[41] In January 1898, reference is made to the gathering of materials for a temple in Jerusalem.[42] The same month Gaebelein published a letter he received from his Russian friend Joseph Rabi-

---

[37] Arno C. Gaebelein, "Fulfilled Prophecy a Potent Argument for the Bible," in *The Fundamentals: A Testimony to the Truth*, ed. Reuben A. Torrey (Chicago: Testimony Publishing Co., 1910), 11:60-61. The story about Frederick the Great's question to the court chaplain made the rounds frequently in fundamentalist circles. Gaebelein may have first heard it from James Brookes. See Rausch, *Zionism*, 270.

[38] Ibid., 62.

[39] Ibid., 62-65.

[40] Arno C. Gaebelein, *The Annotated Bible*, (New York: Publication Office "Our Hope," 1913), 1:432.

[41] Rausch, *Zionism*, 237.

[42] Arno C. Gaebelein, "Material For the Temple Ordered," *Our Hope* 4 (January 1898): 242.

nowitz. In the letter Rabinowitz complained about the two-edged sword the Zionist movement appeared to be.

> At first glance it seems as if Zionism is a sign of the times by which the work in the Lord's vineyard could be helped, because they feel their national need. But alas, it is a pity to say, the Jews in general become very arrogant under the speeches of the ungodly leaders of the congress [on Zionism] and one can see from the Jewish papers that Zionism is at present very hostile to Christianity, leaning entirely towards Turkey and Islam. The Zionists desire to be a kind of Messiah themselves, to possess a State, a land, and a Zion, but without Jehovah.[43]

Thus, Gaebelein at an early date was filled with mixed feelings about the Zionist movement.

However, most comments are positive. Later in the same year Gaebelein spoke in accepting terms as he noted that the "national awakening of the Jews in our country becomes very marked."[44] Following the progress of the Zionist movement in detail, Gaebelein gave the following significant remarks in 1905:

> As known to most of our readers who are interested in the Jewish question, England made an offer to Zionism last year to permit Hebrews to settle in East Africa and establish there an independent "Jewish State." Orthodox members of the great Zionistic movement protested at once against this scheme, though in certain quarters it was highly recommended. We believed and stated before that the East-African scheme would be completely abandoned. This has now come to pass. The Federation of American Zionists assembled lately in Philadelphia with almost 250 delegates. The convention declared that Palestine was the only place for the colonization of Hebrews. They also adopted a resolution that the coming Zionistic Congress, to be held this month in Basle, should reaffirm the original programme as laid down by Dr. Herzl in 1897. This Congress will undoubtedly bury the East Africa project forever out of sight. This is significant. It proves that Zionism is alive and moving in the right direction.[45]

[43] Arno C. Gaebelein, "The Hope of Israel Movement," *Our Hope* 4 (January 1898): 246.

[44] Arno C. Gaebelein, "Jewish Notes," *Our Hope* 5 (December 1898): 287.

[45] Arno C. Gaebelein, "Editorial Notes," *Our Hope* 12 (August 1905): 71.

76

This observation by Gaebelein is typical of the numerous comments given periodically in the pages of *Our Hope*. One can see Gaebelein's identification of two forces working in the Zionist movement, the orthodox Jews who sought a home in Palestine and the non-orthodox Jews who simply sought a homeland regardless of location. This dichotomy within Judaism which Gaebelein perceived fits with his understanding of the battle with Communism discussed in a previous section. In addition, the report by Gaebelein raises the question of what is legitimate Zionism. For Zionism to be "alive and moving in the right direction" it must be a Zionism focused on the literal promised land in Palestine. Gaebelein's scriptural expectations would allow no other options.

Gaebelein's understanding and use of Zionism was most clearly shown in two of his books. *Hath God Cast Away His People?* (1905) and *Hopeless, Yet There Is Hope* (1935). The two books, separated by thirty years, demonstrate that Gaebelein's approach to the Jewish Question and the settling of Palestine did not significantly change during the course of his ministry.

Hath God Cast Away His People?

In *Hath God Cast Away His People?*, Gaebelein began with nine expository chapters on Romans 11.[46] The first verse of Romans 11 supplied the name of the book. At the outset Gaebelein plainly defined the issue at hand:

> In it [Romans] the Holy Spirit unfolds the purposes of God concerning the earthly people He has chosen for Himself. The knowledge of Israel's place and position in God's revealed plan is of incalculable importance. All the confusion in doctrine and practice we see about us, is more or less the result of a deplorable ignorance which exists throughout Christendom about Israel's place and future. The carnalizing of the professing church has been the sad fruit of this ignorance.[47]

---

[46] Arno C. Gaebelein, *Hath God Cast Away His People?* (New York: Gospel Publishing House, 1905), 7-81.

[47] Ibid., 7.

The future of God's earthly people, the nation of Israel, must be understood. It is one of the central truths of the Bible.

Following the exposition of Romans 11, Gaebelein gave a survey of prophetic passages in the Psalms involving Israel, a detailed discussion of the prophecies about Israel given by Balaam in the Book of Numbers, and an exposition of Isaiah 11 and 12.[48] In all of these Gaebelein's goal was to establish that the ethnic, political nation of Israel has a future.

Four chapters provided a correlation of the scriptural promises discussed in Romans 11, the Psalms, Balaam's prophecies, and Isaiah 11-12 with current events. The first one of these was dedicated to the beliefs of orthodox Jews. Showing his great depth in Jewish literature outside of the Bible, Gaebelein cleverly demonstrated that orthodox Jewish expectations are often rooted in the Bible and should be respected.[49] Specifically, mention was made of the return of the Jews back to their homeland in Palestine as an act of God. With respect to the contemporary Zionist movement Gaebelein's analysis was that

> The restoration which we are privileged to see in our times in the Zionistic movement seems to be a mock restoration—that is, one in unbelief—which is likewise foretold in prophecy. The true restoration will come after the King has been manifested in His glory.[50]

In addition, two chapters gave population statistics for Jews living throughout the world and in Palestine.[51]

A significant chapter, entitled "Zionism, The Great Jewish National Movement,"[52] was begun joyfully by Gaebelein, "Never has there been such a

---

[48] Ibid., 85-152.

[49] Ibid., 153-78.

[50] Ibid., 172-73.

[51] Ibid., 205-28.

[52] Ibid., 179-204. Three postscript chapters are added by Gaebelein. One written by himself identifies the power of the North in biblical prophecy as Russia (231-41). Note that this is pre-

78

wonderful and worldwide movement for national restoration among the Jews, since the day when Jerusalem fell, at the beginning of this Christian age."[53] He recited a history of the Zionist movement and briefly surveyed the life and attainments of Theodor Herzl, the founder of the modern Zionist cause. Several pages were given over to addresses made by Herzl at the various Congresses of the Zionist movement as well as excerpts from Herzl's *Der Judenstaat*.

Finally, Gaebelein furnished his assessment of the whole matter.

> What significance has this great national revival among the Jews for us Christian believers? Has it any prophetic meaning? Is there anything in the prophetic Word, which foretells such a movement? These are the questions often asked by interested students of the Word of God. That Israel is to be restored to the land of the fathers, and a remnant of His people to possess the land and receive the long promised blessing, has been clearly proven by the Scripture expositions contained in this volume. Zionism, we wish to say, is not the divinely promised restoration of Israel. That restoration is brought about by the personal, visible and glorious coming of the Son of Man. Zionism is not the fulfillment of the large number of predictions found in the Old Testament Scriptures, which relate to Israel's return to the land.[54]

Thus, Gaebelein unmistakably denied that the contemporary political movement of Zionism was fulfilling the Old Testament promises of the restoration of Israel to the land. He lamented the absence of the Word of God from the leadership of the movement and the political rather than religious overtones of the effort. The movement was one of "unbelief and confidence in themselves instead of God's eternal purposes."[55] Only the return of Christ would usher in the real restoration of the nation of Israel.

Bolshevik. One article by Scofield on the Messianic Question is added (245-70). Adoniram J. Gordon's "Three Weeks with Joseph Rabinowitz" marks the end of the book (273-79).

[53] Ibid., 181.

[54] Ibid., 200.

[55] Ibid., 201.

In light of such statements one wonders why Gaebelein would focus on the Zionist movement at all. Fortunately, he clarified the issue.

> If Zionism succeeds, and no doubt it will, it will be a partial return of the Jews in unbelief to their land. Is such a return anywhere foretold in the Scriptures? We do not know of a single passage which tell us that such should be the case and yet it is evident by all the predicted events which fall into the closing years of this present age, that in order that these events can be fulfilled, a part of the Jewish nation must be back in the land; while among them is the believing remnant, the great majority will be unbelieving.[56]

Gaebelein then noted the future building of a Jewish temple which was necessary for prophecy to be fulfilled (Dan. 11:31). Passages from Zechariah, Daniel, Ezekiel, and Matthew were also cited as requiring part of the Jewish people to be in Palestine.[57]

Consequently, while the overall thrust of the Zionist movement did not demonstrate the ultimate situation that must be attained for biblical prophecy to be realized, there were inferences from the prophecies that a partial restoration leading up to the final and full restoration was possible and perhaps likely.

Hopeless Yet There is Hope

Gaebelein's 1935 book entitled *Hopeless Yet There is Hope* demonstrated the balance between pessimism and optimism that the writer attempted to maintain. Part I dealt with the hopeless state of affairs for the twentieth century as Gaebelein saw it.[58] Gaebelein first traced the decline of morality in the early 1900s, the rise of socialism, and the buildup of military armament before World War I. Second, he outlined the gruesome events of the World War itself. A third chapter focused on the years from 1922 to 1928 in which Soviet terrorism along

---

[56] Ibid.

[57] Ibid.

[58] Arno C. Gaebelein, *Hopeless Yet There is Hope: A Study in World Conditions and Their Solution*, (New York: Publication Office "Our Hope," 1935), 13-149.

with the rise of crime in the United States dominated current events in the opinion of Gaebelein. He also spoke out against the continuing inroads made by liberalism in Christian institutions.

The next chapter mentioned the financial crash of 1929 and continued a discussion of the Soviet attempt to spread world revolution along with the rise of anti-Semitism under Hitler in Germany. Two final gloomy chapters combined fears of Soviet advancement in light of American recognition of that country, moral and religious decline, and the failure of the New Deal. In short, the Depression days of the 1930s justified in Gaebelein's eyes, both at home and abroad, a dismal outlook. In his mind, the postmillennial optimism at the turn of the century had completely been demolished by current events.

Fortunately, Gaebelein added the second part to his book. Optimism was possible based on an understanding of three points outlined in the three remaining chapters. First, Israel continued to be the nation of hope.[59] In light of the morbid picture Gaebelein had painted, he showed that the survival of the Jewish longing for a home land through centuries of persecution pointed out that the "Jewish Hope is a never dying Hope."[60] In this example, the world should take hope.

However, the world should take hope precisely because the fulfillment of the hope of Israel was flickering on the horizon. In the second chapter of this section on optimism Gaebelein again broached the topic of Zionism. A detailed chronology of the movement through 1935 was provided for the reader. Interestingly, Gaebelein acknowledged some theological communication between himself and early elements of the Zionist cause.

> The writer had a special deep and sympathetic interest in the Jewish people during the years 1889 to 1899, giving them a Gospel testimony, and also in welfare work. He met from time to time orthodox Hebrews, Bible-believing and Messiah-expecting, who were members of the *"Choveve*

[59] Ibid., 153-65.

[60] Ibid., 157.

Zion" (lovers of Zion) organization. This society had come into existence in 1884 in Kattowitz, we believe, and was composed mostly of orthodox Jews. Branches sprang up everywhere. When traveling in Russia in 1895 we conversed with some of them and they were delighted to find a Gentile who believed in the Jewish Hope ... The Choveve Zion Societies were the harbingers of the greater, now world-wide organization known as *"Zion-ism."*[61]

This shows that Gaebelein was influenced by contact with Zionists just a few years after his conversion to premillennialism in 1887.

As in his earlier work, Gaebelein here rejected the modern political Zionist cause as the ultimate fulfillment of biblical prophecy about the restoration of the nation of Israel.

We state at once without any further arguments that Zionism is *not* the re-alization of the great "Hope of Israel," nor will it result in bringing the ful-fillment of the promise made to Abraham, "In thee shall all the families of the earth be blessed."[62]

He gave two conditions that were necessary concerning the return of Israel to the land. Without these the ultimate fulfillment has not arrived. The first was the "whole-hearted return of Israel to the Lord, expressing faith in and obedience to Him."[63] The modern Zionist movement failed on this point since its character was overwhelmingly secular and political without reference to Jehovah God of the Old Testament although individuals existed within the group who believed the prom-ises of the Old Testament.[64]

The second condition involved the Messiah as "acknowledged by the or-thodox Jewish interpretations of the Old Testament Scriptures."[65] It was impera-

---

[61] Ibid., 166-67.

[62] Ibid., 172.

[63] Ibid., 173.

[64] Ibid., 174.

[65] Ibid.

tive that "Messiah must come and through Him and His power, through His enthronement and reign as King, Israel's blessing and glory will be accomplished."[66] For Gaebelein Jesus would have to return to earth before he would acknowledge that the national restoration of the Jews according to the Bible was fulfilled. However, Gaebelein would add that the presence in Palestine of unbelieving Jews by the hundreds of thousands constituted evidence that the day of the Lord, a day of tribulation and calamity, was not far away. This day of tribulation was to be followed by the coming of the Messiah.[67]

In summary, Gaebelein throughout his ministry watched the Zionist movement with the understanding that it was not the national restoration of Israel which would lead to world blessings. It was only the foreshadowing of an ultimate restoration based upon the coming of Christ. A pessimistic world could look with hope at the partial restoration knowing that the biblical return to the land with the accompanying promises of blessing could not be far off.

Conclusion

Four observations can be made concerning the influence which the Zionist movement had on Gaebelein's thinking. First, as was shown above, there can be no question that in the early formative days of his premillennialism, Gaebelein had contact with Zionists. This was a normal by-product of his outreach to Jews in New York City, many of whom were orthodox Jews who longed for the restoration of Israel. Furthermore, the spirit of Gaebelein's discussions about Zionism betray a camaraderie with these people that he did not reserve for even some Bible-believing premillennialists like Robert Cameron, the posttribulationist.

Second, and related to this, is the reliance of Gaebelein, at times, upon the orthodox Jewish interpretations of the Old Testament which overlapped Zionist

---

[66] Ibid.

[67] Arno C. Gaebelein, *World Prospects, How is it All Going to End? A Study in Sacred Prophecy and Present Day World Conditions* (New York: Publication Office "Our Hope," 1934), 52-53.

tendencies. As noted earlier, Gaebelein's reading of Guers was coupled with his constant contact with the Jewish understanding of the Old Testament posed by his Jewish friends. Both forced him to reexamine the Old Testament prophecies as they touched upon the nation of Israel. Zionism, as part of this overall thrust, would undoubtedly cause him to focus on the future restoration of the nation of hope.

Third, Zionism with its partial restoration was one of many current events which constituted the signs of the times. The coming of the Lord with the attendant events would come about in a premillennial fashion just as the Bible declared, according to Gaebelein's understanding. In the same way that the day of the Lord or tribulation was foreshadowed by the rise of anti-Semitism, the national restoration of Israel was typified by the political movement of Zionism. Thus, Zionism served a confirmatory use in Gaebelein's mind.

Fourth, Gaebelein's interest in Zionism also points one in the direction of influence from another quarter. The early 1890s saw Gaebelein's first contacts with the men of the Niagara Bible Conference. Those men were already alert to the possibilities of a future national restoration of Israel and the developing Zionist ideas among the Jewish people in the nineteenth century. Rausch has shown that Gaebelein's interest in Zionism was not an isolated one in fundamental premillennial circles.[68]

The fact that Gaebelein was in the mainstream of fundamentalism in this matter is bolstered by the fact that Gaebelein was one of over a dozen speakers at a Bible conference at the end of World War I sponsored by the Chicago Hebrew Mission. The entire conference was given over to "The Jew in History and Prophecy."[69] As Rausch noted, Jewish interests in general and Zionism in particular

---

[68] Rausch, *Zionism*, 53-270.

[69] *The Jew in History and Prophecy: Addresses Delivered at a Conference on Behalf of Israel,* with a Foreword by Robert M. Russell (Chicago: The Chicago Hebrew Mission, 1918).

constituted part of the fabric of fundamentalism.[70] Thus, Gaebelein's interest in Zionism reflected his growing attachment to the Bible Conference movement in the 1890s as well as his own contacts with the Jews.[71]

The Influence of the Niagara Conference on Gaebelein

Introduction

The Niagara Bible Conference movement provided the environment in which Gaebelein's ministry came to dwell. The roots of the movement can be found in the formation of a private conference in New York City in 1868 headed up by James Inglis, an editor of the premillennial periodical, *Waymarks in the Wilderness*.[72] After the death of Inglis and other leaders in the early 1870s, the annual meetings had to be reconstituted in 1875 under the leadership of James H. Brookes, the "founding father and controlling spirit" of the conferences which came to be named after the usual location of the annual meeting, Niagara-on-the-Lake, Ontario.[73]

As seen in the last chapter, Gaebelein was noticed by the men of the Niagara movement in the middle of the 1890s primarily because of his outreach ministry to the Jews of New York City. The men of that significant group became the

---

[70] Rausch, *Zionism*, 53.

[71] Ariel underestimated the influence of Zionism in Gaebelein's thinking and gave only a short section on it. See Yaakov S. Ariel, *On Behalf of Israel: American Fundamentalist Attitudes Toward Jews, Judaism, and Zionism. 1865-1945*, with a Preface by Martin E. Marty, Chicago Studies in the History of American Religion, no. 1 (Brooklyn: Carlson Publishing, 1991), 114-16. He did not like the passivity of Gaebelein when compared to other fundamentalists like William Blackstone who actively lobbied to help the Jews find a homeland. It is true that Gaebelein's interest remained primarily theological and theoretical. Most likely the influence of the orthodox Jews he encountered played a role here. Since the Zionist movement was primarily political and not religious, Gaebelein kept his distance. Yet it must be remembered that a theological friend is still a friend. Gaebelein did not lack compassion on the Jews as his welfare work in New York City and his continual warning about the Holocaust and anti-Semitism prove.

[72] Sandeen, *Roots of Fundamentalism*, 133.

[73] Ibid., 134. Sandeen gave a good summary of locations and dates for the conferences. They were held at Niagara-on-the-Lake, Ontario, from 1883 to 1897.

closest ministerial friends which Gaebelein would have although he would outlive virtually all of them by many years. Among them were Ernst F. Stroeter, George C. Needham, William J. Erdman, James H. Brookes, Arthur T. Pierson, Adoniram J. Gordon, William G. Morehead, James M. Gray, and Nathaniel West. Articles written by such men frequently found their way to the pages of *Our Hope*, often posthumously.

It is difficult to pinpoint any specific influence regarding these men on Gaebelein, Acknowledgments were usually given in general terms.[74] Yet some specific individuals deserve investigations in this regard. By the time Gaebelein stood in the pulpit of Niagara in 1898, he was approaching major changes in his ministry which have been outlined in the previous chapter. That those changes occurred in the context and influence of Niagara there can be no doubt. Of special interest then will be Ernst F. Stroeter, a maverick in the group who worked side by side with Gaebelein until their parting over Messianic Judaism in 1899, James H. Brookes, whose position as leader of the group makes him a likely candidate for influence upon Gaebelein, the Plymouth Brethren among the group, who among other things introduced Gaebelein to Darby, and C. I. Scofield, who, together with Gaebelein, wore the mantle of leadership in the premillennial fundamentalist cause in the first two decades of the twentieth century.

Ernest F. Stroeter

In his autobiography Gaebelein recalled how Ernst F. Stroeter came to join him in the Jewish outreach ministry in New York City:

> During the summer of 1893 Professor Ernst F. Stroeter, Ph.D., visited New York and attended one of my Saturday services. Dr. Stroeter was professor in the Denver (Colorado) University; an able scholar and Christian gentleman and above everything an ardent believer in prophecy, the premillennial Coming of the Lord, and the restoration of Israel. While I preached, the tears were streaming down his face and one could see how

---

[74] For example, see Arno C. Gaebelein, *Autobiography*, 79.

deeply he was moved. I had met him before. His first question was: "Do you think there would be a place for me in this work? I will gladly resign my professorship in Denver and join you in this glorious work." What he suggested materialized the following year, and he became the Secretary of the Hope of Israel Movement of which I had been appointed Superintendent. The Jews also heard him gladly.[75]

Stroeter went on to help Gaebelein establish *Our Hope* magazine in 1894 and continued with him until the split over Messianic Judaism occurred in 1899. In spite of the rift between the two, Gaebelein maintained respect for Stroeter as the above description of the professor as "an able scholar and Christian gentleman" testified. Later in his autobiography Gaebelein recalled with fondness Stroeter's European ministry when he remarked that "he continued to do an excellent work among Jews and Gentiles, also editing a German paper, till the Lord called him home."[76]

The five years that the emotional Stroeter spent working with the fiery Gaebelein must have sparked many interesting conversations about theology, especially prophetic topics. Yet there is no indication in any of Gaebelein's writings that Stroeter influenced him in any way concerning specific theological points. However, on two scores a positive influence from Stroeter can be surmised. Gaebelein's assessment of Stroeter as an "ardent believer in prophecy, the premillennial Coming of the Lord, and the restoration of Israel" betrays a possible direction.[77] Gaebelein was still young in his premillennial faith, having been converted to it in 1887 through contact with the orthodox Jews and reading Guers' *La Future D'Israël*. It is probable that the older and long-time premillennialist Stroeter helped to deepen Gaebelein's understanding of that approach to Scripture. A cor-

---

[75] Ibid., 44.

[76] Ibid., 67.

[77] Ibid., 44.

ollary of this would be Stroeter's interest in Zionism and castigation of the Gentile church for its anti-Semitism.[78]

Secondly, Stroeter, a German Methodist like Gaebelein, must have supplied his colleague with some fruitful contacts within the overall Bible Conference movement. As noted in the last chapter, Stroeter was on the conference scene at least as early as 1886 when he spoke at the International Prophetic Conference in Chicago. He was listed as a professor at Central Wesleyan College in Warrenton, Missouri.[79] This places Stroeter in close proximity to James Brookes in St. Louis. In addition, Stroeter continued his speaking schedule at the prophecy conferences after his association with Gaebelein began. In 1895 he was on the schedule at the Third International Prophetic Conference in Allegheny, Pennsylvania.[80] It is possible that Gaebelein attended that conference although, by his own admission, Gaebelein did not speak at a prophetic conference until 1898.[81]

Stroeter's influence upon Gaebelein was probably limited to providing contacts and solidifying Gaebelein's premillennial stance because of the maverick nature of his ministry. His belief in Messianic Judaism, the idea that a Jew who becomes a Christian still receives the future blessing of the nation of Israel and does not have to give up his present Jewish traditions, was contrary to the mainstream position within the Bible Conference movement.[82] Rausch noted this mainstream dominance of the opposing viewpoint while discussing Gaebelein's abandonment of Stroeter's position in 1899:

---

[78] Rausch, *Irenic Fundamentalist*, 27-32.

[79] Donald Dayton, ed. *The Prophecy Conference Movement*, (New York: Garland Publishing Co., 1988), 3.

[80] Rausch, *Irenic Fundamentalist*, 27.

[81] Gaebelein, *Autobiography*, 71.

[82] The Hope of Israel Movement during Stroeter's alliance with Gaebelein was criticized by the Mildmay Mission to the Jews on precisely this point showing that the position was not readily accepted within fundamentalist circles (Rausch, *Irenic Fundamentalist*, 40-41).

As he became intricately involved with the fundamentalist Bible conference circuit, Arno Gaebelein was pressured to wrestle with the fundamentalist teaching that a converted Jew becomes part of the true Christian
church and therefore is no longer a Jew. A change of view on this topic
was bound to have radical implications for the Hope of Israel movement,
because it was alien to the founding principles which Gaebelein had written himself. Nevertheless, he came to believe that the fundamentalist conference circuit interpretation was the correct biblical teaching, and he gave
up his former interpretation.[83]

Stroeter's inability to sway Gaebelein on the most fundamental point of the outreach to the Jews may show how little theological persuasion he had over Gaebelein's thinking. It is to the credit of the two that Gaebelein and Stroeter remained friends in spite of the difference.

James H. Brookes

The giant and guiding hand of the Bible Conference movement was James
Brookes, a Presbyterian pastor from St. Louis.[84] His shadow hung over the conferences even after his death in 1897.[85] Brookes wrote a doctrinal statement outlining fourteen points in 1878 which served as a general set of guidelines and was
later adopted in 1890 as the official articles of faith by the Niagara group.[86] Although the article discussing millennial questions was couched in general terms,
the majority of men at the Niagara meetings followed Brookes' lead in teaching
Darbyite dispensationalism.[87] Sandeen, commenting on one of Brookes' addresses
at the 1882 conference, gave an instructive analysis.

---

[83] Rausch, *Irenic Fundamentalist*, 56-57.

[84] Sandeen, *Roots of Fundamentalism*, 132-35.

[85] Note Gaebelein's marking of the absence of Brookes in the 1898 Niagara conference at Lake
Chautauqua (*Autobiography*, 71).

[86] Sandeen, *Roots of Fundamentalism*, 140-42.

[87] Ibid., 139-41. Sandeen described the Niagara conference as "Darby's concept of the church
adapted to the American environment" (136).

From this outline it is quite apparent that Brookes was teaching not only by the Brethren method [of Bible teaching], but also the Darbyite any-moment coming. In Brookes' other writings it is clear that he accepted most of Darby's dispensationalism, including the secret rapture of the church and the distinction between the spiritual role of the church in this age and the earthly role of the Jewish nation. Brookes never acknowledged any intellectual debt to the Plymouth Brethren, suggesting only that he became a premillennialist by reading the prophetic passages of the Bible. However, in his periodical the *Truth* he regularly recommended the writings of the Brethren, and he did visit B. W. Newton in about 1862 on his only European visit. We have already discussed the possibility that Brookes may have met Darby on one of Darby's visits to Saint Louis.[88]

The characteristic of not passing on the source where one first received the truth may be the reason that Gaebelein did not see the Darby connection early on in his contacts with the Niagara men. Yet, if Sandeen is correct, and there is no reason to judge otherwise, Brookes was influenced by Brethren or Darbyite views.[89] Consequently, any influence of Brookes upon Gaebelein, like Guers, was the passing on of Darbyite dispensationalism without Gaebelein knowing the source.[90]

Nevertheless, an examination of available records shows that the most reasonable conclusion is that Gaebelein was impacted by the atmosphere and doctrinal teaching of the Niagara Conference more than any direct personal influence from Brookes. Gaebelein met Brookes in late 1893 although it is not clear where. His recollections of that first meeting reveal some measure of indebtedness to Brookes.

We shall never forget our first meeting together. It was in the presence of Professor Morehead of Xenia, Ohio. Knowing that I was German and being suspicious of German rationalism, he made me pass an examination. He wanted to know what I believed about the authorship of the Penta-

---

[88] Ibid., 139.

[89] Ibid., 74, 139.

[90] Just because someone acknowledges a source other than the Bible for his views does not necessarily cast doubt upon the validity of his position. It seems that in the cases of Brookes and Gaebelein, the contacts with the Brethren forced them to reexamine prophetic passages, certainly a positive influence regardless of the outcome of such reevaluation.

teuch, whether it was Mosaic or documentary. Then came questions about the Book of Isaiah, the authenticity of Daniel, and the historicity of Jonah. Finally Dr. Brookes turned to Morehead and said, "He is all right!" He took me literally under his wings.[91]

In some measure it seems that Brookes was satisfied where Gaebelein already stood on theological issues although no record of any eschatological questions is given.

The last statement by Gaebelein that "he took me literally under his wings" is an enigmatic one. The advertising of Gaebelein's ministry in Brookes' periodical, *The Truth*, and the help Brookes gave the young magazine *Our Hope* has been touched upon in the previous chapter. However, one is hardpressed to see how the phrase "under his wings" is to be taken when the two ministered so far apart geographically. Gaebelein did make regular monthly visits to St. Louis at least by 1898, the year after Brookes died.[92] It is certain that Gaebelein made earlier visits as well.

> My first visit to Missouri was made in 1896, for it was in this year that I first came to St. Louis. During the time of my activity among the Jewish people, a branch of the Hope of Israel had been opened in this city. Mrs. C. D. Ely was instrumental in bringing this about. She rented an old church building on Morgan Street, and for several years I made almost monthly visits to St. Louis, speaking to Jews and Gentiles. Dr. James H. Brookes was still living, and he had a very warm heart for any effort to give the Gospel to the Jews.[93]

In spite of the periodic, personal contact between Gaebelein and Brookes during the final year of the latter's life, the statements indicating doctrinal tutelage under the elder premillennial statesman should be taken as hyperbole. In the context of the Bible Conference movement, this may have been an accepted way to indicate minor personal contact coupled with major doctrinal and philosophical agreement.

---

[91] Gaebelein, *Autobiography*, 39-40.

[92] Ibid., 71.

[93] Ibid., 153.

In addition, Gaebelein claimed that *Our Hope* was the heir apparent to *The Truth*.[94] Furthermore, over forty years after the death of Brookes, he published an article in *Our Hope* entitled "Israel in the Gospels" written by Brookes.[95] Thus, Gaebelein demonstrated a long-standing respect for the doctrinal teachings of Brookes in an area which Gaebelein would consider his own area of expertise.

However, major points of change in Gaebelein's ministry did not directly involve Brookes. Gaebelein was already a premillennialist when they first met. Beyond that, Brookes' death took place two full years before Gaebelein's abandonment of Messianic Judaism. Gaebelein's great soul searching on the nature of the church had begun in 1898. No doubt the Conference environment, including the preaching ministry of Brookes, played a role.[96] However, when Gaebelein discussed that tumultuous year in his theological pilgrimage, the name of James Brookes is missing.[97] In its place are the names of Plymouth Brethren.[98]

The Plymouth Brethren

Much was said in the last chapter about the encounter Gaebelein had with certain Brethren men through the Bible conferences beginning in 1898.[99] Men like

---

[94] Ibid., 45-46.

[95] James H. Brookes, "Israel in the Gospels," *Our Hope* 50 (December 1943): 395-407.

[96] It is probably better to indicate some interrelationship between Brookes and Gaebelein concerning the passing on of Brethren Darbyite teaching than to ignore it all together as apparently Crutchfield did. See Larry V. Crutchfield, *The Origins of Dispensationalism: The Darby Factor* (Lanham, MD: University Press of America, 1992), 212. The truth is somewhere between major influence and its absence altogether.

[97] Of course, Gaebelein may be practicing Brookes' (and the whole fundamentalist movement's) way of not revealing the particular sources for theological influence. That is why many of the conclusions in this matter must remain tentative.

[98] Gaebelein, *Autobiography*, 75-85.

[99] The influence of the Brethren upon Gaebelein was through direct personal contact as much as through the writings of Darby (and others) or indirectly through C. I. Scofield. Crutchfield only gave the latter aspect in his diagram of interrelationships (*Dispensationalism*, 212).

92

Francis Fitch, John T. Pirie, and Alwyn Ball were laymen in the Brethren movement who had become involved with some of the conferences. The impact of these men can be seen in three connections.

First, these Brethren became the strong financial supporters of the ministry of Gaebelein.[100] Sandeen remarked that Gaebelein "never seems to have lacked funds for his projects."[101] He noted that these same gentlemen were the ones who financed much of Scofield's expenses when he worked on the *Scofield Reference Bible*.[102] Their support may have been necessary for Gaebelein's ministry to advance nationally as it did. It is unlikely, without major giving from a few sources, that Gaebelein could maintain *Our Hope* without advertising or keep up the hectic traveling schedule which became the trademark of his ministry.

Second, as stated before, through these men, Gaebelein learned of the Brethren movement and the writings of their leading lights, especially John Nelson Darby.[103] One must take seriously Gaebelein's claim that this was his first direct contact with the Brethren. Although the Darbyite view of the distinction between Israel and the church had already become dominant in the Niagara Conferences,[104] Gaebelein noted major changes in his ministry in conjunction with his contact with these particular Brethren.[105] The theological impact was revealed through these major changes: 1) the rejection of Messianic Judaism, 2) the aban-

---

[100] This is implied, but not explicitly stated in Gaebelein's *Autobiography* (83).

[101] Sandeen, *Roots of Fundamentalism*, 223.

[102] Ibid.

[103] Gaebelein, *Autobiography*, 84-85.

[104] Sandeen showed that this could be true even without direct involvement of the Brethren in all of the conferences. He noted that in the early 1878 conference, no Brethren were known to have attended compared to a conference in Mildmay where they were prominent (*Roots of Fundamentalism*, 156).

[105] Again, see Arno C. Gaebelein, *Autobiography*, 75-85. This is by far the most important chapter in his autobiography for understanding his theological development.

donment of denominationalism, and 3) the emphasis on the pretribulational rapture of the church.[106] All of these points can be tied to Gaebelein's newly adopted view of the nature of the church. The first two followed, in Gaebelein's thinking, from the nature of the church as one body in Christ.[107] Gaebelein's view of the rapture question was based, in part, on his understanding of an absolute distinction between the nation Israel and the body of Christ, the church.[108]

Third, these Plymouth Brethren may have been the ones who introduced Gaebelein to a pastor and Bible teacher named Cyrus I. Scofield. Gaebelein met Scofield some time between 1895 and 1898 although the specific time cannot be ascertained.[109] Most likely it was near the end of that time when the two Bible teachers finally crossed paths. The Brethren layman Francis Fitch may have been the instrument. He knew Scofield and had become the printer for the Bible Correspondence Course which was an ongoing project of Scofield.[110] At least, it is possible to say that, with the establishment of Fitch as the printer of *Our Hope*, Gaebelein, Scofield, and the Plymouth Brethren from the Niagara Conference formed a kind of triumvirate of fellowship. The contributions of Scofield make it necessary to explore the influence he my have had on Gaebelein.

---

[106] All three of these points were discussed in detail in the last chapter.

[107] Ibid., 76-78.

[108] A later chapter will develop Gaebelein's argumentation in the rapture question. It will be found in general that he partly argues for a pretribulational rapture based on the theological concept of an absolute distinction between Israel and the church. The bifurcation between the two keeps the church from involvement in the tribulation period because it is a Jewish period in God's dealing.

[109] A general statement by Gaebelein noted that he met Scofield about the time he took the pastorate of the East Northfield Church. That was in 1895. See Arno C. Gaebelein, *History of the Scofield Reference Bible* (New York: Our Hope Publications, 1943), 26. By 1899 Scofield was close enough to Gaebelein to give him advice about his decision to leave the Methodist Church (Gaebelein, *Autobiography*, 81-82).

[110] Gaebelein, *History of the Scofield Reference Bible*, 37.

Cyrus I. Scofield

Attempting to track down the specific influence of Scofield on Gaebelein leads to similar results as that of James Brookes. Specific acknowledgements of dependence in theology are not found. In the case of Scofield, some evidence does exist to show that influence went from Gaebelein to Scofield as much as from the former lawyer to Gaebelein.

Converted to faith in Christ while a lawyer in St. Louis in 1879,[111] Scofield quickly came under the watchful care of James Brookes who pastored in the same city.[112] Trumbull's assessment echoed the sentiments of Scofield himself.

> There were probably few if any men of the last fifty years in North America who did as much to influence and guide the Bible study and Christian life of the sound Christian leaders of our generation as James H. Brookes.

---

[111] Charles G. Trumbull, *The Life Story of C. I. Scofield*, (New York: Oxford University Press, 1920), 35. Joseph M. Canfield, a harsh critic of Scofield and his brand of dispensationalism, has suggested that Trumbull's account, one that was reviewed by Scofield before publication, was not true concerning the conversion date for Scofield (*The Incredible Scofield and His Book*, [Asheville, NC: Joseph M. Canfield, 1984], 78-83). In general, Canfield, who often gave painstaking details from research, adopted the posture that Scofield altered the story of his life to make himself more palatable to the dispensational public. Apparently, Canfield saw many conflicts between various sources concerning the life of Scofield. For example, he cited Gaebelein as contradicting himself when he places Scofield in Switzerland from 1904 to 1906 and at the same time produced a letter from Scofield dated 2 September 1905 written on stationery from the Lotus Club in New York City (Gaebelein, *History of the Scofield Reference Bible*, 32-33, 56-57; Canfield, *The Incredible Scofield*, 186). However, the use of stationery from one particular place is not sufficient evidence to locate the origination of a letter with certitude. Canfield was simply too hasty in his conclusion. However, the massive volume of chronological details which Canfield gave warrants further investigation. For a review of Canfield's work, see John D. Hannah, "A Review of *The Incredible Scofield and His Book*," *Bibliotheca Sacra* 147 (July-September 1990): 351-64. One of the problems in Scofield research, as with other dispensationalists, is the paucity of resources. See BeVier's complaints along these lines ("C. I. Scofield: Dedicated and Determined," *Fundamentalist Journal* 2 [October 1983]: 37-38 and "A Biographical Sketch of C. I. Scofield," [M.A. thesis, Southern Methodist University, 1960], 1).

[112] Trumbull and Canfield are in apparent agreement on the influence of Brookes on Scofield in spite of the fact that there is no detailed information about this relationship. Both took Scofield's word on this point (Trumbull, *The Life Story*, 35-38 and Canfield, *The Incredible Scofield*, 71-74). There is no reason to deny Scofield's testimony about his contact with Brookes who ministered in the same city.

He was peculiarly blessed of God in making plain dispensational truth and the great fundamentals of the prophetic study of God's Word.[113]

Scofield often went to the home of Brookes to study the Bible under the leadership of the national figure.[114] This time of intense tutelage under Brookes lasted a little over two years until Scofield took the pastorate of a Congregational church in Dallas, Texas, in the summer of 1882.

Gaebelein was aware of the dependence of Scofield upon Brookes.

> But the most important event after his [Scofield's] conversion was his early acquaintance with the outstanding Bible teacher of the day, Dr. James H. Brookes . . . Dr. Brookes was an able scholar and editor of *The Truth*. He was a firm believer in prophecy, an ardent premillenarian who knew how to divide the Word of truth rightly.
>
> At the feet of this choice servant of Christ, Scofield took his place. Here he learned what he could not have learned in any of the theological seminaries of that time. Being instructed by Dr. Brookes in Bible study, he soon mastered, with his fine analytical mind, the ABC's of the right division of the Word of God, which he later embodied in a small brochure, *Rightly Dividing the Word of Truth*. From Dr. Brookes' instructions he became acquainted with the high points of sacred prophecy relating to the Jews, the Gentiles, and the Church of God.[115]

Gaebelein and Scofield must have often talked about Brookes in their frequent meetings from 1898 until 1902 when Scofield returned to Texas.[116] Gaebelein's itinerary during that time took him quite often through New England towns.[117] In Boston, Gaebelein held an annual Bible conference and had monthly meetings in the Park Street Congregational Church beginning in 1901 which lasted for

---

[113] Trumbull, *The Life Story*, 35.

[114] Ibid.

[115] Gaebelein, *Scofield Reference Bible*, 22.

[116] Ibid., 39-40.

[117] Gaebelein, *Autobiography*, 71.

twenty-eight years.[118] With Scofield in Northfield until 1902, this gave Gaebelein and Scofield ample opportunity for contact and, presumably, theological discussion.

The implication of such discussions would be the sharing of Brookes' teaching which consisted, as shown above, of Darbyite dispensationalism. In light of the older Scofield's longer association with Brookes and the time he had to internalize the message, one might easily expect Gaebelein to assume the same posture to Scofield that Scofield had held with respect to Brookes. When Scofield and Gaebelein attempted to resurrect the Niagara Conference idea through the Sea Cliff conferences, Gaebelein seemed in control of its orchestration, but Scofield appeared to be the spiritual father of at least the first meeting in 1901 with four messages entitled "Where Faith Sees Christ."[119] In this conference Gaebelein acknowledged the central role for Scofield.[120]

There were several other ways that Gaebelein showed his appreciation of, if not dependence on, C. I. Scofield. Articles by Scofield often appeared in *Our Hope*. Gaebelein on three occasions included either a book or chapter written by Scofield in a volume written and published by Gaebelein himself.[121] A collection of messages or lessons by Scofield was also published by Gaebelein.[122] In addi-

---

[118] Ibid., 104-5.

[119] Ibid., 117.

[120] Ibid.

[121] Although published by Our Hope Publications as a book, Gaebelein's *Our Age and Its End* is actually a fifteen page forward (i-xv) or introduction to Scofield's *Lectures on Prophecy* (3-134). See Arno C. Gaebelein, *Our Age and Its End* (New York: Our Hope Publications, 1940 [?]). Also, a small article entitled "The Messianic Question" written by Scofield appeared in two of Gaebelein's books: *The Jewish Question* (New York: Publication Office "Our Hope," 1912 [?]), 105-37, and *Hath God Cast Away His People*, 245-70. In both of these books, Scofield's article takes on the form of an appendix.

[122] Arno C. Gaebelein, ed., *Things New and Old: Old and New Testament Studies by Dr. C. I. Scofield* (New York: Our Hope Publications, 1920).

tion, frequent meetings between the two continued into the second decade of the twentieth century.

One interesting area in which Gaebelein and Scofield did not associate is a bit of a mystery. Scofield toyed for a time with the idea of starting a nondenominational assembly in New York City with Gaebelein as a kind of co-leader, and other teachers and associates on staff with a view to a nationwide ministry. Scofield's declining health was cited by Gaebelein as a reason this notion was not pursued.[123] Scofield did help start a church in Douglaston on Long Island, New York, in 1915.[124] However, it never became the center for a nationwide ministry of sending out Bible teachers and Gaebelein was never associated with it. With the help of William Pettingill, a Bible teacher from Philadelphia, Scofield's original idea was partially realized with the founding of the Philadelphia School of the Bible in 1914.[125] Evangelist Lewis Sperry Chafer became one of the teachers and helped to develop the curriculum.[126] There is no evidence that Gaebelein assisted Scofield in either the church in Douglaston or in the development of the school. It may have been that Gaebelein's own itinerant ministry representing *Our Hope*, which he had considered a special call at the turn of the century, prevented his later association with Scofield in these ministries.

Perhaps the most forceful way in which Gaebelein showed his homage to the great Bible teacher was through his active defense of Scofield against attacks after Scofield's death. An illustration of this is a letter from Gaebelein to Lewis

---

[123] Gaebelein, *History of the Scofield Reference Bible*, 64.

[124] Canfield, *The Incredible Scofield*, 250.

[125] Ibid., 245-47. See also BeVier, "Biographical Sketch", 87-88 and John D. Hannah, "The Social and Intellectual History of the Origins of the Evangelical Theological College," (Ph.D. diss., University of Texas at Dallas, 1988), 127-35. Hannah has shown that the Philadelphia School of the Bible was really an outgrowth of Scofield's development of a nontraditional school in New York in 1911 which consisted largely of a traveling conference ministry on the part of Scofield and Lewis Sperry Chafer.

[126] Hannah, "Evangelical Theological College," 133.

Sperry Chafer, president of the Evangelical Theological College (now the Dallas Theological Seminary) and an understudy himself of Scofield, in April 1931.

Dear Brother:-

You will find on a separate sheet certain utterances made by Professor George L. Robinson, of McCormick Seminary, Chicago, Illinois.

There is no mistake about it, he made these statements in Bluffton College. Most reliable witnesses vouch for them. If he uttered these miserable slanders there he probably will repeat them elsewhere. Inasmuch as he is a speaker of Dr. Biderwolf's Summer School of Theology, it is my opinion that something must be done about this lying tongue.

I have written him a letter and asked him two questions.

(1) I quoted the words attributed to him and asked him if he said these things.

(2) I requested him to bring his proofs and evidences that Dr. Scofield wrote a good part of the Reference Bible in jail.

If he refuses to answer, or if he gives (as he probably will) a defying answer, I shall take the whole matter into the Court of Christian public opinion and charge him with being a slanderer.

I just want to ask your brotherly advice, if you think this should be done. And if I go ahead with it will you stand by me and give me your moral support?

With best wishes,

Yours,
A. C. Gaebelein[127]

That Gaebelein took the attack upon Scofield as an attack on the whole premillennial position is clear when he summarized for Chafer the statements of Professor Robinson.

Dr. Scofield was a drunkard, he divorced his wife and he was in jail, where a good part of the Scofield Bible was written. He then denounced all premillennialists as being not even Christians at all. He singled out Drs.

---

[127] Letter, Arno C. Gaebelein to Lewis Sperry Chafer, 21 April 1931, New York City, New York, Arno C. Gaebelein Papers, Archives, Dallas Theological Seminary (hereafter cited as ADTS).

Torrey and Gray especially. He also said that Dr. D. L. Moody did not teach the premillennial Coming of Christ.[128]

Chafer's response placed Scofield in a place where others in the past had placed Brookes. He told Gaebelein of his delight to fellowship with one who had shared in the heritage of the organizer of the Scofield Reference Bible notes.[129]

Yet the influence does not seem to be all one-sided in the Scofield-Gaebelein relationship. Gaebelein, as an associate editor of the Scofield Reference Bible, participated in at least three meetings of the group of consulting editors and was involved in a large amount of correspondence with Scofield and others in the group.[130] With pride Gaebelein wrote in his autobiography that he had promised Scofield "every possible assistance by taking over certain sections of the Bible, furnishing the analysis of certain books and assisting in prophetic interpretations."[131] He added a letter written to him by Scofield which gives much of the credit for the prophetic portions of the notes in the Scofield Bible to Gaebelein.

> My beloved Brother: By all means follow your own views of prophetic analysis. I sit at your feet when it comes to prophecy and congratulate in advance the future readers of the Reference Bible on having in their hands a safe, clear, sane guide through what to most is a labyrinth.
> Yours lovingly in Christ,
> C. I. S.[132]

---

[128] Ibid.

[129] Letter, Lewis Sperry Chafer to Arno C. Gaebelein, 29 April 1931, Dallas, Texas, Arno C. Gaebelein Papers, ADTS. Another opportunity arose for Gaebelein and Chafer to defend Scofield. In 1934, Chafer took the lead, on Gaebelein's request, at giving a lengthy written response to charges against Scofield by B. W. Baker including a claim that Scofield denied the infallibility of the Bible (Letter, Lewis Sperry Chafer to Arno C. Gaebelein, 26 May 1934, Dallas, Texas, Lewis Sperry Chafer Papers, ADTS). Baker was a Southern Presbyterian minister who strongly accused both Scofield and Chafer of heresy ("Is There Modernism in the Scofield Bible? A reply to L. S. Chafer," *Presbyterian of the South* 111 [18 March 1936]: 1-4). Also, see Hannah, "Evangelical Theological College," 360.

[130] Trumbull, *Life Story*, 99.

[131] Gaebelein, *Autobiography*, 94.

[132] Ibid.

100

Such statements indicate that Gaebelein was honored in his own right in the area of prophetic interpretations. It may have been that his contacts with the orthodox Jews and his knowledge in the area of Jewish backgrounds brought a depth to the topic that others lauded.

In summary, generalizations can be made and inferences drawn as to the relationship between Gaebelein and Scofield. They shared in the pretribulational controversy with Cameron and West at the turn of the century and in fellowship with the Plymouth Brethren who walked in the Niagara circles. The general heritage of James Brookes and Darbyite dispensationalism was reinforced in Gaebelein by this relationship. However, no specific theological turning can be proven to be the result of specific Scofieldian influence. The duo shared in each other's ministry. The joy of this sharing is sensed when Gaebelein remarked that Scofield "followed my ministry more closely than anybody else."[133]

Conclusion

In the previous chapter a general framework of influence upon Gaebelein was established from the flow of his life. In this chapter, more investigation of Gaebelein's relationships was undertaken. Primary sources for study appeared to be 1) Émile Guers, whose book, *La Future D'Israël*, played such a pivotal role in Gaebelein's conversion to premillennialism, 2) the political movement known as Zionism, which Gaebelein initially came in contact with through his outreach to mostly orthodox Jews in New York, and 3) the Niagara Bible Conference movement.

The book by Guers proved to be a source of Darbyite theology for Gaebelein, although at the time he was not aware of it. It also forced Gaebelein to examine methodology, not just dogma, in his study of prophecy. The Niagara Conference influence on Gaebelein was also primarily a Darby source. Gaebelein

---

[133] Ibid., 103.

actually came to hear of Darby through some Plymouth Brethren associated with Niagara. Through Brookes, Scofield, and these Brethren, Gaebelein inherited a detailed understanding of Darby's views on eschatology and ecclesiology.

The distinction between Israel and the church in the Darby system helped Gaebelein move toward three conclusions: 1) Messianic Judaism violates the New Testament understanding of the church, 2) the sectarian spirit within denominationalism violates the New Testament understanding of the church, and 3) the New Testament understanding of the church leads one to an acceptance of the Darby view of a two-phase Second Coming in which the church does not share in the Jewish time of tribulation to come on the face of the earth.

Zionism strengthened Gaebelein's faith in the Bible promises about the national restoration of Israel. Consequently, his premillennial thinking was enhanced, and in his mind, verified by world events, especially those involving the Jewish people. It is also true that Gaebelein encountered Zionism not only through his personal contacts with Jews, but also from the environment of the Niagara Conference where it was heartily welcomed.

Guers and the Niagara men placed in his hand a theology from Darby which correlated with a somewhat Jewish understanding of the Old Testament promises. Current events, especially those related to Zionism, confirmed the theological package. In the final analysis, the two historical fountains which fed the stream of Gaebelein's theological thinking consisted of Orthodox Judaism with its hope for national restoration and the methodology of John Nelson Darby and the Plymouth Brethren.

CHAPTER 4
THE LITERAL HERMENEUTIC

Introduction

Marsden referred to Gaebelein as a "thoroughgoing literalist."[1] He cited Gaebelein's refusal to believe that German ambitions during World War I represented the beginnings of a revived Roman Empire which was predicted in the Bible. The Roman Empire of biblical days simply did not include the territory of modern, national Germany.[2] Gaebelein was expecting an exact correlation in modern times to the biblical presentation. Such literalism as that pointed out by Marsden, whether to be lauded or not, does not capture the full range of methodological principles practiced by the editor of *Our Hope*.[3]

In this chapter and the next, it will be shown that Gaebelein approached the Bible with two basic interpretational rules. The first is the literal one as mentioned by Marsden above which Gaebelein selectively applied to the Bible. The

---

[1] George Marsden, *Fundamentalism and American Culture: The Shaping of Twentieth-Century Evangelicalism, 1870-1925* (New York: Oxford University Press, 1980), 143.

[2] Ibid.

[3] Oswald T. Allis, a non-dispensational contemporary of Gaebelein, noted that "there is probably no more ardent literalist living today than A. C. Gaebelein" (*Prophecy and the Church* [Phillipsburg, NJ: Presbyterian and Reformed Publishing Co., 1945], 290). Allis complained in the next sentence about Gaebelein's description of "a spiritual resurrection of a literal Israel" in Daniel 12:2. See Arno C. Gaebelein, *The Prophet Daniel: A Key to the Visions and Prophecies of the Book of Daniel* (New York: Publication Office "Our Hope," 1911), 200. Allis correctly recognized that there was more than literal interpretation practiced in the theology of Gaebelein.

second is dispensational integration which has differing aspects related to theology, typology, and application. An underlying unity based on Gaebelein's understanding of the progress of revelation ties all three facets together. Both literal hermeneutics and dispensational integration can be defined, in part, from Gaebelein's own use of the words *literal* and *dispensational*, respectively.

Before one can assess Gaebelein's literal hermeneutic, one must distance himself to some degree from more recent discussions concerning the use of the term *literal* as applied to the debate between dispensationalism and covenant theology. In the 1940s and 1950s antagonists from both sides, like dispensationalist Dwight Pentecost and amillennialist Oswald T. Allis, operated under the assumption that the crucial dividing line between the two theological systems was literal versus allegorical interpretation.[4] In 1965, Charles Ryrie made the significant claim that a consistently applied literal hermeneutic was the foundation for the essence of dispensationalism.[5] Discussions in the 1980s attempted to draw attention away from literal hermeneutics in the debate.[6] Gaebelein's use of literal interpretation would fit more closely with the Pentecost-Allis salvos concerning literal as opposed to allegorical interpretation. However, as will be seen in later discussions, his readiness to add to literal interpretation, especially through types, makes him somewhat of a stranger to the consistent literalist that Ryrie pictured for dispensationalism. However, Gaebelein usually follows Ryrie in literal interpretation of prophecy.

---

[4] Dwight Pentecost, *Things To Come* (Grand Rapids, MI: Zondervan Publishing House, 1958), 1; Allis, *Prophecy*, 244.

[5] Charles C. Ryrie, *Dispensationalism Today* (Chicago: Moody Press, 1965), 43-47. In this assessment, Earl Radmacher concurred ("The Current Status of Dispensationalism and Its Eschatology," in *Perspectives on Evangelical Theology* ed. Stanley N. Gundry and Kenneth S. Kantzer [Grand Rapids, MI: Baker Book House, 1979], 163-76).

[6] See David L. Turner, "The Continuity of Scripture and Eschatology: Key Hermeneutical Issues," *Grace Theological Journal* 6 (Fall 1985): 275-87; Robert Saucy, "The Crucial Issue Between Dispensational and Nondispensational Systems," *Criswell Theological Review* 1 (Fall 1986): 149-65; Craig A. Blaising, "Development of Dispensationalism by Contemporary Dispensationalists," *Bibliotheca Sacra* 145 (July-September 1988): 254-80.

In addition, one must come to grips with the precise meaning of the word *literal*. Poythress complained that the word carries with it some intellectual packaging that may lead a person to view it as the opposite of figurative.[7] The concept of literal interpretation has been used to refer to various ideas such as first-thought meaning which is opposite to figurative, a kind of flat interpretation which recognizes only obvious figures of speech, and the aim of grammatical-historical interpretation.[8] Usually what is meant is grammatical-historical interpretation. Poythress urged the elimination of the term in the discussions because of this ambiguity.[9]

However, this writer is not yet willing to surrender the use of the idea of literal interpretation to describe what is taking place in various hermeneutical approaches to the text. One only needs to recognize two levels of use in the discussion.[10] Roy Zuck insightfully clarified this truth in the following way:

> Figurative speech ... is a picturesque, out-of-the-ordinary way of presenting literal facts that might otherwise be stated in a normal, plain, ordinary way. Saying that "The argument does not hold water" is an unusual way of saying the more ordinary sentence, "The argument is weak." Both sentences convey a *literal* fact. One conveys it in a figurative fashion, the other in a nonfigurative way ... The figurative is a colorful vehicle for presenting literal truth ... Figurative language then is not antithetical to literal interpretation; it is a part of it. Perhaps it is better not to speak of "figurative versus literal" interpretation, but of "ordinary-literal" versus "figurative-literal" interpretation. Therefore in this book *figurative* means figurative-literal, and *literal* means ordinary-literal. Both are part of what

---

[7] Vern Poythress, *Understanding Dispensationalists* (Grand Rapids, MI: Zondervan Publishing House, 1987), 71-86.

[8] Ibid., 82-85.

[9] Ibid., 84-85. The sense of ambiguity in the use of the word *literal* is one reason for the study of Gaebelein. An understanding of how dispensationalists have defined and used literal interpretation throughout the history of the movement would enable scholars to identify those features of literal interpretation that are unique to dispensationalism and those which stem from influences within the broader history of evangelical interpretation.

[10] Poythress' two categories of first-thought meaning and flat interpretation would best be described as differing degrees for the same category. See Poythress, *Dispensationalists*, 82-85.

is normally meant by "literal interpretation." Rather than saying, "Figurative is the opposite of literal," it may be preferable to say, "ordinary-literal is the antithesis of figurative-literal," while understanding that both are legitimate means of communicating literal truths—truths to be interpreted in their normal, historical, grammatical sense without making them say something not intended by the word.[11]

One use of literal, then, has to do with the style of a statement. At this level one is distinguishing literal from figurative. The second level deals with the message of the text, that is, what is conveyed regardless of the style of the text. At this level one focuses on literal interpretation as the aim of grammatical-historical interpretation. It is at this level that discussions most frequently come up in terms of literal versus allegorical interpretation.[12] In light of the above qualifications, the specific discussions to follow will venture to give a descriptive presentation of how Gaebelein defined and used literal interpretation.[13]

General Definition and Use of Literal Interpretation

Gaebelein frequently used the word *literal* when discussing various interpretations. On many occasions he affirmed a literal approach without definition.

The literal meaning of the Word is often attempted to be destroyed. If the Word of God does not mean literally what it says, what then does it mean?

---

[11] Roy Zuck, *Basic Bible Interpretation* (Wheaton, IL: Victor Books, 1991), 147.

[12] Elliott E. Johnson also saw two basic understandings of literal interpretation (*Expository Hermeneutics: An Introduction* [Grand Rapids, MI: Zondervan Publishing House, 1990], 9). The first use of literal is in opposition to what is figurative. The second use, corresponding somewhat to Zuck's grammatical-historical interpretation, is that approach to the text that allows the text to provide the basis of interpretation. His favorite phrase in this connection appears to be "textually based" (31). He established in technical terms how true interpretation is based upon proper grammatical, historical, textual design (genre), and theological considerations (31-53). Premises regarding these are all grounded in the foundational truth of the literal premise or rule: "Literal affirms that the meanings to be interpreted are textually based. This premise sets the framework for the system. All the other premises are derived from and developed within the scope of what literal affirms" (21).

[13] In this presentation the emphasis is on a descriptive rather than prescriptive presentation. A single violation of literal interpretation by Gaebelein should not be taken as an indictment of the view that literal interpretation is the cornerstone of dispensationalism. The issue is much larger than that as this chapter will show.

... The history of the Jews is witness to the fact that God fulfilled literally His words of threatening ... Still, in our day, an adulterous generation, professing to believe in God and His Word, turns away from the living Word and the written Word and denies the literal meaning of prophecy.[14]

Unfortunately, Gaebelein never impressed upon his readers a technical definition of what he meant by literal interpretation. Usually, the context of his use of the term revolved around the nation of Israel. In both Old and New Testaments, Israel referred to the "literal descendants of the sons of Jacob."[15] In other words, Israel was always to be taken as a reference to the Jewish people.

Literalism was a simple, yet highly significant, matter to Gaebelein.

Now, it is no small matter whether the Word of God, especially the word of prophecy, is allowed to stand for just what it declares, according to its plain meaning, or whether its plain, obvious reading is to be discarded and another substituted.[16]

Gaebelein here equates literal with plain or obvious language. He charged that acceptance of nonliteral interpretation would be acknowledgement that "God in His Word declares one thing, but He means quite another thing."[17] Declaration and meaning should match in his thinking. He felt that readers clearly grasped his discussions along these lines and needed little further explanation. Literal interpretation would be obvious by simply reading the text.

If by literal interpretation is meant the aim of grammatical-historical interpretation, then, on occasion, Gaebelein is an excellent practitioner. His expositions of Philippians and Galatians give classic examples of solid grammatical-

---

[14] Arno C. Gaebelein, "Jehu, Jehoshaphat, Nimshi," *Our Hope* 8 (October 1901): 222.

[15] Arno C. Gaebelein, *Meat in Due Season: Sermons, Discourses and Expositions of the Word of Prophecy* (New York: Arno C. Gaebelein, Inc., n.d.), 178.

[16] Ibid., 179.

[17] Ibid., 180.

historical interpretation.[18] Within other commentaries, John 8 and 11, along with Matthew 23, provide cases where Gaebelein followed this kind of literalism within the context of a book in which he sees much typology.[19] The *Annotated Bible*, a commentary on the entire Bible, also tended, at times to tone down typology and emphasize literal exposition when compared to Gaebelein's commentary on the same passages elsewhere.[20]

Other concerns of grammatical-historical interpretation were important to Gaebelein as well. He used the word *literally* in the common way to correct faulty translations.[21] He made conscious decisions about the manuscript variants and, in one case, devoted several pages to corrections for the Book of Revelation.[22] He was aware of the need to look carefully at the context of a passage.[23]

Context was especially important when the nation Israel was the topic under consideration.

---

[18] Arno C. Gaebelein, "The Epistle to the Philippians" *Our Hope* 9 (September 1902): 148-64; *The Epistle to the Galatians: A Complete Analysis of Galatians with Annotations* (New York: Our Hope Publication Office, n.d.).

[19] Arno C. Gaebelein, *The Gospel of Matthew: An Exposition* (New York: Our Hope Publication Office, 1910), 452-62; *The Gospel of John: A Complete Analytical Exposition of the Gospel of John* (Wheaton, IL: Van Kampen Press, 1936), 154-68, 193-218.

[20] For example, compare Gaebelein's approach to 2 Kings 9-10 in "Jehu, Jehoshaphat, Nimshi," *Our Hope* 8 (October 1901): 219-222 and in *The Annotated Bible* (New York: Publication Office "Our Hope," 1915), 2:325-30.

[21] For example, see Arno C. Gaebelein, *The Prophet Ezekiel: An Analytical Exposition* (New York: Our Hope Publication Office, 1918), 42, 145, 161. Gaebelein was, however, not beyond correcting a translation for theological reasons. He rejected the *Twentieth Century New Testament* translation of Romans 11:25 because it supported postmillennial doctrine ("The Twentieth Century New Testament," *Our Hope* 8 [August 1901]: 59).

[22] Arno C. Gaebelein, *The Revelation: An Analysis and Exposition of the Last Book of the Bible* (New York: Our Hope Publication Office, n.d.), 210-25.

[23] For example, Gaebelein rejected the prevalent use of 1 Corinthians 2:9 ("But as it is written, eye hath not seen, nor ear heard, neither have entered into the heart of man, the things which God hath prepared for them that love Him") to speak of unseen things in the future. His basis was the next verse: "But God hath revealed them unto us by His Spirit." See Arno C. Gaebelein, *The Prophet St. Paul: The Eschatology of the Apostle to the Gentiles* (New York: Our Hope Publication Office, 1939), 24.

Some time ago we stopped in a small place holding several meetings. In giving an address on dispensational truths we mentioned the Word of the Lord "Jerusalem shall be trodden down by the Gentiles until the times of the Gentiles are fulfilled." A person came to us after the meeting and said, "but you don't mean that the same Jerusalem over in Palestine is to be built up again? It can't be that Jerusalem, but the New Jerusalem in Heaven." It did not take us long to convince the friend that it is the same Jerusalem which is now being trodden down by the Gentiles. This incident illustrates the foolish method of commentators, who will take a verse and apply it literally to the Jews or Jerusalem, and the next verse they spiritualize and apply to the church, when the context proves that it belongs to the same people and city of which the previous verse speaks.[24]

In this attention to textual and grammatical detail, Gaebelein never articulated a theoretical basis for his handling of the Bible. The closest he comes is when literal interpretation is referred to as "the law of sound exegesis."[25]

A hint of Gaebelein's historical concerns can also be seen with respect to his interest in the nation Israel.

It may not be altogether out of place to say whom we mean by Israel. There is so much wrong teaching about, that one is forced to refer almost constantly to the most simple foundation truths. The fact is that the most popular interpretation of the Bible makes Israel mean the church. Thus it has come to pass that all these wonderful prophecies which speak of a restoration of Israel and the blessing in store for them have been claimed to mean the "spiritual Israel," the church, and that this present age sees the fulfillment of these promises. This is totally wrong. This method of spiritualizing promises which relate exclusively to one people and one land has thoroughly carnalized the church. When God says Israel He means Israel and not the church. When God reveals the mystery hid in former ages, unknown in the Old Testament, the mystery of the church or assembly and His gracious purposes concerning this body, He does not mean Israel. So let us understand that Israel *is* Israel, namely, the descendants of Abraham, God's ancient people, the earthly people of God. When we speak therefore of the restoration of Israel, and cite from the Scriptures prophecy after

---

[24] Arno C. Gaebelein, "Notes on Prophecy and the Jews," *Our Hope* 9 (February 1903): 487. The passage under consideration is Luke 21:20-24.

[25] Gaebelein, *Prophet Paul*, 110. The issue under consideration is the meaning of the word *Israel* in Romans 11.

prophecy, we mean that which God the Holy Spirit meant, the literal fulfillment of all these prophecies in the literal Israel to whom their own
prophets transmitted these oracles of God.[26]

Thus, Gaebelein viewed literal interpretation in the sense that the Israel of the Old

Testament would have taken the promises in its own historical context without

any New Testament revelation.[27] Again, there is evidence of commitment at times

to the aim of grammatical-historical interpretation.

In addition, as some of the quotations above suggest, Gaebelein gave clues

about his use of literal by the critical labels he placed on rival views. For example,

while discussing the meaning of Acts 3:19-21, he commented: "If we interpret the

Word of Prophecy literally and cease spiritualizing it, we shall have no difficulty

to behold the full meaning of the times of refreshing and the restitution of all

things."[28] He frequently complained that erroneous expositors had "spiritualized

these glorious visions" of the future kingdom for Israel.[29] Gaebelein's exposition

of the vision of the man with the inkhorn in Ezekiel 9 referred to the fact that the

command was to be carried out literally. He noted that "God's judgments are al-

ways carried out to the letter; there is no such thing as a 'spiritual' fulfillment of a

---

[26] Arno C. Gaebelein, *The Harmony of the Prophetic Word* (New York: Fleming H. Revell
Co., 1907), 118-19.

[27] This emphasis on the nation Israel in this connection will be a major topic to be discussed in
a later section. For now the main point is that interest in the proper historical context and setting of
certain passages was maintained by Gaebelein in some areas. Another routine example of his
interest in contextual and historical factors can be found in his commentary on Acts 3:19-21.
"These are very interesting words and of great importance. They can only be understood in the
right way if we do not lose sight of the fact to whom they were addressed, that is to Jews, and not
to Gentiles. They are the heart of this discourse, and as such a God-given appeal and promise to
the nation. If this is lost sight of, the words must lose their right meaning" (*The Acts of the Apostles: An Exposition* [New York: Our Hope Publication Office, 1912], 78).

[28] Gaebelein, *Acts*, 79.

[29] Arno C. Gaebelein, "The Biblical Logic of Premillennialism," *Our Hope* 36 (December
1929): 347.

judgment of God."[30] In all of these examples, 'spiritual' means something beyond the word or letter of the text. The implication is that Gaebelein viewed literal interpretation as accepting the letter of the text.[31]

Less frequent was Gaebelein's reference to allegorical interpretation by which he meant the same approach as the spiritual one above. Concerning the last nine chapters of Ezekiel, he discussed four overall viewpoints: 1) the chapters were fulfilled in the return from captivity, 2) the descriptions are ideal explanations which cannot be defined, 3) the allegorical interpretation, and 4) the literal interpretation connected to the restoration of Israel in the future. With respect to the third approach he noted the following:

> The third interpretation of these chapters is the allegorical which spiritualizes everything and claims that the Christian church, its earthly glory and blessing, is symbolically described by the prophet ... But this theory gives no exposition of the text, is vague and abounds in fanciful applications, while the greater part of this vision is left unexplained even in its allegorical meaning, for it evidently has no such meaning at all.[32]

Here Gaebelein equates allegorical and spiritual interpretation.[33] It is also associated with a symbolic interpretation of those chapters. Gaebelein accuses this erroneous view of ignoring exposition so that the text had no value on its own without the fanciful creativity of the interpreter. Technically, literal interpretation would not necessarily be the opposite of allegorical in this case since more than two views are presented. However, the general implication is that the true interpretation, a literal one, would be exposition without symbolic overtones and with no creativity on the part of the expositor.

---

[30] Arno C. Gaebelein, *The Prophet Ezekiel: An Analytical Exposition* (New York: Publication Office "Our Hope," 1918), 63.

[31] This emphasis taken by itself would correspond to Poythress' description of a flat interpretation or interpretation that is literal if possible. See Poythress, *Dispensationalists*, 83.

[32] Gaebelein, *Ezekiel*, 272-73.

[33] Gaebelein used the term *spiritual* much more frequently than *allegorical*.

112

Another word associated with the spiritualizing of scripture which Gaebelein used is *phantomized*. In a discussion about the kingship of Christ and the
literal nature of the coming kingdom of Israel, he complained about one writer in
this way:

> A certain prolific writer has branded Christ's coming as King a dangerous
> perversion of the Scriptures. The same writer has continued in his denials
> of dispensational truths to such an extent that now he also fights the
> earthly hope of Israel, as if God did not intend to keep His oath-bound
> covenants. All is now spiritualized—one might say—phantomized by
> him.[34]

This latter term appears to highlight Gaebelein's belief that the spiritual approach
to the interpretation of prophecies is characterized by the absence of supportive
evidence in the text itself. In fact, he is saying that such an approach actually denies what exists in the text.

Gaebelein also referred to the literal approach as one opposed to a view of
accommodation.

> I believe that the literal sense of Old Testament prophecy has been far too
> much neglected by the churches, and is far too much neglected at the pre-
> sent day, and that under the mistaken system of *spiritualizing* and *accom-
> modating* Bible language, Christians have too often completely missed its
> meaning.[35]

A key to what Gaebelein meant by the word *accommodating* is given when
Scofield, in an article in *Our Hope*, used the same terminology.[36] The restoration
of Israel predicted in Isaiah 11 did not take place at the end of the Babylonian
captivity. The warrant for such a view appears to be, in this case, a rejection that
the passage could be using hyperbolic language. There is nothing in the text itself

---

[34] Arno C. Gaebelein, "Editorial Notes," *Our Hope* 37 (April 1931): 585. See also Gaebelein,
"Biblical Logic," 348.

[35] Gaebelein, *Meat*, 13.

[36] C. I. Scofield, "The Israel of God" *Our Hope* 8 (June 1902): 634.

which must be construed as hyperbolic unless one has already ruled out a future fulfillment of its message.[37]

Thus, Gaebelein indirectly defined literal interpretation in two ways. First, it is the opposite of spiritualizing, allegorizing, or phantomizing a text. Literal interpretation does not seek a secondary, spiritual meaning. The substance for its expositional decisions is in the text itself and requires no imagination on the part of the interpreter. Second, literal interpretation does not look for language that goes outside of the boundaries of normal, plain language as opposed to hyperbolic or symbolic language.

In general, both of these views were found in the context of statements primarily relating to the restoration of the nation Israel. Note that Gaebelein appears to mix the two categories which Zuck had outlined.[38] The first definition above corresponds to the aim of grammatical-historical interpretation while the second matches the view that literal is the opposite of figurative or symbolic. Gaebelein is imprecise in his use of the term *literal* and moves freely between categories in his own interpretations.

Examples of Nonliteral Interpretation

In spite of his frequent references to literal interpretation, Gaebelein allowed nonliteral interpretation in many cases. This is especially true of his use of

[37] Scofield pointed out that the predictions about the restoration of Israel referred to the future because the passage does not correspond in scope to the remnant which returned after the Babylonian captivity. To prove this he quoted Nehemiah 9:36 which describes the returning remnant as servants in their own land ("Israel," 634). Thus, he compares other passages to help in determining the stylistic possibilities of the one being interpreted. This appears to be an application of the analogy of faith principle which will be discussed in more detail later concerning Gaebelein's dispensational integration.

[38] Even though the two categories given by Zuck and Johnson are useful for the discussion, it must be recognized that the two levels sometimes overlap.

dispensational integration as it relates to types found in the Bible.[39] However, even apart from that large category in Gaebelein's thinking, one can easily note his acceptance of the nonliteral in the text. In this way, he can be seen as an interpreter who avoided wooden literalism.[40]

First, Gaebelein admitted the extensive use of symbols in the biblical text. In the Book of Revelation, one filled with symbolic overtones, he quite expectedly allows room for symbols although the basis for each case may be different. The identification of the 144,000 from the twelve tribes of Israel given in Revelation 7:4-8 and 14:3 gave Gaebelein opportunity to demonstrate his reasoning concerning symbols. In his commentary on chapter fourteen, he noted that

> The 144,000 are the same company which was sealed in chapter vii, but they also include the distinctly Jewish remnant which suffered more specifically in Palestine. The number 144,000 being symbolic and not actual permits such an interpretation. In one word they represent the "all Israel" saved by the coming of the deliverer out of Zion (Rom. xi:26).[41]

That the identification of the 144,000 has nothing to do with the church is grounded on an understanding of the "unfolding of the book."[42] The literalness of the Jewish tribes is accepted by Gaebelein but not the literalness of the number 144,000. It is an indefinite number consisting of all the Jews who will be saved when Jesus comes.[43]

---

[39] Gaebelein's use of dispensational-typological integration actually forms his most used category of interpretation. As such, it deserves its own discussion in detail when dispensational integration as a whole is studied.

[40] The claims of Marsden and Allis cited earlier about the ardent nature of Gaebelein's literalism might lend itself to the charge of a wooden or strict literalism which refuses to accept figurative language. If this is what is meant, the charge is without merit in Gaebelein's case.

[41] Arno C. Gaebelein, *The Revelation: An Analysis and Exposition of the Last Book of the Bible* (New York: Our Hope Press, 1915), 86.

[42] Ibid.

[43] Gaebelein takes the 1,000 years in Revelation 20 literally and not as an indefinite time period (*Revelation*, 132). He attempts no justification in his commentary. He appears to leave himself open to the charge of inconsistency on this particular point.

The basis for his understanding is found in numerology.

> The number, 144,000, that is, 12,000 out of each tribe, must be looked upon as symbolical. It speaks of the complete government, which as to the earth, is invested in a redeemed and restored Israel.[44]

The number 12 (or 12 multiplied by 10, 100, or 1000) represented divine government and led Gaebelein to view the 144,000 (a multiple of 12,000) as symbolic and indefinite.[45] There appears to be no textually based reason for the choice unless it is seen as inherent in the number itself.

Gaebelein also denied the literalness of the characteristics of the 144,000 but on different grounds.

> The characteristics of the 144,000 are next given. Verse 4 must not be interpreted in a literal sense. Those who apply it to a first fruits of the church

---

[44] Gaebelein, *Revelation*, 58.

[45] The number twelve as divine government plays a major role in Gaebelein's exposition of the New Jerusalem in Revelation 21-22 (*Revelation*, 162). An example of the arbitrary nature of Gaebelein's use of numerology is given in his commentary on Ezekiel 40:5-16 (*Ezekiel*, 278-79). In the temple vision, a man measures the height and the breadth of the wall as six cubits each. Gaebelein interpreted the number of measurements taken (two) multiplied by the actual measurement itself (six) to give the number of divine government (twelve). Clearly there is no textual basis for such a procedure. Although numerology comes into the exposition of Gaebelein, one must be cautious to note that it is not primary in his thinking when exegeting passages in the Bible. The approach of Gaebelein resembles what John Davis has characterized as a "mystical" use of numbers (*Biblical Numerology* [Grand Rapids, MI: Baker Book House, 1968], 125-49). The source of Gaebelein's thinking about numerology is unknown. One likely place is the traditional Judaism he encountered in his ministry to orthodox Jews. Davis noted that "number symbolism was also a prominent feature of the Talmudic and Midrashic literature of the Jews" (*Biblical Numerology*, 115). Gaebelein was also aware of E. W. Bullinger who wrote on that subject in 1894 during Gaebelein's ministry to the Jews (*Number in Scripture*, 4th ed. [London: Eyre & Spottiswoode Ltd., 1921]). Gaebelein generally viewed Bullinger and his followers as extremists (*Prophet Paul*, 58; *Acts*, 67). However, no specific mention of Bullinger's work on numerology was ever cited by Gaebelein to this writer's knowledge. Gaebelein's use of numerology is certainly not as extensive as that of Bullinger. However, the most likely source for Gaebelein's numerology was Frederick W. Grant, leader of the Montreal faction of the exclusive Brethren (H. A. Ironside, *A Historical Sketch of the Brethren Movement* [Grand Rapids, MI: Zondervan Publishing House, 1942]). Grant authored a book giving a survey of numerical significance in the Bible (*The Numerical Structure of Scripture* [New York: Loizeaux Brothers, 1899]). In addition, he published an unfinished commentary of several volumes on the entire Bible dedicated to its numerical perfection (*The Numerical Bible* [New York: Loizeaux Brothers, 1904]). Gaebelein referenced the latter work in his commentaries with an occasional commendation. For example, see Gaebelein, *Matthew*, 90; *Annotated Bible*, 1:296.

> have done so and it has led to much confusion and even worse things. Literal impurity is not in view. If it had a literal meaning this company would consist of men only. The woman, the great harlot Babylon and her daughters, the God-less and Christ-less religious world-systems (chapter xvii) are then on earth. They did not defile themselves with the corruptions and idolatries prevalent on the earth. They kept themselves from spiritual fornication. They are the firstfruits and the earnest of the blessings soon in store for the earth.[46]

No numerology affects this exegetical decision. A literal approach would, in Gaebelein's view, lead to an absurdity, Jewish men going into the Millennium without Jewish women. Consequently, literalism is rejected in this case.

Gaebelein also rejected a literal interpretation of Babylon given in Revelation 17-18.

> There are many who believe that the literal Babylon is in view here in these two chapters. It is claimed that literal Babylon on the banks of the Euphrates is to become once more a large city and the seat of government during the end of this age. Literal Babylon never was a part of the Roman empire, and as the Babylon of Revelation xvii and xviii is seen in closest identification with the empire, and for a time at least is its center and capital, the Babylon in Asia is ruled out at once.[47]

Here, in Gaebelein's mind, is a conflict between two potentially literal ideas, the literally revived Roman empire (developed from other passages) and Asian Babylon. The latter was out of place geographically as the capital of a literally revived Roman empire. Gaebelein uses the context of the two present chapters and the idea that "along with the revival of the Roman empire there will be a revival of Papal Rome" to identify Babylon as the "Papal system in its final power and control in the world."[48]

---

[46] Gaebelein, *Revelation*, 86-87.

[47] Ibid., 97.

[48] Ibid., 97-99.

One final example in which Gaebelein showed an acceptance of symbolism was Ezekiel's vision of the dry bones.[49] Gaebelein rejected a literalism which viewed the dry bones coming to life as a picture of physical resurrection.[50] The vision speaks of a valley of dry bones which are covered with sinews and flesh as well as the coming of a breath of life (Ezek. 37:8-10). A later explanation speaks of graves which are opened (Ezek. 37:12-13). The picture given is one of physical resurrection. However, Gaebelein sees the physical resurrection as symbolic of the national resurrection or restoration of the nation of Israel.[51] However, he justifies this view by the context. The symbolism is revealed in verse eleven when God explains that the bones are the whole house of Israel.[52]

Three other arguments figure in his logic on this point. First, he noted that some elements in the text cannot be explained in a literal fashion.

> When we read here in Ezekiel of graves it must not be taken to mean literal graves, but the graves are symbolical of the nation as being buried among the Gentiles. If these dry bones meant the physical dead of the nation, how could it be explained that they speak and say, "Our bones are dried up, and our hope is lost?"[53]

---

[49] Passages such as the ones discussed throughout this section could be multiplied by the hundreds. Those who view Gaebelein (or any dispensationalist of that time period) as a thoroughgoing literalist who virtually ignores symbolism has simply not read the literature. Another example of how Gaebelein arbitrarily assigned symbolic meaning is the symbolic nature of the book of Life and the other books which are opened in Revelation 20:11-15 at the judgment of the great white throne (*Revelation*, 147-48).

[50] Here the issue is not that the dry bones are symbolic. The question is the reference. Three choices seem to emerge: physical resurrection of believers (either Jewish or Christian or both), national resurrection or restoration of Israel as a nation, and spiritual blessings upon the church. The first one might be classified as a wooden or strict literalism. The last one would be an example of allegorization. Gaebelein opted for the second.

[51] Gaebelein, *Ezekiel*, 245-47.

[52] Ibid., 245.

[53] Ibid., 246.

The fact that the bones speak *before* the resurrection demonstrates that the text is dealing with the symbolic. Second, John 5:28-29 teaches that there is a twofold resurrection, one for the just and one for the wicked. If an actual resurrection from the dead is allowed here, in Gaebelein's view, a third resurrection would be added thereby producing a contradiction.[54] Third, parallel passages use physical resurrection in a figurative way, even to speak of the national restoration of Israel.[55]

Such examples show that Gaebelein readily admitted to symbolism in the text. They also demonstrate that he often used *literal* as the opposite of *figurative*. He was not a strict literalist in this sense, although literalism in one part of a passage could lead him to reject literalism in another part. Theological conclusions from other passages and similar usage in parallel passages were also used by him to reinforce the existence of figurative language. Absurdities in the text on the basis of literal interpretation obviously indicated symbolism. The most surprising departure from literal interpretation was the incorporation of numerology, from a traditional or theological motivation, into interpretation. For the most part, Gaebelein's understanding of the figurative elements as opposed to the literal elements of a passage, fit into Zuck's analysis of what encompasses grammatical-historical interpretation.

Emphases of Literal Interpretation

Gaebelein did not apply literal interpretation, in the sense of grammatical-historical interpretation, with equal rigor to all the Bible. There were selective targets which were chosen as primary. A literal interpretation of these passages is

---

[54] Ibid.

[55] Ibid., 246-47. Here Gaebelein mentioned the prodigal son who was dead and then alive (Luke 15:24). He was clearly not physically dead and then resurrected. Another example used by Gaebelein is Romans 11:15 (*Prophet Paul*, 129-30). There Paul asks the question, "For if the casting away of them (Israel) be the reconciling of the world, what shall the receiving of them be, but life from the dead?" The phrase "life from the dead" in this context speaks of the national restoration of Israel in analogous terms to the figure of the dry bones in Ezekiel.

crucial for understanding the entire Bible. In fact, much of Gaebelein's dispensational integration is built upon an understanding of these passages in the light of
the literal hermeneutic.

Old Testament Prophecy

Prophecy in general held an overpowering attraction for Gaebelein. He
noted that it leads believers, if properly understood, close to the heart of God.[56]
The disastrous neglect of prophecy stole from the saint the "true knowledge of
Him and His redemption work who is the one theme of all prophecy."[57] While
Gaebelein did not bypass New Testament prophecy, there is an emphasis within
his prophetic interpretation upon Old Testament prophecy and its literal interpretation.[58]

The first way that literal interpretation of the Old Testament prophecy is
emphasized by Gaebelein can be seen in his view of the restoration of Israel in
what has come to be called the millennium. He viewed the Old Testament as con-

[56] Arno C. Gaebelein, "The Wonders of Progressive Prophecy," *Our Hope* 46 (April 1940): 665.

[57] Ibid.

[58] The nondispensationalist, Oswald T. Allis, noticed this emphasis among dispensationalists like Gaebelein. "A further important result of the claim of Dispensationalists that prophecy must be interpreted literally, that so understood it is perfectly intelligible and if unconditional must be literally fulfilled, is the tendency to exalt the Old Testament at the expense of the New Testament, to insist that its predictions stand, we may say, in their own right, and are in no sense dependent upon the New Testament for amplification, illumination, or interpretation ... The assumption that underlies these statements is that anything but literal fulfillment would be tantamount to abroga-tion or modification ... In short, Paul's words must be interpreted in such a way as not to conflict with the hopes and claims of the Zionists!" (*Prophecy*, 48-50). Allis exaggerates the misunder-standing and nonuse, at times, of the New Testament (compare Arno C. Gaebelein, *Will There Be A Millennium? When and How?: The Coming Reign of Christ in the Light of the Old and New Testaments* [New York: Publication Office "Our Hope," 1943], 20-35, 59-72). However, he has captured the sense of the centrality (for dispensationalists like Gaebelein) of literal interpretation of the Old Testament text, taken by itself, in prophetic matters. George Ladd, also a nondispensa-tionalist, recognized this central role of the literal interpretation of the Old Testament for a dispen-sationalist, "Dispensationalism forms its eschatology by a literal interpretation of the Old Testa-ment and then fits the New Testament into it" ("Historic Premillennialism," in *The Meaning of the Millennium: Four Views*, ed. Robert G. Clouse [Downers Grove, IL: InterVarsity Press, 1977], 27).

120

taining hundreds of unfulfilled promises about the coming restoration of Israel which must literally be fulfilled.[59] The kingdom is clearly a literal, earthly kingdom. The interpretation of Old Testament passages simply could not be spiritualized, "The kingdom which Israel expected was not the unrevealed present dispensation, nor was it the Church, but the literal kingdom."[60]

Not only did Gaebelein believe the centrality of the Old Testament on this point, he found nothing in the New Testament "which would authorize us to say this great theme of the Old Testament prophetic Word meant events in connection with a spiritual Israel."[61] The first place that Gaebelein examines to prove biblical truth about the millennium is the Old Testament.[62] For him, this was a logical first step.

> Every intelligent student of the Bible has discovered that the character of this future age, call it the Millennium, or the kingdom age, is most clearly revealed in the Old Testament and not in the New Testament.[63]

In addition, Gaebelein commented that the Book of Revelation, the one New Testament book dedicated totally to prophecy has its basis largely in the truth of the Old Testament.

> Not only what is revealed in the New Testament, but also Old Testament prophecies are restated once more in this majestic book which leads us from time into eternity. One of the reasons why the prophetic message of the Revelation has been so much misunderstood and misinterpreted is the

[59] Gaebelein, *Ezekiel*, 247.

[60] Gaebelein, "Editorial Notes" *Our Hope* 37 (April 1931): 586.

[61] Gaebelein, *Harmony*, 158. See also Gaebelein, "The Harmony of the Prophetic Word," *Our Hope* 9 (September 1902): 132.

[62] Gaebelein, *Millennium*, 19.

[63] Ibid., 20. Gaebelein also noted that such truth was "fully" revealed in the Old Testament and not in the New Testament (47).

ignorance of expositors as to the contents of the prophetic Word in the Old Testament and God's revealed purposes.[64]

Gaebelein ridiculed the criticism which claimed that there was just slender support for the idea of a literal millennium given in only one chapter of the Bible (Revelation 20). That chapter in Revelation gave the only reference to the duration of the millennium, but the nature of the kingdom age was clearly spelled out throughout the Bible, especially in the Old Testament prophecies.[65]

A second way in which Gaebelein highlights a literal interpretation of Old Testament prophecies is through a comparison of fulfilled and unfulfilled prophecy.[66] One comparison involves the dispersion of Israel which had already occurred and the restoration of the nation yet to take place. In a commentary on Deuteronomy 30, he affirms that "if the prediction concerning their fall and punishment has been so literally fulfilled the prediction of their restoration will most assuredly be fulfilled in the same way."[67]

Gaebelein also compared predictions about the suffering of Messiah with those concerning the coming glory of Christ.

> The whole path of the babe born in Bethlehem to the sufferings on the cross, His humiliation and rejection, was made known through the prophets; all these predictions have found in our Lord their *literal* fulfillment. The literal fulfillment of prophecies relating to the humiliation of the Christ is a warrant for the literal fulfillment of the prophecies relating to the glories of the same Lord and Christ who suffered. How ridiculously inconsequent are most interpreters of the prophetic Word in that they de-

[64] Arno C. Gaebelein, *The Return of the Lord* (New York: Publication Office "Our Hope," 1925), 94. See also, Gaebelein, *Millennium*, 44.

[65] Gaebelein, *Annotated Bible*, 9:266.

[66] In his article for *The Fundamentals*, Gaebelein relies almost exclusively on the literal interpretation of Old Testament prophecy to prove the inspiration of the Bible. A subtheme of this article appears to be this point of comparison. See Arno C. Gaebelein, "Fulfilled Prophecy, a Potent Argument for the Bible," in *The Fundamentals* ed. Reuben A. Torrey (Chicago: Testimony Publishing Co., 1910), 11:55-86.

[67] Arno C. Gaebelein, "Notes on Prophecy and the Jews," *Our Hope* 8 (July 1901): 42.

122

fend the literal fulfillment of the sufferings in Christ and then spiritualize the prophecies which speak of the glories afterwards. The sufferings were literal, the glories are literal also.[68]

To make sure that his readers understood he was dealing with Old Testament interpretation, Gaebelein continued by noting that there was no basis in the New Testament for "spiritualizing of the Old Testament predictions of the coming glories." In fact, the New Testament "endorsed the literal fulfillment of unfulfilled Old Testament prophecy."[69]

In this connection, a favorite passage appears to be the predictions given to Mary by the angel Gabriel.

> And behold thou shalt conceive in thy womb, and bring forth a son, and shalt call His name Jesus. He shall be great, and shall be called the Son of the Highest; and the Lord God shall give unto Him the throne of His Father David, and He shall reign over the house of Jacob for ever, and of His kingdom there shall be no end (Luke 1:31-33).

Gaebelein commented in the following way.

> How literally the first part of this announcement has been fulfilled is well known. The second part, relating to the throne of David, His reign over the house of Jacob and His kingdom, is generally declared to be sa piritual [sic] throne of David in heaven, and a spiritual reign, and a spiritual kingdom. When God made a covenant with David He did not promise him a spiritual throne in heaven, nor a spiritual kingdom, but an earthly throne and an earthly kingdom. The return of our Lord, the Son of Man and the Son of David, will bring the realization of the promised throne and the promised kingdom.[70]

The passage is, of course, a New Testament one. However, in Gaebelein's mind he is viewing the birth of Christ in light of its fulfillment of the Old Testament predictions such as Isaiah 7:14. The unfulfilled nature of the Davidic promise in the passage is based upon 2 Samuel 7:14-17. The Davidic promise, in a literal,

---

[68] Gaebelein, "Harmony," 132.

[69] Ibid.

[70] Gaebelein, *Return*, 31-32.

earthly sense, will be fulfilled just like the birth of Christ was fulfilled in a literal, earthly sense.[71]

Several examples of Old Testament passages could be given to demonstrate specific usage by Gaebelein concerning the emphasis upon literal interpretation of prophetic texts. In the controversial passage which gives Peter's sermon on Pentecost, Acts 2:14-28, Gaebelein justified a Jewish understanding of the text by the reference to Joel 2:28-32. That is, the prophecy in Joel is addressed to Judah and Jerusalem and has Jewish, not Christian implications.[72] Furthermore, the details of Joel 2:28-32 such as the wonders in heaven (sun turned to darkness, moon turned to blood) did not take place on the day of Pentecost. Therefore, the passage in Acts cannot be stating a Pentecost fulfillment for the Joel passage. Gaebelein's primary reasoning centers around fulfillment of literal details in the Old Testament text.[73]

---

[71] Gaebelein also alluded to this passage with similar argumentation elsewhere. See Gaebelein, *Millennium*, 59-61, and "Editorial Notes," *Our Hope* 8 (June 1902): 618. Such use of this passage must have been common in dispensational premillennial circles. William Blackstone, a contemporary of Gaebelein and a like-minded dispensationalist who ministered to Jews, began a chapter on literal interpretation with a discussion of this passage. He used it by noting that a Christian could not honestly witness to a Jewish person with this passage if he did not take the second part about the Davidic promise literally in the same way he took the first part about Jesus (*Jesus is Coming*, [Chicago: Fleming H. Revell Co., 1908], 20-21). See similar discussions in the light of Jewish missions in Émile Guers, *Israël aux Derniers Jours De L'Économie Actuelle ou Essai Sur La Restauration Prochaine De Ce Peuple, Suivi D'Un Fragment Sur Le Millénarisme* (Genève: Émile Beroud, 1856), 28 (hereafter cited as *La Future D'Israël*). Gaebelein would have easily agreed with this approach in the context of Jewish evangelism.

[72] Gaebelein, *Acts*, 52.

[73] Ibid., 53-54. Gaebelein on that basis noted: "That which they saw and heard was indeed the outpouring of the Holy Spirit, but not in the full sense as given in the prophecy of Joel. What took place is a pledge that in due time all prophecy contained in the book of Joel would be fulfilled." Later he noted that "Pentecost was only the earnest of what is yet to take place in Jerusalem." The important truth to note is that Gaebelein lets his literal understanding of Joel 2 govern his thinking in Acts 2. Another passage in which his reasoning is similar is Hebrews 8:7-13 concerning the new covenant. On the basis of Old Testament passages like Jeremiah 31:31-34, Gaebelein interprets the new covenant in terms of the nation of Israel. Thus, when he comes to the Hebrews passage, he does not see the church at all. Some of the present blessings of the church are similar but are not part of the new covenant blessings promised for Israel. It is interesting that in the *Annotated Bible*, Gaebelein ignores the mention of the new covenant in 1 Corinthians 11:25 (3:121-22)

124

The last chapter of Daniel provides another example of Gaebelein's literalism in Old Testament prophecy. The references to 1,260 and 1,335 days given in
Daniel 12:11-12 are taken literally without symbolism.[74] However, in Ezekiel 4:1-
9, Gaebelein takes the references to 40 and 390 days as equal to 40 and 390 years,
respectively. In the Ezekiel passage one should note that Ezekiel himself does
literally lay on his left side for 390 days and on his right side for 40 days. The
significance of the passage is the demarcation of prophetic years with respect to
Israel and Judah. Gaebelein clarified that

> Some have concluded on account of this passage, that throughout the pro-
> phetic word wherever "days" are mentioned, they mean "years." This is
> incorrect. The "year-day" theory is not a scriptural one. Where we find
> days, it means days unless the text itself, as it is here in Ezekiel, explains
> the days as years.[75]

Thus, even in a prophetical passage where symbolism is seen, Gaebelein sought a
textually based way of looking at the symbols.

Perhaps the most revealing passage for understanding Gaebelein's emphasis upon the literal interpretation of Old Testament prophecy is Deuteronomy 28-
32. The first chapter in this section gives, according to Gaebelein, an outline of
"the history of the scattered nation (Israel), all their suffering and tribulations, as
it has been for well nigh two millenniums."[76] He clearly believed that history has
demonstrated that the curses for disobedience found in Deuteronomy 28:15-68

---

and in the Synoptics (3:53-56, 101, 168-69). The new covenant in 1 Corinthians 3:1-18 is, for
Gaebelein, apparently a synonym for the gospel (3:160-64).

[74] One can note the comparison to symbolism in the 144,000 of Revelation 7. Numerology was
used, as discussed above, to take that number as figurative. Daniel is also a book of many symbols
(e.g., Daniel 2, 7). Apparently, these numbers in Daniel 12:11-12 do not come close to some special numerical meaning, Jewish or otherwise. Gaebelein appealed to the New Testament for con-
firmation of the literalism he found in this Old Testament passage (*Daniel*, 206-7).

[75] Gaebelein, *Ezekiel*, 38. Verse six teaches that each day was to represent a year.

[76] Gaebelein, *Annotated Bible*, 1:427.

were literally fulfilled in the nation.[77] Even the minute predictions, as well as the general ones, have been fulfilled in precise terms.[78] Deuteronomy 29 repeats the same message.

The next chapter (Deut. 30), assuming a dispersion, promises a return of the nation to the land. This message of hope for Israel can only be taken, in Gaebelein's view, as a literal hope for the nation. The Jews will not be assimilated into the nations around them and will one day be brought back to the land which God had promised them through Abraham.[79] His placement of the fulfillment of these passages in the future is based upon a literal view of the detailed promises in the text in comparison with historical events from the past.

> These magnificent promises of blessing are not for a spiritual Israel, as people sometimes term the church, but for the literal Israel. Some say, the return predicted by Moses and the other prophets was fulfilled when a remnant of Jews came back from Babylon. This is incorrect for neither were the people scattered among all the nations, nor did the small remnant, which came back from the Babylonian captivity, enjoy the glories and blessings predicted in the prophetic Word. Another return will take place, when their once rejected King comes back.[80]

Deuteronomy 31:1-30 gives few details for Gaebelein to discuss although the warning of God's judgment and the delivering of the Law are cited.

It is the next chapter (Deut. 32) with its song of Moses which summarizes the entire section. In this, "the song of Moses embraces the entire history of Israel, past, present and future."[81] The past judgments of God upon disobedient Israel are

---

[77] Ibid.

[78] Ibid. Gaebelein took the reference to the nation coming as an eagle (Deut. 28:49) as Rome. Although this individual term is taken as symbolic, the overall message of oppression given in the passage was taken as literal.

[79] Ibid., 1:430-31. Gaebelein correlated this passage with several other Old Testament predictions and promises (Jer. 32:37-38, Isa. 24, 60-62, Ezek. 36:24).

[80] Ibid., 1:431-32.

[81] Ibid., 1:435.

126

especially detailed in Deuteronomy 32:19-33.[82] Verse twenty-six gives a prediction of the scattering of the nation into the far corners of the earth. The gloomy
portrait of 32:34-42 describes God's final dealing with the nation Israel in the
special time of a Great Tribulation to come upon the earth.[83] Gaebelein was careful to note the inclusion of the Gentiles in this time of judgment (32:40-42).[84] The
final verse of the song (32:43) foresees the "glorious consummation" when the
nation will be brought back to the land in restoration.[85] Gaebelein allowed a
"spiritual" application of some of the text to believers in the church today.[86]

However, primary was the minute fulfillment of the details in the history
of the nation of Israel.[87] This sequence or pattern traced, for Gaebelein, the history
of Israel from its rejection of God to its national restoration. That this sequence
played a major role in Gaebelein's use of Scripture is seen by the fact that, not
only did he refer to the song of Moses as a "great prophecy,"[88] it was, in fact, "the
key to all prophecy."[89]

In summary, Gaebelein selected Old Testament prophecy, especially as it
relates to the nation of Israel, for employment of literal interpretation (usually as
the aim of grammatical-historical interpretation). Of particular interest was his

---

[82] Past with respect to the present age but future with respect to Moses as he spoke these
words.

[83] Gaebelein, *Annotated Bible*, 1:435. Gaebelein compared 32:39 with Hosea 5:15-6:3 to support his contention in this section.

[84] Ibid.

[85] Ibid.

[86] Ibid., 1:436. Note Gaebelein's comments on 32:9-14.

[87] Ibid., 1:437. This minute fulfillment was, for Gaebelein, evidence for inspiration of the Bible.

[88] Ibid., 1:435.

[89] Ibid., 1:437. It is the sequence itself that is the key, not the particular passage giving the pattern.

observation of the outline of Israel's history given in Deuteronomy 28-32. Later this sequence will be seen as a major part of Gaebelein's development of his dispensational integration. In relation to the literal hermeneutic, two points emerge: 1) it is the basis for finding the sequence of Israel's prophetic history in Old Testament narrative and 2) it leads in several passages to an emphasis on the future restoration of Israel as a nation to the land of Palestine. The importance of the latter is echoed by Gaebelein's statement that "the Old Testament is practically a sealed book to every person who does not believe in a literal restoration of Israel to their land."[90]

Ephesians

The second area of the Bible for which Gaebelein emphasized literal interpretation is the Book of Ephesians. Justification for this determination begins by noting the special place that the entire book had in Gaebelein's thinking. This standing is partly dependent upon Gaebelein's exegesis of Colossians 1:25.

> In the Epistle to the Colossians Paul makes the statement, "Whereof I am made a minister, according to the dispensation of God which is given to me for you, to fulfill the Word of God" (Col. i:25). To fulfill the Word of God does not mean, as often stated, that Paul fulfilled his ministry and was faithful in it. It means rather that to him was given the revelation which makes full, or completes, the Word of God. The highest and most glorious revelation, which the God and Father of our Lord Jesus Christ has been pleased to give, He communicated through the Apostle Paul. The two prison Epistles to the Ephesians and Colossians embody this completion of the Word of God. The Ephesian Epistle holds the place of pre-eminence. The revelation which is given in this Epistle concerning believing sinners, whom God has redeemed by the blood of His Son, and exalted in Him into the highest possible position, is by far the greatest revelation.[91]

---

[90] Ibid., 1:432.

[91] Arno C. Gaebelein, *God's Masterpiece: An Analytical Exposition of Ephesians I-III* (New York: Our Hope Publication Office, 1913), 2-3. See also *Annotated Bible*, 7:234, and *Acts*, 48. Gaebelein's interpretation of Colossians 1:25 was shared by the dispensationalist H. A. Ironside (*Lectures on the Epistle to the Colossians* [Neptune, NJ: Loizeaux Brothers, 1929], 56-57). For a survey of other exegetical views of Colossians 1:25 see John Eadie, *Commentary on the Epistle of*

128

The same sentiment was repeated in several other works by Gaebelein. Ephesians is the "greatest of all the Pauline Epistles."[92] It is the "richest portion of God's Word."[93] The Apostle Paul was used to fill up or finish the revelation of God in terms of content.[94]

Gaebelein never used the word *literal* in his exposition of the text of Ephesians. However, there are several points at which literalism leads him to rather significant conclusions. There are two tracks in his exposition to be examined, truth about redemption and statements about the church. He characterized the Ephesians presentation of redemption with these words: "The revelation which is given in this Epistle concerning believing sinners, whom God has redeemed by the blood of His Son, and exalted in Him into the highest possible position, is by far the greatest revelation."[95] Ephesians 1 with its outline of the Trinity's involvement in the redemption of sinners, motivated Gaebelein's statement.[96]

The crucial verse is Ephesians 1:3 ("Blessed be the God and Father of our Lord Jesus Christ, who blessed us with all spiritual blessings in heavenly *places* in Christ"). The blessings which individual believers receive are "spiritual blessings

REDEMPTION + CHURCH.

Paul to the Colossians (n.p.: Richard Griffin & Co., 1856; reprint, Minneapolis, MN: James and Klock Christian Publishing Co., 1977), 93-94.

[92] Gaebelein, *Return*, 59.

[93] Gaebelein, *Annotated Bible*, 3:273.

[94] Concerning books of the Bible which were written after Ephesians, Gaebelein would note that such revelation, though needed, did not introduce new topics per se. See Gaebelein, *Prophet Paul*, 67-78.

[95] Gaebelein, *Masterpiece*, 2-3.

[96] Ibid., 16-49.

in heavenly places in Christ." Gaebelein takes the word *spiritual* here in a literal sense.[97]

> Then in the *third* place we read of the blessings, what kind of blessings they are, spiritual blessings; they are therefore communicated by the *Holy Spirit*. And how many such blessings has He given? Our authorized version states "with all spiritual blessings." The correct rendering is "with *every* spiritual blessing." There is then no blessing whatever, which God can give, which He has kept back from those who are in Christ. All God, the God and Father of our Lord Jesus Christ, can give in spiritual blessings, He has given. It is a most blessed fact! God has now come forth and revealed what He can do for such as we are and how great are the exceeding riches of His Grace. In Old Testament times God had His people Israel. To them He promised earthly blessings. But greater than the blessings of the earth are the blessings He has given to us in Christ.[98]

Thus, these spiritual blessings refer to the realm of the Spirit and not to the sphere of the material or earthly. The nature of the idea of *spirit* inclined Gaebelein in that direction. Such blessings are also greater than Old Testament blessings which, although given by God, deal with the earth and material things.

The next part of that phrase helps to qualify what Gaebelein did with the passage. Those blessings are given "in heavenly *places* in Christ." Again the literal sense of the words can be found in Gaebelein's comments.

> The phrase "in heavenly places" should be translated "Heavenlies." It is peculiar to this Epistle. We find the Heavenlies mentioned five times. Chapter i:3, 20 [sic]; ii:6; iii:10 and vi:12. It has a twofold meaning, the nature of the blessings which are ours in a risen and ascended Christ, and the locality where our Lord, the Head of the body is. In the Heavenlies where He is now, the church will be with him.[99]

---

[97] One should be careful not to confuse this use of the word *spiritual* with the idea of spiritual or allegorical interpretation, a secondary or deeper meaning, which is opposed to literal interpretation, the primary meaning.

[98] Ibid., 21.

[99] Ibid., 21-22.

130

He clarified the first aspect of this definition in his commentary on Ephesians 1:20. The meaning is that the power of the Holy Spirit, the power of heaven, is available for Christians.[100] In this sense, it is taken in a somewhat figurative way.

The second aspect of the definition, however, demonstrates an understanding of the literal, physical location of Christ in heaven. Gaebelein's commentary on its use by Paul in Ephesians 2:6 ("made us sit together in heavenly places in Christ Jesus") expanded this perspective.

> Besides giving us life and placing us in the blessed position as sons in resurrection, He has seated us in Christ Jesus in the heavenly places. Quite often the statement is quoted as "made us sit together in heavenly places *with* Christ Jesus." This is incorrect. We are not seated with Christ, but *in* Christ. When He comes again, we shall be with Him and share His glory. Here we have the very summit of Christian position. We are not alone representatively, but also virtually, sitting in Christ in the highest Glory. Not alone have we life in Him, but He *is* our life. Therefore our life is hid with Christ in God. In Him, who is our life, we are seated in the heavenly places.[101]

Here the importance of a literal understanding of the preposition *in* can be seen. As a result, the Christian believer is virtually in Christ in the location of heaven. Implied in this view is a vital union with the Savior. The word *virtually* in this discussion almost carries the idea of *literally*. Christ does not merely represent believers. They are literally united to Him. This does not mean that Gaebelein saw Christians in heaven in any bodily, physical sense. His exposition reveals, however, that in some sense believers are actually there. They are not represented by proxy.[102]

---

[100] Ibid., 58-59.

[101] Ibid., 77.

[102] Gaebelein did not comment on the significance of the use of *heavenlies* in Ephesians 3:10 and 6:12. In 3:10 he refers to the principalities and powers as unfallen angels who live in the heavenly places (*Masterpiece*, 131). In 6:12 he sees the subjects as fallen angels who live in the "sphere above the earth, the aerial heavens and beyond" (*Annotated Bible*, 3:268-69). In either case, the dichotomy which separates the term *heavenlies* from the earth is maintained.

Besides this emphasis of literal interpretation involving redemptive truths, Gaebelein also stressed such an approach with respect to truth taught in Ephesians about the church, which he referred to as "God's Masterpiece."[103] The key passage is Ephesians 3:1-7 in which the Apostle Paul explains the mystery of Christ. Gaebelein in outline fashion goes through each phrase of the passage. Paul had received a special revelation of the mystery of Christ. This mystery was not known in other ages but now has been made known to the Apostle (3:5). The mystery is defined in Ephesians 3:6, according to Gaebelein, as "the risen Christ, who has a body composed of believing Jews and Gentiles."[104] He added that the "Head, Christ, and the Body, the Church, composed of believing Jews and Gentiles, joint-heirs, joint-members, joint partakers—this is the mystery."[105]

The emphasis of the passage appears to be on the inclusion of the Gentiles along with Jews in God's dealings. However, as Gaebelein noted, the Old Testament contains several passages which predict the future promises of the Gentiles in connection with Israel.[106] These Old Testament promises, in Gaebelein's view, even speak of a day when "the Gentiles will join themselves to Israel."[107] How, then, could this revelation be something not known in previous ages and just now revealed to the Apostle?

Gaebelein's way of dealing with the question was to refuse to allow the Old Testament passages to dictate the precise nature of this joining of Gentiles and Jews.[108] He chose instead to use the context of the Ephesian letter to define

---

[103] Gaebelein, *Masterpiece*, 61, 79.

[104] Ibid., 119.

[105] Ibid. 123.

[106] Ibid., 122. Gaebelein cited Isaiah 60:3-5 as an example.

[107] Ibid.

[108] This, of course, is not a denial on Gaebelein's part of the literal interpretation of those Old Testament passages. He allows a future fulfillment of them in his scheme. The point here is that

132

what he considered to be a brand new entity.[109] Before Paul's description of the mystery, he reminded the Ephesians that he had written about it before in a few words (Eph. 3:3-4). Gaebelein correctly points back to Ephesians 1:9-12 where Paul describes the mystery of the Father's will concerning Christ and the age to come. God's purpose was "that in the dispensation of the fulness of times he might gather together in one all things in Christ, both which are in heaven, and which are on earth" (Eph. 1:10).

Similar terminology is used in the latter verses of the same chapter. Christ has ascended to the right hand of the Father in heavenly places (1:20) and has a position of rulership, not only in the present age, but in the age to come (1:21). The section is capped with the statement "And hath put all things (recall 1:10) under his feet, and gave him to be the head over all things to the church, which is his body, the fullness of him that filleth all in all" (1:22-23). Connecting these three passages, Ephesians 1:8-10, 1:20-23, and 3:1-7, Gaebelein concluded that the church, as part of Christ, is included in the mystery. The church was, therefore, an entity that was not made known in the Old Testament. It is part of the special revelation given to Paul. When the full context of Ephesians 2:11-22 is added with its mention of the reconciling of Jew and Gentile into one body, one can easily see how Gaebelein would see a consistent presentation in Ephesians 1-3 concerning the mystery.[110] The mystery included the church. The church, then, was a New Testament truth.

Gaebelein is willing to let each testament stand alone in its presentation if there is no precise correlation between the Old Testament passage and that in the New.

[109] Ibid., 118-19.

[110] In this analysis, Gaebelein is correct. It would be a mistake to restrict discussions of the content of the mystery to Ephesians 3:1-7 and conclude that only the nature of the inclusion of the Gentiles with Jews in one body was unrevealed in the Old Testament. It seems that taking the book of Ephesians as a whole leads one to the conclusion that the existence of the church was also unrevealed. Gaebelein, on these particular points, appears to be following grammatical-historical interpretation of the first three chapters.

In summary, two tracks of literal interpretation have been seen in Gaebelein's emphasis upon Ephesians. First, with respect to the redemption of the individual believer, there exists a positional truth in which the saint is, in some sense, literally in Christ in the heavenly domain. Second, the context of Ephesians 1-3, taken as a unit, led him to the conclusion that the church was a mystery not made known in the Old Testament. Both of these emphases play a significant role in Gaebelein's theological formulations.

Synthesis of Old Testament Prophecy and Ephesians

The first major category of literal interpretation for Gaebelein involved Old Testament prophecy, especially as it related to the future restoration of Israel to the land of Palestine. In comments on this issue, Gaebelein frequently used the word *literal* to describe his view. The practice of literal interpretation as the aim of grammatical-historical interpretation was also found in Gaebelein's approach to Ephesians. Three basic outputs were seen as the result of these emphases: 1) the literal future restoration of the nation of Israel (and historical events leading up to it), 2) the literal position of the believer in Christ in heaven, and 3) the church as a new truth unrevealed in the Old Testament.

As Gaebelein looked at both testaments in the light of these facts (derived from literal interpretation), he drew one basic conclusion. There was an absolute distinction between Israel and the church. Truth about one could not be mixed with truth about the other. In essence, God had two dealings, two programs, and two peoples of God.[111]

> Now as we begin to talk on the other phase of the second coming of Christ, the return of our Lord Jesus Christ to this earth, which is the Hope of Israel, the Hope of the nations and the Hope of creation, we go back to the Old Testament, to the unfulfilled prophecies in the Old Testament Scriptures. It is very sad to think that that which is written there has been

---

[111] Recall that this was one of the interpretive principles of Émile Guers (*La Future D'Israël*, 29-37).

so much spiritualized and altogether wrongly interpreted in Christendom. What is the reason? Surely if the heavenly calling and the wonderful ending of the church—church truth as we term it—were understood, it would be impossible to spiritualize that which is in the Old Testament. How truthfully one of the greatest teachers of the Bible of the last century has said "The interpretation is one in the Old Testament, and can only be one, and that is the literal interpretation; the application is manifold.[112]

Gaebelein's statement simply means that Old Testament truth about the future of Israel should be allowed to stand on its own apart from interference from church truth (the allusion to Ephesians). In short, distinctions between Israel and the church should be allowed to stand or confusion in interpretation would result.[113]

The distinction between Israel and the church is worked out in several areas by Gaebelein. First, Israel and the church have separate purposes. He noted that many Christians had told him that

the right key for the Bible was put into their hands when they saw Israel means Israel and not the church, when they understood God's loving purpose concerning that people whom He, in His sovereign mercy, chose to be His people ... If we begin to divide the Word of Truth rightly concerning the Jews, the Gentiles, and the church of God, and see that God has His plan clearly outlined in His Word for each of the three, and has fully revealed that when He began to take out of the nations a people for His name, the gathering of the church, He has not completely and finally cast away His earthly people Israel, we shall then surely have the right key which opens up all in God's Word.[114]

---

[112] Arno C. Gaebelein, "The Coming of the Lord, the Hope of Israel, and the Hope of the Nations and Creation," *Our Hope* 8 (September 1901): 194.

[113] There is no circular reasoning on the part of Gaebelein. He is not saying that literal interpretation leads to the distinction and then using the distinction to justify literal interpretation. It is better to view his statement in reciprocal fashion. They go together. One cannot exist without the other. If literal interpretation is abandoned, there is no basis for the distinction. If the distinction has not been seen, then an abandonment of literal interpretation is involved.

[114] Gaebelein, *Harmony*, 119. Gaebelein also noted that the believer who practices literal interpretation enters into the fact of distinction between Israel and the church and "enters into the thoughts and purposes of God" (37). See also *Acts*, 17-18, and *Meat*, 178.

Second, Israel and the church have separate blessings, earthly blessings for Israel and heavenly or spiritual ones for the church. This would relate to the Christian believer's virtual position in Christ in the heavenlies.[115] Third, Israel and the church were chosen by God in different ways. Israel was chosen in time out from among the existing nations while the church was chosen before the foundation of the world.[116]

Finally, the destiny of Israel and that of the church differ. Israel has an earthly inheritance while the church has a heavenly destiny.[117] Gaebelein commented on this in clear fashion.

> Now the fact is, when the millennium comes it will not be an age of blessing *for the church* in the earth, for the church is then passed out of the world and rules and reigns with Christ, her Lord, in the heavenlies. The church has no promise of a millennium, but the blessings of the coming age are for Israel, the nations and creation.[118]

Such distinctions form the basis for the dispensational-theological integration which Gaebelein used in several passages. It is in this way, as will be shown later, that one can say that Gaebelein's dispensational understanding of the text is based on literal interpretation.

Christ in Old Testament Passages

One other area in which Gaebelein emphasized literal interpretation involves New Testament passages which validate the exercise of seeing Christ in the Old Testament. Unlike Old Testament prophecy and Ephesians which provide a rather large context in which to operate, here one finds Gaebelein interpreting isolated verses.

---

[115] Gaebelein, *Masterpiece*, 21-22.

[116] Ibid., 26-27.

[117] Ibid., 27.

[118] Gaebelein, *Harmony*, 188.

136

Four passages used by Gaebelein in this way are Luke 24:27, 44; John 5:39, Revelation 19:10 and 1 Peter 1:10-11. In Luke 24, Jesus appeared unknown to the two disciples on the road to Emmaus. Then "beginning at Moses and all the prophets, he expounded unto them in all the scriptures the things concerning himself" (Luke 24:27). Luke 24:44 adds that the statements about Jesus in the Old Testament could be found in the law of Moses, in the prophets, and in the Psalms, that is in all of the Old Testament as the Jews understood it. In this context, Gaebelein exclaimed, "What a marvelous fact is the harmonious witness of all Scripture to the Person of our divine Saviour."[119]

The universal nature of these verses was reinforced by John 5:39, "Search the scriptures; for in them ye have eternal life: and they are they which testify of me." Concerning the presence of Christ in the Old Testament in light of this verse, Gaebelein commented that "All God is and all God has revealed is like Himself inexhaustible. All our searching can never exhaust the revelation of His person. There remains always something new to be discovered about His matchless person as revealed in the Old Testament."[120]

In a similar way Gaebelein used Revelation 19:10, "The testimony of Jesus is the spirit of prophecy." According to this passage, Gaebelein asserted that "we are told that when the Holy Spirit in the Old Testament speaks in Prophecy He bears witness to the blessed, holy, worthy and glorious Name—the Name of Jesus, Jehovah-Saviour. This testimony includes everything concerning Himself, past, present, and future."[121] In the discussion to follow, Gaebelein viewed "everything" as including prophecy about the attributes and work of Christ, the plan of

---

[119] Arno C. Gaebelein, *The Church in the House* (New York: Our Hope Publication Office, n.d.), 49. See also Gaebelein, "Wonders," 740 and *Millennium*, 48.

[120] Gaebelein, *Church*, 48.

[121] Gaebelein, *Millennium*, 25.

redemption, and the history of the nations.[122] Another passage, 1 Peter 1:10-11, teaches that the prophets of the Old Testament proclaimed the suffering and glory of Israel's Messiah. This twofold testimony, in Gaebelein's mind, was an expansion of Revelation 19:10.[123]

Such verses were taken at face value by Gaebelein as proof-texts or justification for his exposition of Old Testament passages concerning Christ and associated events which included the nation of Israel. He found this unveiling of Christ in the Old Testament in two forms, direct prophecy and types.[124] Concerning these, Gaebelein noted that

> God has not only spoken by direct prophecies of the Son of His love, His humiliation and His exaltation, His suffering, His atoning death, the gracious results of His sin-bearing work, His resurrection, His priesthood, His return, His judgment work and victory over His enemies, and His world-wide kingdom, but God has revealed these predicted events of the Redeemer in certain persons, whose lives as followers of God foreshadowed parts of His life, in historical events and in Israel's ceremonial laws of sacrifices, offerings and the entire levitical worship.[125]

Thus, Gaebelein took certain New Testament passages concerning Christ in the Old Testament seriously. In doing so, he provided a basis for connecting virtually all direct Old Testament prophecy to Jesus and for using dispensational-typological integration for understanding Christ in the historical portions of the Old Testament.

Conclusion

The literal hermeneutic, in the sense of grammatical-historical interpretation, was defended by Gaebelein almost exclusively with respect to passages that

---

[122] Ibid., 25-26. See also Gaebelein, "Wonders," 740.

[123] Gaebelein, *Millennium*, 26.

[124] Gaebelein, *Listen—God Speaks!* (New York: Our Hope Publications, 1936), 75-76. A discussion of these two forms is given in the context of Gaebelein's use of Revelation 19:10.

[125] Ibid., 76.

138

taught the national restoration of Israel. However, his handling of other texts showed that he was concerned about literal interpretation elsewhere without mentioning the term. Of special note was his literal interpretation of the church in Ephesians as a new entity unrevealed in the Old Testament. As a result, an absolute distinction between Israel and the church emerged as a doctrinal mainstay for his theology. It would have been better for Gaebelein to advocate in writing the grammatical-historical approach for all the Bible rather than selecting a limited scope. Yet his interpretation in the two main areas of the national restoration of Israel and the church as a new entity unrevealed in the Old Testament is essentially accurate.

However, his choices also reflect a keen awareness of major Scriptural themes. Without the literal interpretation of the national restoration of Israel, for example, the biblical covenants to Abraham and David would be divorced from all reality. In addition, the text of Ephesians taken at face value, with its presentation of a framework of dispensations, must not be considered an insignificant addition to theology. Instead, it provided a structure, in conjunction with truth about Israel, for interpreting the entire Bible.[126] In this connection, the literal hermeneutic finds added significance by it relationship to dispensational integration to be discussed next.

---

[126] Elliot E. Johnson, "Hermeneutics and Dispensationalism," in *Walvoord: A Tribute*, ed. Donald K. Campbell (Chicago: Moody Press, 1982), 240-54. Johnson highlighted the teaching of Ephesians as the frame upon which to build the rest of theology.

CHAPTER 5
DISPENSATIONAL INTEGRATION

Introduction

Vern Poythress complained that dispensationalists use a dual hermeneutic, one literal with respect to Israel and one spiritual with respect to the church, while at the same time claiming to be consistently literal.[1] However, it must be noted that Gaebelein, as a dispensationalist, never claimed to apply literal interpretation as his only way of handling or using the Scriptures. At some points, it is foundational. However, his theological decisions most frequently do not directly use the literal hermeneutic.

One can understand why nondispensationalists have trouble understanding the writings of some dispensationalists like Gaebelein. Strong statements on the literal interpretation of prophecy are sometimes mixed with an obvious departure from a literal approach when discussing the same text. The instructive example of Gaebelein's handling of 2 Kings 9-10 is given here at length to demonstrate the possible confusion.

The history of the above two chapters is an intensely interesting one, inasmuch as it foreshadows the judgment which will come at the end of this

---

[1] Vern S. Poythress, *Understanding Dispensationalists* (Grand Rapids, MI: Zondervan Publishing House, 1987), 22-29. Recall this present writer's earlier distinction between hermeneutics proper and integration across various texts. Poythress may be confusing the exegetical statements of dispensationalists with their overall theological synthesis. However, Gaebelein's example, as will be seen in typology, leads easily to questions about inconsistency.

dispensation. The historical books of the Old Testament are too little studied in the light of dispensational truths. These books contain, indeed, history which is far different from the profane history; the historic records we find here were preserved, arranged and written down by the Holy Spirit, and contain, therefore, spiritual and dispensational lessons.[2]

Here Gaebelein strongly relates *dispensational* to *spiritual* indicating that, in some form, a dispensational approach to the passage involves a secondary meaning which is not part of the normal, literal understanding of the text. His comparison of scriptural history to profane history supports this idea. It is doubtful that he uses *spiritual* as a reference to devotional applications of the text. The observation of a foreshadowing or typology in the passage points one in the direction of seeing "spiritual and dispensational lessons" through a use of historical elements as types of future events.

Gaebelein continued the article by rehearsing the historical events of the wickedness of Ahab and Jezebel, the judgment pronounced by the prophet Elijah, the departure of Elijah by way of the whirlwind into heaven, the victory of Jehu over the house of Ahab, and the death of Jezebel. No doubt he accepts the historicity of these events and interprets them literally at that level.[3]

However, Gaebelein added an understanding of typology to the historical occasions. Ahab and Jezebel are types of "a Christ-rejecting world" in the present age.[4] Elijah's departure in the air is seen as a type of the rapture of the church before the judgment of the day of the Lord.[5] The meanings of the names Jehu (Jehovah is He), Jehoshaphat (Jehovah judges), and Nimshi (Jehovah the revealer) show Gaebelein that Jehu is a type of Jesus Christ "who will gather all nations in

---

[2] Arno C. Gaebelein, "Jehu, Jehoshaphat, Nimshi," *Our Hope* 8 (October 1901): 219.

[3] Ibid., 219-221.

[4] Ibid., 220. Gaebelein justified the association of Jezebel with the wickedness of the present world by the use of her name in a discussion of the church of Thyatira in Revelation 2.

[5] Ibid.

the valley of Jehoshaphat and judge them there.[6] The defeat of Ahab's house and the horrible death of Jezebel are a type of the judgment of the nations when Christ returns.[7] These types are more than simple analogies for Gaebelein. He believed that God intended them to be teaching devices in the text of scriptural history.

After outlining these types, Gaebelein emphasized the literal fulfillment of the victory of Jehu. Apparently, he intends for the reader to see the coming judgment of the nations, which Jehu represented in picture form, as also literally fulfilled.

> The literal meaning of the Word is often attempted to be destroyed. If the Word of God does not mean literally what it says, what then does it mean? ... The history of the Jews is witness to the fact that God fulfilled literally His words of threatening ... Still, in our day, an adulterous generation, professing to believe in God and His Word, turns away from the living Word and the written Word and denies the literal meaning of prophecy.[8]

Confusion is heightened even more as Gaebelein, in the next paragraph, again emphasizes types. "We would not overlook in these hints on the typical meaning of the two chapters before us the question which thrice was put to Jehu as his chariot sped on. The question, 'Is it peace?'"[9] Gaebelein comprehended this question as a type of the question to be asked of every person in the present age concerning his own peace with God.[10]

In this discussion, literal interpretation was mixed with the idea of types in the text. The use of types was apparently referred to as a dispensational or spiri-

---

[6] Ibid., 221.

[7] Ibid., 220-21. Gaebelein correlated the type and antitype based partly upon the reference in Revelation 19:17-18. In that passage, immediately after the coming of Christ an invitation is issued to come to the supper of the great God where the flesh of men and animals will be eaten much like the dogs who ate Jezebel's flesh.

[8] Ibid., 222.

[9] Ibid.

[10] Ibid.

tual understanding of the text. In addition, literal interpretation was discussed at two separate points, the historicity of the text being exegeted and the literal fulfillment of the historical events implied by the types.[11]

A second example which demonstrates how reading Gaebelein can produce confusion in the areas of hermeneutics and theological method is found in his analysis of Genesis 5. Of special interest to him are the meanings of names in the text much like that demonstrated with respect to Jehu in the previous example.

> Names in God's Word have a meaning. Correctly traced to their original meaning, they will always help in the understanding of God's ways. Here we have ten names. These names give us a startling revelation.
>
> Adam..............Man.
> Seth ....Set.
> Enosh.............Frailty.
> Cainan ....Deplorable.
> Mahalaleel......The Blessed God.
> Jared ....Descends.
> Enoch ....Teaching.
> Methuselah.....Death sent away.
> Lamech..........To the Distressed.
> Noah..............Rest. Comfort.
>
> As we put them together we have the story of Redemption. What wonderful revelation they give! Man, set (in) frailty, deplorable. This is man's place. Now comes the blessed Gospel itself. The Blessed God (our

---

[11] A similar example is Gaebelein's general approach to the Psalms. He noted that "a closer study of the Psalms and a literal interpretation of all they declare will make this clear to the reader" (*The Harmony of the Prophetic Word* [New York: Fleming H. Revell Co., 1907], 24). The pronoun *this* refers to the experiences in the Psalms being fulfilled in the future as opposed to the experience of David's life. In the next statement Gaebelein added, "Here indeed is a mine of wealth in prophetic foreshadowings which is inexhaustible" (24-25). This mixing of references to literal and typological interpretation is surprising until one understands, at least in this case, that by literal, he refers to the literal fulfillment of what the types represent. The Psalms give many experiences from the life of David, but his life gives, in picture form, the experiences of the nation of Israel. These national experiences are to be taken literally which interpretation is reinforced by the use of the literal hermeneutic in prophetic passages concerning Israel.

Lord)—descends—teaches sending away death; to the distressed, rest and comfort.[12]

Here Gaebelein betrays a penchant for seeking patterns in a text. He seems to have a soteriological-Christological concern and may be practicing his view that Christ can be seen in the Old Testament, not just in predictive passages, but in historical ones through types. Here the men are types individually and corporately. However, the synthesis statement tying all of the meanings together is quite arbitrary.[13]

The first of these two examples more closely follows the mainstream of Gaebelein's method. He definitely practices interpretation in more than one way and allows a single text to be interpreted in two ways simultaneously. To understand the second approach, which is being called dispensational integration, and its relationship to the literal hermeneutic, is the aim of the following discussion. It will begin with a study of 1) Gaebelein's definition of dispensation, 2) his use of patterns and the analogy of faith, and 3) the progress of revelation and God's purposes. These concepts will enlighten the reader to his use of the word *dispensational* which in turn will provide insight into the outworking of Gaebelein's dispensational integration in the areas of theology, typology, and application.

---

[12] Arno C. Gaebelein, "The Fifth Chapter of Genesis," *Our Hope* 9 (May 1903): 631. Gaebelein listed the meanings of names without the synthesis statement attached in *The Annotated Bible* (New York: Publication Office "Our Hope," 1913), 1:28.

[13] Gaebelein indicated that in looking at this passage he had the help of an orthodox Jewish rabbi in translating the names (*As It Was—So Shall It Be, Sunset and Sunrise: A Study of the First Age and Our Present Age* [New York: Our Hope Publication Office, 1937], 61). This Jewish influence may indicate indebtedness to midrashic formulas of some kind. An interest in the meanings of names is certainly consistent with some Jewish commentaries on Genesis (Gen. R. 6:4). However, the Christian summary provided by Gaebelein would not be thought of by a Jewish commentator. Gaebelein, more than likely, was simply creative. These kinds of interpretations by Gaebelein, although consistent with his search for patterns in the Bible, do not appear to be part of the major methodological rules (literal and dispensational) which are practiced. An investigation of midrashic formulas is beyond the scope of the present study although such a study in the light of Gaebelein's interests might be profitable.

144

The Definition and Scheme of Dispensations

Gaebelein defined the concept of a dispensation partly in terms of the word *age*.[14]

> The meaning of this word, as used in Scripture, is not the duration of a life-time, but it has an entirely different meaning. An age in Scripture is a definite period of time, the bounds of which are marked off as to beginning and end by our omniscient God. Each age has a definite beginning and a definite end. During each age God carries out His own eternal purposes, and these are the purposes of redemption. In each He dispenses something which fits in with these purposes and He does in each age a certain work. That is why an age has also been called "a dispensation."[15]

A dispensation is associated with a definite period of time. However, the idea goes beyond the time period to what takes place during the time period from a divine perspective. God has eternal purposes which are worked out or dispensed during each age in the area of redemption.[16] Concerning this working out of God's

---

[14] Arno C. Gaebelein, *Our Age and its End* (New York: Our Hope Publication Office, n.d.), ii-iii and *Studies in Prophecy* (New York: Publication Office "Our Hope," 1918), 7. Lewis Sperry Chafer appeared to emphasize the time element, but included the stewardship idea to be discussed below (*Systematic Theology* [Dallas: Dallas Seminary Press, 1947], 1:40, 7:121-23). J. Dwight Pentecost apparently preferred the word *age* to the word *dispensation* (*Things to Come*, [Grand Rapids, MI: Zondervan Publishing House, 1958], 129-34).

[15] Gaebelein, "Wonders," 235.

[16] This emphasis on redemption goes counter to the complaint that Ryrie voiced about covenant theology's same emphasis. Ryrie sought a doxological purpose as central to God's working throughout the dispensational scheme. Covenant theology, in Ryrie's view, perceived God's working in history as primarily soteriological. See Ryrie, *Dispensationalism*, 46-47. Superficially read, Gaebelein sides with the covenantalists on this point. He noted that "we might call these ages the history of redemption from start to finish" (*Our Age*, ii). Ryrie's attempted comparison certainly has diminishing support (Craig A. Blaising, "A Development of Dispensationalism by Contemporary Dispensationalists," *Bibliotheca Sacra* 145 [July-September 1988]: 267-69). Nonetheless, Ryrie's contrast may need to be reconsidered. See Michael D. Stallard, "Prophetic Hope in the Writings of Arno C. Gaebelein," *The Journal of Ministry and Theology* 2 (Fall 1998): 190-210, as well as the discussion of prophetic hope in the next chapter of this present work.

purposes, Gaebelein used the words *administration* and *stewardship* as synonyms for *dispensation*.[17]

Beyond the basic definition, Gaebelein described a dispensation or age in the following way: "Each age as revealed in Scripture has a beginning manifesting the supernatural but in its progress each age declines, degenerates and finally ends in another display of the supernatural in divine judgment. The eternal age alone has no such end."[18] This description corresponds somewhat to Ryrie's list of primary and secondary characteristics of a dispensation.[19] The statement by Gaebelein emphasizes the negative aspects which can be associated with the secondary elements listed by Ryrie (test, failure, and judgment).[20] However, Gaebelein qualified the idea of judgment at the end of every dispensation.

> It is frequently said and written that every Dispensation closes up in judgment. We can but give a qualified assent to that oft-repeated statement. This present age is the most lengthened of the Dispensations. It is one full of Gospel light and grandly lit up with the moral glories of the Cross unutterable in expression ... The age has its finale in the triumphant shout of the redeemed ... Such is the cry of the conquering host caught up to meet the Lord in the air. On the other hand, the translation of the heavenly saints seals the doom of Christendom. The truth is that the Dispensation closes in triumph on one hand and judgment on the other. Every past and future age has its dark and bright, its night and day.[21]

---

[17] Gaebelein, *God's Masterpiece: An Analytical Exposition of Ephesians I-III* (New York: Publication Office "Our Hope," 1913), 35-36, 116 and *The Church in the House* (New York: Publication Office "Our Hope," n.d.), 93.

[18] Gaebelein, *Our Age*, iii. Compare C. I. Scofield's description of a dispensation as "a period of time during which man is tested in respect of obedience to some specific revelation of the will of God" (*The Scofield Reference Bible* [New York: Oxford University Press, 1909], 5).

[19] Ryrie, *Dispensationalism*, 36-39.

[20] This pessimism with respect to each age (especially for the present age) is one reason that dispensationalism has been criticized as a negative theology. See John H. Gerstner, *Wrongly Dividing the Word of Truth: A Critique of Dispensationalism* (Brentwood, TN: Wolgemuth & Hyatt Publishers, 1991), 155-59.

[21] Gaebelein, *Meat*, 108-9.

146

The exact number and specific classification of dispensations in biblical history seemed unimportant in Gaebelein's presentations. In fact, he noted that there was more than one way to outline the dispensational scheme of the Bible. While making sure not to criticize the seven dispensations of the Scofield Reference Bible, he introduced a classification of three dispensations.[22]

First, there is the Age of Preparation which begins with the fall of man and the first promise of hope given in Genesis 3:15. Part of this age sees the calling of the nation of Israel in God's redemptive plan. Second, the Age of Participation starts with the coming of the Holy Spirit on the day of Pentecost and ends with the rapture of the body of Christ as outlined in 1 Thessalonians 4:17-18. This dispensation takes its name from the invitation which God gives to sinners in this age to become participants in the death and resurrection of Christ.[23] The third dispensation is the Age of Consummation (also Age of Glory) which corresponds to the kingdom age. It commences with the return of Jesus Christ to earth. The seven-year tribulation period after the rapture of the church and before the coming of Christ is a kind of introduction to this kingdom age. The kingdom age will, after one thousand years, merge into eternity.

A second outline Gaebelein considered valid was similar to the one above.[24] The first age is called the Jewish Age and starts with Abraham. The second and present age is once again called the Age of Participation. It concludes at the close of the tribulation period rather than with the pretribulational rapture.

[22] Arno C. Gaebelein, "The Dispensations," *Our Hope* 37 (December 1930): 341-46. The discussion to follow will primarily rely on this article.

[23] Ibid., 342.

[24] Arno C. Gaebelein, "The Wonders of Progressive Prophecy," *Our Hope* 47 (October 1940): 235-41.

Although the name of this dispensation is the same as in the scheme above, its name is derived here from the participation of the Gentiles in the Gospel.[25]

Another scheme listed five dispensations: 1) before law, 2) law, 3) the present grace dispensation, 4) fullness of times or dispensation of glory, and 5) eternity.[26] In another work, he emphasized the three dispensations of law, grace, and the fullness of times.[27] All of the various schemes are similar with only minor variations and emphases. Of most concern to Gaebelein in all of these appears to be the progression of the three dispensations which could be labeled law-Israel, grace-church, and kingdom. In the light of the second scheme above, Gaebelein remarked that "surely these three ages, or dispensations, are clearly marked in Scripture. The teacher who rejects them cannot be a safe and sound teacher."[28]

Patterns and the Analogy of Faith

Daniel Fuller criticized recent dispensationalists for returning to the analogy of faith, the principle of theological interpretation or using one passage of Scripture to interpret another.[29] In his view, earlier dispensationalists had used it unwisely while later dispensationalists had, temporarily at least, seen the dangers of theological interpretation. Indeed, a study of dispensationalists of the Scofield era reveals that the principle was believed and practiced by earlier dispensationalists.[30] What Fuller may have been singling out was the general dislike of the proc-

---

[25] Ibid., 238. In this scheme, the last dispensation of the kingdom is not discussed, but assumed in Gaebelein's writeup.

[26] Gaebelein, *Our Age*, iii.

[27] Gaebelein, *Church*, 92-93.

[28] Gaebelein, "Dispensations," 343.

[29] Daniel P. Fuller, *Gospel and Law: Contrast or Continuum?* (Grand Rapids, MI: William B. Eerdmans Publishing Co., 1980), 61-64. By "recent dispensationalists" is meant post-1960 dispensationalists.

[30] For example, Gaebelein, as will be shown in the following discussion, and his friend, Lewis Sperry Chafer, held the view that interpreting Scripture by Scripture was appropriate if all of the

ess of using later or simpler passages to interpret a particular text.[31] Nonetheless, the analogy of faith has been defined in such a way that it can be seen as a major part of the dispensational integration used by Gaebelein.

Four nuances of meaning have been assigned to the analogy of faith since the days of the Reformation.[32] First, the meaning of a text must harmonize with traditional faith expressed in the Apostles' Creed or in the understanding of the church. Second, analogy of faith has meant the procedure whereby difficult texts were understood on the basis of clear texts on similar topics. Third, it has been used to intend the notion that a single passage must be interpreted in light of the specific doctrinal theme or themes associated with it. Fourth, the analogy of faith has usually meant the idea of understanding an individual text in the light of the entire Bible. Behind this last idea is the belief that the whole Bible is coherent and various passages can, therefore, be harmonized.

Gaebelein's theological method moves freely in the arena of the last three ideas with the concept of interpreting in the light of the entire Bible especially prominent. He attempted to prove the validity of the analogy of faith from Scripture itself.[33] The phrase, "no prophecy of the scripture is of any private interpretation," given in 2 Peter 1:20, "teaches that no prophecy explains itself as such,

---

passages in the entire Bible on a certain theme were included in the process. See Chafer, *Systematic Theology*, 1:117-18.

[31] For example, see Ryrie's statement that "new revelation cannot mean contradictory revelation. Later revelation on a subject does not make the earlier revelation mean something different" (*Dispensationalism*, 94).

[32] Henri Blocher, "The 'Analogy of Faith' in the Study of Scripture," *Scottish Bulletin of Evangelical Theology* 5 (Spring 1987): 17-38. See also Walter C. Kaiser, "Hermeneutics and the Theological Task," *Trinity Journal* 12 (Spring 1991): 3-14.

[33] The passage traditionally used to support an analogy of faith is Romans 12:6 ("so as to have sound judgment, as God has allotted to each a measure of faith"). Kaiser showed that this text cannot be used to justify the analogy of faith ("Hermeneutics," 4-6). Gaebelein ignored this passage in his argumentation.

none stands for itself."[34] He added that "God's purposes are revealed in it progressively from beginning to end. Holy men of God spake, and each of them and all of them were moved by the same Spirit, therefore the entire prophetic Word *must* be harmonious, and it must be studied as a whole, comparing Scripture with Scripture."[35] Several key concepts converge in this discussion by Gaebelein. He believed strongly in the divine origin of the Bible as the bedrock for a corollary faith in the unity of the Scriptures. He saw God's purposes revealed progressively throughout the whole Bible leading one to conclude that the entire canon had to be involved in the study of a single passage. Any interpretation which did not measure up to the overall unity of the Bible must be rejected.

A second passage used to prove the correctness of a theological interpretation is 1 Peter 1:10-13 which taught, according to Gaebelein, that Old Testament prophets did not have a full understanding of what they wrote because they could not view it in light of the entire written revelation that was later to be completed.[36] He went on to declare his purpose of showing "the harmony of the prophetic Word relating to the glories and events still future, tracing them through the entire Word."[37]

In fact, Gaebelein's book, *The Harmony of the Prophetic Word*, is devoted totally to the exercise of the analogy of faith applied to prophetic passages. After the introductory chapters, the biblical themes such as the day of the Lord,[38] the

---

[34] Arno C. Gaebelein, "The Harmony of the Prophetic Word," *Our Hope* 9 (September 1902): 130-31. This idea grates somewhat against the literal hermeneutic emphasized by Gaebelein in previous discussions, especially when Old Testament passages about Israel were not to be interfered with by New Testament passages. They basically stood alone.

[35] Ibid., 131. See also Gaebelein, *Harmony*, 12-14.

[36] Gaebelein, "Harmony," 131-32. See also *Harmony*, 14-15. The book cited here, *Harmony of the Prophetic Word*, is a later expansion of an article in *Our Hope* by the same name.

[37] Gaebelein, "Harmony," 132.

[38] Gaebelein, *Harmony*, 17-40.

Great Tribulation,[39] the judgment of the nations,[40] the Antichrist,[41] the Christ's second coming,[42] the conversion and restoration of Israel,[43] and the millennial kingdom[44] are studied inductively with the entire Bible and every mention of the topic theoretically in mind, even if space did not allow complete discussion.

Gaebelein made specific application of the analogy of faith to the book of Revelation.

> For the study of this New Testament Prophetic Book the knowledge of the chief content of the Old Testament Prophetic Word is ... an absolute necessity ... (2 Peter 1:20-21) means that the interpretation of prophecy must be done by comparing Scripture with Scripture ... To understand any prophecy is only possible by taking the entire Prophetic Word into consideration.[45]

General statements to the same effect abound in the writings of Gaebelein.[46]

In connection with this belief that Scripture should interpret Scripture, one finds in Gaebelein an emphasis on the idea of patterns or sequences. Discussing

---

[39] Ibid., 41-55.

[40] Ibid., 56-76.

[41] Ibid., 77-98.

[42] Ibid., 99-116.

[43] Ibid., 117-58.

[44] Ibid., 159-208.

[45] Arno C. Gaebelein, *The Revelation: An Analysis and Exposition of the Last Book of the Bible* (New York: Our Hope Publications, n.d.), 11.

[46] For example, "It is always proper in reading and interpreting the Word of God, to see if not elsewhere in the Bible terms or things to be interpreted are used, so that through them the right meaning can be ascertained" (Arno C. Gaebelein, *The Acts of the Apostles: An Exposition*, [New York: Publication Office "Our Hope," 1912; reprint, Neptune, NJ: Loizeaux Brothers, 1961], 121). See also Arno C. Gaebelein, *The Return of the Lord* (New York: Publication Office "Our Hope," 1925), 13, and "The Whole Prophetic Word" *Our Hope* 8 (July 1901): 2. Another example is his statement that the meaning of symbols in Ezekiel cannot be fully understood without a comprehension of the historical books of 2 Kings and 2 Chronicles (*The Prophet Ezekiel: An Analytical Exposition* [New York: Publication Office "Our Hope," 1918], 107).

the "dispensational" chapters, Romans 9-11, Gaebelein correlated the salvation experience of Paul with the future conversion of the nation of Israel.[47]

> He refers twice to his experience when he was saved on the road to Damascus, and these two references give us the key. "But for this reason mercy was shown me, that *in me first*, Jesus Christ might display all long-suffering, for a pattern of those that should hereafter believe on Him to eternal life" (1 Tim. 1:16). Now the word "pattern" (Hypotyposis) means a sketch, an outline, a delineation. It is an outline of what is going to happen some day on a larger scale when the nation, to which Paul belonged will be saved, as he was saved.[48]

Typology is part of this pattern which Gaebelein expected to find in the lives of all major Bible characters.[49] For now, the point is that he was willing to view the Bible with patterns.

In the specific case above, the life and conversion of Paul with all its details was placed side by side with the prophetic passages throughout the Bible which spoke of the future conversion and restoration of Israel.[50] Paul's experience helps interpret the passages dealing with the future experience of the nation. Thus, the pattern (in this case through typology) is a specific application of the analogy of faith.

In a discussion of future events about the nation of Israel, Gaebelein reveals the importance of the idea of a pattern in terms of sequence. There are three great events which are in the future: 1) Christ's literal second coming, 2) the conversion and national restoration of Israel, and 3) the Gentile nations turning to God.[51] Concerning these events Gaebelein affirmed that "the order cannot be re-

---

[47] Arno C. Gaebelein, *The Prophet St. Paul: The Eschatology of the Apostle to the Gentiles* (New York: Publication Office "Our Hope," 1939), 115. His use of the word *dispensational* highlights the fact that these discussions involve dispensational integration.

[48] Ibid., 115-16.

[49] Ibid., 146.

[50] Ibid., 146-55.

[51] Ibid., 128.

152

versed. It is the divine program. To prove these points we would have to go through the prophetic books of the Old Testament and the Psalms citing hundreds of passages. Read as striking proofs Zechariah 2:6-13; Isaiah 59:20,21; Isaiah 60."[52] Gaebelein went on to note how this sequence, seen throughout several passages, related to the church age. He then noted, "now we shall be able to understand the dispensational 'much more.'"[53] Hence, the idea of a sequence or pattern seen by comparing many Scriptures with each other, is part of what it means to have a dispensational understanding of the Bible.

A final example of how patterns are seen in relation to Gaebelein's use of the analogy of faith can be found in his interpretive approach to the individual passage in John 10:9, "I am the door; by Me if any man enter in, he shall be saved, and shall go in and out, and find pasture."[54] A pattern of scriptural uses of the word *door* combine to produce an interpretation. The expected result is that "these different doors will illuminate this simple and blessed word of the Friend of Sinners."[55]

Beginning with the first occurrence of a door given with respect to Noah's ark and continuing with an analysis of the blood-marked door in the Passover, the scarlet thread of Rahab, the door of hope in the valley of Achor, and the door of the Tabernacle in the wilderness, the following conclusion is adopted:

> If it meant death and judgment for those in the Old Testament who passed through that veil into the presence of God, it now means death and judgment for all who refuse to come unto God by this new and living way ... What I have said shows the meaning of the word of our Lord, "I am the Door." Through Him we enter into the presence of God. Believing on Him we are saved. In Him judgment cannot reach us; in Him we are cov-

[52] Ibid.

[53] Ibid., 129.

[54] Gaebelein, *Church*, 132-42.

[55] Ibid., 133. In this context, Gaebelein referred to them as illustrations. Many of the examples are types.

ered by the righteousness of God; in Him we are safe and secure; in Him is our shelter, our peace and our glory.[56]

It is clear that the judgment aspects of the Old Testament examples given in the pattern of usage are inserted into John 10:9. Gaebelein's statements seem to imply more than making a list of various truths throughout the Bible and presenting them individually. Some passages actually inform the meaning of other passages. This is another example of the analogy of faith.

One specific aspect of Gaebelein's use of the analogy of faith centers around his dependence upon the location which has the fullest explanation of a certain doctrine. Associated with this is the importance of the idea of silence in various parts of the Bible on any given topic. While discussing the possibility that Ezekiel 16:35-59 teaches the future restitution of the wicked dead, he begins by noting that "the Old Testament is not that part of the divine Revelation where teachings and doctrines about the future state are given."[57] An exegesis of Old Testament passages shows the national restoration of Israel, but little hint, in Gaebelein's view, of the physical resurrection of individuals.[58]

Consequently, a second principle is stated. "Should we find anything in the Old Testament concerning the future state, the state of the righteous and the unrighteous after death, such a hint or statement can only be rightly understood and interpreted by the great doctrine concerning the future state as revealed in the New Testament."[59] Gaebelein clarified what he did not mean by this statement in case there was any misunderstanding.

By this, of course, we do not say that the Old Testament needs correction by the revelation of the New, nor do we say that the Old is inferior to the

---

[56] Ibid., 140.

[57] Gaebelein, *Ezekiel*, 112.

[58] Ibid., 112-13.

[59] Ibid., 113.

New; all *is* the Word of God. However, as the Old Testament does not show man's condition after death, any passage which appears to relate to such a condition must be interpreted by the full light as given in the New Testament.[60]

This appears to be a specific case of letting the clear and full teaching of passages (in the New Testament in this case) dictate any controversial passages elsewhere (as in the Old Testament) which have little support in their own context.

In the third principle mentioned in the discussion, Gaebelein turns to the issue of silence in the New Testament. "If such passages as Ezekiel xvi:53 and Ezekiel xxxvii:1-14, etc., teach the restitution of the wicked by resurrection for another chance, we must then find such a doctrine of the restoration of the wicked dead for another chance to accept salvation most clearly and fully revealed as one of the great doctrines of the New Testament."[61] From a slightly different perspective, the silence of the New Testament, in this example, appears to inform alleged interpretations in the Old Testament. Earlier the relative silence of the Old Testament with respect to these alleged interpretations was also informed by the New Testament's fuller understanding. In both cases, the more comprehensive understanding presented in New Testament teaching is to be used to make an exegetical decision in Old Testament passages concerning the second probation doctrine.

Is Gaebelein in these examples simply reading the New Testament back into the Old? The comparing of Scripture with Scripture done by Gaebelein should most often be taken as a search for patterns rather than a simple priority of the New Testament. Earlier discussions about the literal hermeneutic and an emphasis on Old Testament prophecy point away from an over-simplistic view of Gaebelein's approach. Instead, as hinted at in some of the examples above, a better place to look for clarification is Gaebelein's view of the progress of revelation.

---

[60] Ibid.

[61] Ibid.

The Progress of Revelation and God's Purposes

The context for which Gaebelein discussed the idea of dispensations and in which he used the analogy of faith was provided by his understanding of the progress of revelation. Adolf Saphir, a frequent contributor during the early years of *Our Hope*, probably presented one of the best explanations of the dispensationalist's understanding of progress of revelation. He does so with the blessing of Gaebelein as editor. Concerning revelation in the Bible, he wrote:

> Every part is complete, containing the seed, the germ; and though subsequent parts contain a much fuller unfolding of the germ, they do not render their predecessors superfluous or antiquated. Thus the whole Gospel is in Genesis; even in Gen. iii. the Protevangelion contains the whole counsel of God in germ. More fully in Leviticus, more fully in David's Psalms, more fully in Isaiah's prophecy, more fully in Paul's epistles. As Israel developed and grew in stature and wisdom (or rather the revelation of Christ in Israel, for the nation always fell short of the glory of God), so the Scripture develops. It is not that something is added to the old stock (as one stone is a collection of small stones), but the plant, the organism, the body, *grows*. Beautiful and benign arrangement of our great and blessed God! Abraham rejoiced, and David rejoiced, and Isaiah rejoiced, and Paul rejoiced; because to each there was given *all*, though on a different scale, in different degree and measure.
>
> But though Paul possesses this whole more perfectly than David and Moses, does he throw aside David and Moses as a scaffolding is thrown aside when the building is finished? By no means: and, among many reasons, for this reason also—that in Genesis and the Psalms and the prophets, there is a great revelation of a great comprehensive plan, the fulfillment of which reaches into the ages to come; so that without the previous portions of the Word, we and future generations cannot be perfect; there is much of this whole which yet remains to be unfolded, and manifested in reality and actual existence. Thus the Apocalypse returns to Genesis, and the eleventh chapter of Paul's epistle to the Romans leads us back to Moses and the prophets.[62]

The key idea is development in the revelation. A key word is *unfolded*. Later revelation has a fuller understanding of the truth given in earlier stages, but the later unfolding cannot undo any previous presentation of the truth. In addition,

---

[62] Adolf Saphir, "Christ and the Scriptures," *Our Hope* 8 (July 1901): 31-32.

revelation given in the Bible is not composed of a simple collection of data items which form a whole. They are organically related like a plant that is growing. As a result there is "a great revelation of a great comprehensive plan."[63]

Gaebelein believed the harmonious nature of this unfolding was evidence of the supernatural inspiration of the Bible.[64] The overall goal of the progress of revelation was the unveiling of the purposes of God.[65] Bible interpretation becomes the analyzing of the "progressive development of the doctrine" under consideration.[66] In this, one would expect to find teachings which were not known in Old Testament times but have been given in the New Testament.[67]

One specific element in Gaebelein's view of the unfolding of God's revelation is the idea of God's purposes in history. These purposes are most clearly revealed in prophecy.

> Prophecy has often been explained as being *History prewritten*. And so it is. But it is something deeper than that ... *It is the revelation of the plan of redemption as planned by our omniscient God, who knows the end from the beginning. This plan of redemption was made by Him before the foundation of the world. It makes known the eternal purposes of God. It reveals His thoughts of eternal love and grace and makes known the great goal of consummation which He has appointed for His eternal glory.*[68]

Prophecy makes known God's eternal purposes which involve God's plan of redemption.

---

[63] Ibid., 32.

[64] Arno C. Gaebelein, "The Wonders of Progressive Prophecy" *Our Hope* 46 (May 1940): 747.

[65] Gaebelein, "Harmony," 131.

[66] Gaebelein, *Return*, 14.

[67] Gaebelein, *Will There Be A Millennium: When and How?: The Coming Reign of Christ in the Light of the Old and New Testaments* (New York: Publication Office "Our Hope," 1943), 20.

[68] Gaebelein, "Wonders," 664-65. Emphasis is Gaebelein's.

Gaebelein made it clear that prophecy, as is true of all Bible doctrines, is progressive.[69] Furthermore, prophecy must be studied via the analogy of faith. "And as we compare Scripture and believe all the prophets have spoken we are led on from knowledge to knowledge, and at the same time keeping close to that which is written, we are kept from perversion, from fanciful interpretations and fanatical guesses for which the study of Prophecy has been such a fertile soil."[70] In this way, progressive revelation in prophecy is combined with God's purposes and the analogy of faith in interpretation. The purposes are worked out in the context of the dispensations or ages.[71] Each dispensation is a portion of the unfolding of God's progressive revelation and possesses its own "peculiar revelation" which denotes the purpose of the age.[72]

Gaebelein saw a chiastic structure to the unfolding of God's purposes.

The Bible presents four great lines of revelation in the outworking of the divine purpose of redemption, viz.: *Creation*; the *Gentiles* or nations; *Israel*; the *Church*. This is the Old Testament order in its historical unfolding. The New Testament reverses the order and presents first the calling and destiny of the Church; then follows the restoration of the kingdom to Israel under the sway of Messiah's sceptre on David's throne; next the calling of the Gentiles or nations, and last the deliverance of creation from the bondage of corruption.[73]

The divine order is found in Acts 15:13-18.[74] Concerning this passage, Gaebelein wrote:

---

[69] Ibid., 666.

[70] Ibid.

[71] Gaebelein, *Our Age*, ii.

[72] Ibid., vii.

[73] Arno C. Gaebelein, *Meat in Due Season: Sermons, Discourses and Expositions of the Word of Prophecy* (New York: Arno C. Gaebelein, Inc.), 19-20.

[74] Ibid.

It has rightly been called the divine program. It is significant that in this first great gathering in Jerusalem, the Holy Spirit lays down the exact plan of how God works in this present age and what will follow after the special purpose of God in this age is accomplished. And this great truth of the dispensations, so necessary to understand the Word of God, is almost unknown today. What would Christendom be if the divine plan and program as uttered by James were believed? How different the work of the great denominational gatherings, if the dispensational facts so prominent in the whole Bible and so fully stated here, were taken into consideration![75]

To view the Bible without keeping these progressively revealed divine purposes in mind is, to Gaebelein, tantamount to questioning the veracity of God who has made promises in "oath bound covenants."[76] In addition, such a denial attacks the divine unity provided by the one author of Scripture, the Holy Spirit.[77] Consequently, the nature of progressive revelation in the unfolding of God's plan and purposes throughout the dispensations of the Bible was a tremendously significant concept for Gaebelein.

The importance of progressive revelation is also seen in the general presentation of much of Gaebelein's theological writings. For example, in a series of articles on progressive prophecy, he began by announcing Genesis 3:15 as the astonishing germ of all prophecy."[78] He then traced the "progressive development of this key-prophecy" through Isaac, Jacob, Jesse, David, Solomon, and then Christ.[79] The next article in the series shows a sequence of brides which serve as

---

[75] Gaebelein, *Acts*, 265. Gaebelein's outline of the dispensational facts in this passage are 1) the calling out of a people from among the Gentiles (the church), 2) the Second Coming of Christ, 3) the establishment of the Davidic Kingdom (assuming the conversion of the Jews), and 4) the conversion of the Gentiles (265-69).

[76] Gaebelein, *Meat*, 181.

[77] Ibid., 226.

[78] Gaebelein, "Wonders," 666.

[79] Arno C. Gaebelein, "The Wonders of Progressive Prophecy," *Our Hope* 46 (May 1940): 740-47.

types. Beginning with Eve, Gaebelein traced a picture of the church through Rachel, Asenath, Rebekah, and the daughter of Pharaoh (bride of Solomon).[80] He also saw a pattern with respect to the use of the term *the third day*. Taking examples from creation, Isaac, Joseph, Moses, Hezekiah, Esther, Jonah, and Hosea, Gaebelein presented a "progressive line of types clustering around the *third day*, predictive of the *third day* when He (Christ) arose from the dead."[81] A progressive study of Melchizedek beginning in Genesis 14 compares various Old Testament prophecies and New Testament promises which point to the glory of Christ and the church.[82] The remaining articles in the series are primarily devoted to drawing the outline for the history of Israel throughout the Bible including the Abrahamic Covenant, judgment on the nation, and its ultimate conversion and blessing.[83]

A peculiar aspect of Gaebelein's concerns with respect to progressive revelation is the area of double fulfillment of prophecy. For example, he remarked: "In the prophet *Amos* we find predictions against nations. This prophet began his prophetic office by pronouncing judgment against the enemies of Israel. They had sinned against Israel and done evil to them. There has been a fulfillment

---

[80] Arno C. Gaebelein, "The Wonders of Progressive Prophecy," *Our Hope* 46 (June 1940): 815-20.

[81] Arno C. Gaebelein, "The Wonders of Progressive Prophecy," *Our Hope* 47 (July 1940): 21-27.

[82] Arno C. Gaebelein, "The Wonders of Progressive Prophecy," *Our Hope* 47 (August 1940): 91-97.

[83] See Arno C. Gaebelein, "The Wonders of Progressive Prophecy," *Our Hope* 47 (September 1940): 161-67; 47 (October 1940): 235-41; 47 (November 1940): 305-10; 47 (December 1940): 380-85; 47 (January 1941): 449-53 and 47 (March 1941): 591-94. Other theological works by Gaebelein which show dependence upon the idea of progressive revelation for the method of presentation are *The Work of Christ* (London: Alfred Holness, n.d.), *The Conflict of the Ages: the Mystery of Lawlessness* (New York: Publication Office "Our Hope," 1933), 22-68, *Harmony of the Prophetic Word, As It Was, The Hope of the Ages* (New York: Publication Office "Our Hope," 1938), 11-53, *Things to Come*, and *World Prospects, How is it All Going to End? A Study in Sacred Prophecy and Present Day World Conditions* (New York: Publication Office "Our Hope," 1934).

160

unquestionably of these judgments, yet a final fulfillment of it is yet to come."[84] A more specific sample of this is Gaebelein's discussion of Enoch's prediction of the coming judgment of the Lord given in Jude 14–16. Gaebelein commented about the intent of the message.

> But what was his message? What coming of the Lord did he mean? Many prophecies have a near fulfillment, but with it the final fulfillment is still in the future. No one would deny that the prophecy of this first prophet of God's word had a meaning for that first age, as it was nearing its appointed end. Enoch announced the approaching end of that age, that it would end with the coming of the Lord, Who would appear and bring holy ones with Him, and that His coming would bring judgment. But this does not by any means exhaust another fulfillment of which Enoch probably knew but little. The epistle of Jude, written by Jude, the brother of James, refers to Enoch and his prophecy. It directs our attention both backward and forward. Backward to the closing days of the first age; forward to the end of our own age.[85]

The message had a double application or double fulfillment with respect to the same preaching. Both the age of Enoch and the present or church age were in view when God gave these words through the prophet Enoch.

Furthermore, Gaebelein observed that many prophecies should be treated this way. This means that, within the context of the progress of revelation, the unfolding of truth about one dispensation can be applied to the revealing of truth regarding a later age. Both applications can be made simultaneously. Such an approach opens the way for both the dispensational-typical and dispensational-applicatory integration to be discussed later.[86]

---

[84] Gaebelein, *Harmony*, 62-63.

[85] Gaebelein, *As It Was*, 74.

[86] In addition to the significance for dispensational-applicatory integration, this last example points one in the direction of discussions about the use of the Old Testament in the New. Gaebelein was aware of the importance of this issue. Wilbur M. Smith, teacher at Moody Bible Institute at the time of Gaebelein's death, recalled a conversation with the editor of *Our Hope* in which the latter revealed, "I never realized until this morning how much of the Old Testament the apostle Paul uses in his Epistle to the Romans. It is just filled with the Old Testament. I must make a special study of this" (*Arno C. Gaebelein: A Memoir*, New York: Our Hope Press, 1946), 9. A helpful survey of the issue can be found in Darrell Bock, "Evangelicals and the Use of the Old Testament

Dispensational Truth

Gaebelein's use of the word *dispensation*, his practice of the analogy of faith, and the overarching progress of revelation which appears to govern both, all contribute to his understanding of dispensational truth. At times the word *dispensational* in Gaebelein's writings approaches the general idea of "truth about the Second Coming" or "eschatological truth."[87] However, at other times the word takes on more detailed significance.

In the introduction to Gaebelein's commentary on Matthew, within a span of thirteen pages the word *dispensational* occurs at least ten times.[88] One would expect a generally consistent use by such a knowledgeable writer. The context of the presentation shows the word used as an adjective in such phrases as "the dispensational Gospel" (twice), "the dispensational truths" (three times), "the dispensational character of Matthew," "dispensational teachings," "the dispensational point of view," "dispensational parts" which are prominent in Matthew, and the "dispensational outline." The primary idea associated with each is a distinction between various biblical elements in the progress of revelation.

For example, Gaebelein introduced a statement of caution when approaching the book of Matthew.

> Because it is the Jewish Gospel, it is *dispensational* throughout. It is safe to say that a person, no matter how learned or devoted, who does not hold the clearly revealed dispensational truths concerning the Jews, the Gentiles and the church of God will fail to understand Matthew.[89]

---

in the New," *Bibliotheca Sacra* 142 (July-September 1985): 209-23 and 142 (October-December 1985): 306-19.

[87] Gaebelein, *Meat*, 96; *Acts*, 298-99.

[88] Arno C. Gaebelein, *The Gospel of Matthew: An Exposition* (New York: Publication Office Our Hope, 1910; reprint, Neptune, NJ: Loizeaux Brothers, 1961), 4-16.

[89] Ibid., 5.

162

The issue for Gaebelein was proper categories. The most important distinction was that between Israel and the church.[90] The "dispensational parts" of Matthew[91] must be interpreted in their proper sphere within the progress of revelation and in light of proper relationships with other elements. The Gospel of Matthew basically gives the outline of the history of God's dealings with its distinctions in each dispensation.

Within this basic thrust of the word *dispensational*, one can see three definite emphases which relate to the methodology of Gaebelein. The first is theological. Gaebelein understood that theological decisions were to be made in the light of this dispensational understanding, that is, in light of proper distinctions within the progress of revelation. This can be called dispensational-theological integration.

The second emphasis within the basic idea of distinctions behind the word *dispensational* is the concept that these peculiar features can be taught through types. At times in Gaebelein's introduction to Matthew, he related dispensational truths to spiritual unfoldings.[92] The close relationship between the word *dispensational* and the practice of typology can be seen when he noted that virtually all of the content of Matthew is "to be looked upon as foreshadowing and teaching dispensational truths."[93] Therefore, in addition to a theological emphasis with respect

---

[90] Ibid., 12. Compare Gaebelein's equation of the church as a new revelation to dispensational truth ("Rightly Dividing the Word of Truth," *Our Hope* 8 [December 1901]: 297-98). The distinctions with respect to God's purposes were also seen as part of dispensational structure ("Editorial Notes," *Our Hope* 8 [June 1902]: 618). The discussion compares the earthly calling of Israel with the heavenly calling of the church.

[91] Gaebelein listed these as 1) the King, 2) the Kingdom, 3) the rejection of the King and Kingdom, 4) the rejection and judgment of Israel, 5) the mysteries of the Kingdom of the Heavens, 6) the church, and 7) prophetic teachings about the end of the present age (*Matthew*, 8-16).

[92] Ibid., 6-7.

[93] Ibid., 7. Many examples exist in Gaebelein's writings which practically equate the word *dispensational* with *typical*. For example, "dispensationally the Feast of Pentecost typifies the coming of the Spirit of God, to baptize believing Jews and Gentiles into one body" (Gaebelein, *Ezekiel*, 324).

to dispensational integration, one also finds a typological thrust which will be called dispensational-typological integration.

There is a third way in which Gaebelein handled the text in connection with dispensational synthesis. Earlier it was observed that he allowed a double fulfillment of the same prophecy. This principle of double application is utilized in non-prophetic portions of Scripture as well. In comments on the Sermon on the Mount, Gaebelein rejected the overall views of the text which see the application as primarily isolated to society, to the church, or to the Jews.[94] Instead, he decided to accept a double application. The principal use of the text sees it as "the proclamation of the King concerning the Kingdom."[95] This is essentially the application of the sermon to the future Davidic kingdom of the nation Israel. But Gaebelein added that "this *never* excludes application to us who are His heavenly people, members of His body, who will share the heavenly throne in the heavenly Jerusalem with Him."[96] Such an approach to Scripture, in light of distinctive elements sharing application, can be labeled dispensational-applicatory integration.[97]

---

[94] Ibid., 106-10.

[95] Ibid., 110.

[96] Ibid.

[97] Poythress differentiated between "hardline" dispensationalists and "applicatory" dispensationalists (*Dispensationalists*, 30-33). "Hardline" dispensationalists refuse any application of Old Testament or kingdom truth to Christians today while the others are willing to make an effort at application. He leaves the impression that contemporary dispensationalists generally fall in the latter category while earlier dispensationalists, like Gaebelein, were "hardline" dispensationalists. His example is the Lord's Prayer in Matthew 6:9-13. Indeed, Gaebelein follows Poythress' distinction with respect to this passage. However, the rest of the Sermon on the Mount is generally applied by Gaebelein to the church as well as to the kingdom. This would point in the direction that Scofieldian dispensationalists were more open to application in this area then they are usually given credit for. Blaising, a dispensationalist, appears to stress that the difference between modern and earlier dispensationalists in this matter is one of degree ("Development," 258-59). See also, John A. Martin, "Dispensational Approaches to the Sermon on the Mount," in *Essays in Honor of J. Dwight Pentecost*, ed. Stanley D. Toussaint and Charles H. Dyer (Chicago: Moody Press, 1986), 35-48.

Each of these three emphases of dispensational integration needs further investigation. Theological, typological, and applicatory considerations must all be examined to broaden and deepen an understanding of Gaebelein's method in these areas. After several examples are given in each category, one might be surprised to find that the second use of dispensational integration through types is the most widespread in Gaebelein's commentaries.

Dispensational-Theological Integration

Dispensational-theological integration, as it is presented here, is not merely the general use of the analogy of faith. It is a particular employment of the analogy of faith whereby the distinctions seen in the Bible drive the interpretation of various passages. Of particular interest is Gaebelein's theological utilization of the absolute distinction between Israel and the church as a switch to determine the meaning of assorted texts. Several examples will be given to demonstrate that Gaebelein's thinking along these lines is widespread.

First, an examination of Gaebelein's view of the Sermon on the Mount manifests clear indications of this integration principle. "If the dispensational character of Matthew were understood, no ethical teaching from the so-called Sermon on the Mount at the expense of the Atonement of our Lord Jesus Christ would be possible, nor would there be room for the subtle, modern delusion, so universal now, of a 'social Christianity' which aims at lifting up the masses and the reformation of the world."[98] Two theological conclusions are made by Gaebelein concerning Matthew 5–7. One should reject any view which minimizes the work of Christ on the cross (atonement) in favor of an emphasis on the ethical teachings of Christ. In a corollary to this, one should reject a social gospel, presumably, in favor of spiritual conversion. This interpretation is based upon Gaebelein's understanding of the Sermon on the Mount in the context of the entire

---

[98] Ibid., 6.

book. While acknowledging application to the Christian believer today, it is seen primarily as the preaching of the King about the future kingdom. At a basic level it is Jewish. To mix Jewish and church truth (apart from allowances for applications) leads to erroneous conclusions.[99]

The most noticeable part of the Sermon on the Mount which received attention from Gaebelein in this respect is the Lord's Prayer given in 6:8-15. The prayer is not intended for the New Testament Christian, even in application.[100] "This perfect model of prayer was given by our Lord to His disciples to be used by them individually and previously to the gift of the Holy Spirit. It was then all on Jewish ground; they were Jewish *believers* and as such they received this model prayer and used it in the transition state."[101] Not only was it intended for the pre-Christian part of the historical records of the New Testament, the prayer was again to be used during the end times. Gaebelein commented the following way: "When the Church is taken from the earth a believing Jewish remnant will give the witness and preach the Gospel of the Kingdom once more. They will undoubtedly use this prayer during the great tribulation through which they will pass, the tribulation in which the evil one is in the earth and famine and many temptations will abound."[102] In both cases, the era in which the prayer is used is Jewish rather than Christian.

---

[99] Discussing the Sermon on the Mount shows the difficulty in distinguishing between the use of the dispensational-theological or dispensational-applicatory aspect of Gaebelein's dispensational integration. The general rule is that the theological aspect is a use of the Israel-church distinction to prevent violation of the primary meaning of a passage. The applicatory aspect is a recognition of the distinctions while expanding use of the text beyond the primary meaning. One must also understand that these analytical categories are the creation of this writer. Gaebelein, for example, did not always make a strong distinction between theological interpretation and application (*Matthew*, 144).

[100] Gaebelein, *Matthew*, 139.

[101] Ibid., 140.

[102] Ibid., 143.

Gaebelein supported this distinction by comparing the model prayer to other scriptural petitions.[103] In particular, the teaching that prayer is to be done in the name of Jesus (John 17:24-27) is seen as beginning at the time the teaching is given. This takes place after the model prayer is given in Matt. 6:8-15. Furthermore, the Johannine passage shows that a new practice is in view. Such an outlook corresponds with the overall distinction between Israel and the church. Gaebelein then uses the distinction to justify the fact that the Lord's Prayer is not a Christian prayer.[104]

Second, Gaebelein's dispensational-theological integration and interpretation also operated in the context of the Olivet Discourse (Matt. 24–25). The three divisions of the discourse are 1) the end of the age (the tribulation period, Matt. 24:4-44), 2) the Christian era (Matt. 24:45–25:30), and 3) the judgment of the nations (Matt. 25:31-46). Study of these divisions, presumably with their distinctions, must be done to "find out what season or time they refer and after we have cleared away some of the false interpretations and misconceptions, we hope to study each division in detail."[105]

Gaebelein rejected the interpretation of the first part which sees fulfillment within the church age. It has "its origin in a deplorable ignorance of God's dispensational dealings with the Jews and the Gentiles. It leaves nothing for the Jew-

---

[103] Ibid., 140-43.

[104] In two other respects, Gaebelein rejected the Lord's Prayer as genuine Christian prayer. The phrase "thy kingdom come" is a prayer for the coming of the literal, earthly Messianic kingdom which Christians do not have a part in. Second, the request, "forgive us our debts as we forgive our debtors," is considered a "legal" or "Old Testament petition." He noted, "Our forgiveness does not depend upon our relation to each other." The distinction in this case is described in law terms as opposed to grace terms. The Israel-church distinction is still in view. See Gaebelein, *Matthew*, 142-43.

[105] Arno C. Gaebelein, *His Last Words: A Study of the Last Discourse of Our Lord Known as the "Olivet Discourse"* (New York: Publication Office "Our Hope," n.d.), 4-5.

ish nation in the future."[106] Rescue from false interpretation on this point is clearly based on two basic propositions.

> Let one get clear on two important teachings of the word and deliverance from this false interpretation of this part of our Lord's discourse will speedily follow. We mean the teaching of the Scriptures of what the church is, her calling and her destiny. And in the second place the teaching of the prophetic word, that the Lord will call a believing Jewish remnant, which will suffer and witness at the end of the age. If a person, be he a teacher or not, is ignorant of either one of these, he must be confused in his conception of the first part of Matthew xxiv.[107]

Thus, with clarity Gaebelein bases the interpretation of Matthew 24:4-44 on a prior commitment to a synthesis of two truths, the nature of the church and the future of Israel. This synthesis, explored earlier, emphasizes the absolute distinction between Israel and the church. This distinction is a theological truth which is brought to the passage as a switch to help in the determination of theological meaning.[108]

Third, Gaebelein's interpretation of the imprecatory Psalms demonstrates his use of dispensational-theological integration.[109]

> Many Psalms contain the experiences of the God-fearing part of the Jews passing through the tribulation and being delivered out of the hands of their enemies by the coming of the Lord from Heaven. We read of the dangers and perplexities by which this remnant, brought back to the land of their fathers, is surrounded. Their sufferings are clearly portrayed, and we hear their pleadings for divine mercy, deliverance, and interference. The imprecatory prayers, calling God's wrath down upon the enemies,

---

[106] Ibid., 6.

[107] Ibid., 8-9.

[108] Similar theological argumentation can be found in Gaebelein, *Acts*, 78 and *Harmony*, 135.

[109] Gaebelein's commentary on the Psalms is perhaps the most difficult to understand of all of his writings (*The Book of Psalms: A Devotional and Prophetic Commentary* [New York: Our Hope Press, 1939]). The reason is that both dispensational-typological and dispensational-theological integrative aspects are brought together to yield conclusions. More on this will be said about the Psalms in the discussion about Gaebelein's use of typology.

are then in order, and will be answered by the majestic appearing of the heavenly King.[110]

The words of the Psalms are taken as prophetic of future experiences of the nation (the dispensational-*typological* integration).

Then with these literal, future experiences in mind, Gaebelein invokes the dispensational-*theological* integration: "This is the only satisfactory key to these imprecatory Psalms, which call on God to destroy the enemies. Christians cannot use them, for we are to pray for our enemies. The pious Jews living in that time of trouble will utter those words."[111] The distinction between Israel and the church is clear. These particular Psalms are Jewish ground. Church truth cannot be mixed with them although secondary application can be made.[112] It is also interesting to note that Gaebelein allows the minutest distinctions to stand without trying to harmonize them. Dispensational-theological integration allows such an approach since the overall distinction between Israel and the church has already been made.

Fourth, one interesting example is Gaebelein's theological argumentation to support a nonliteral interpretation of Daniel 12:2, "And many of them that sleep in the dust of the earth shall awake, some to everlasting life and some to shame and everlasting contempt." He remarked:

We repeat the passage has nothing to do with physical resurrection. Physical resurrection is however used as a figure of the national revival of Israel in that day. They have been sleeping nationally in the dust of the earth, buried among the Gentiles. But at that time there will take place a national restoration, a bringing together of the house of Judah and of Israel. It is the same figure as used in the vision of dry bones in Ezekiel xxxvii.[113]

---

[110] Gaebelein, *Harmony*, 46.

[111] Ibid.

[112] Gaebelein, *Psalms*, 190.

[113] Gaebelein, *Daniel*, 200.

The passage, in his view, is on Jewish ground. It speaks of the national restoration of believing Jews (the remnant) and the everlasting contempt for those Jews who, in the endtime, will reject God and His Word.[114]

The rationale for this exegetical decision comes from a comparison of this passage with the doctrine of resurrection taught in the New Testament.[115] If a literal, physical resurrection were taught in Daniel 12:2, a contradiction would result. Gaebelein is not precise in the discussion here. He reacts to the view that sees only one general judgment.[116] However, he seems concerned also about any interpretations which would produce a possible third resurrection.[117] The correct outline is given in Revelation 20:5-6, 13 where two physical resurrections are seen separated by one thousand years. The first resurrection is for the righteous while the second is for the wicked dead.[118]

Gaebelein apparently wanted to maintain a strict understanding of the two resurrections. The easiest route is to remove the troublesome passage of Daniel 12:2 from the consideration in the matter. Gaebelein believed that the first resurrection, including both Old and New Testament saints, occurred at the rapture.[119] The second resurrection of the wicked dead occurred at the end of the millennium. In doing this, however, he ignores the chronology of Daniel 11–12 as well as Revelation 19–20.[120] In addition, he abandons his view of an absolute distinction

---

[114] Ibid., 200-1.

[115] Ibid., 200.

[116] Ibid.

[117] Gaebelein, *Ezekiel*, 246; *Annotated Bible*, 5:39-40.

[118] Gaebelein, *Daniel*, 200.

[119] Gaebelein, *Annotated Bible*, 8:112.

[120] Gaebelein's understanding of the latter verses of Daniel 11 places them during the time of the Tribulation (*Annotated Bible*, 36-41). A literal, physical resurrection in the first verses of Daniel 12 would create a chronological problem for the resurrection and rapture of the saints before the tribulation. Similarly, in Revelation 19 the return of the Lord to the earth is seen. Then the

between Israel and the church.[121] Both share in the rapture prior to the tribulation period. In this way, Gaebelein surprisingly places the preservation of the precise distinction between the first and second resurrections ahead of the distinction between Israel and the church. His understanding of this dissimilarity in the resurrections is then incorporated into Daniel 12:2.[122]

Dispensational-Typological Integration

The Definition and Scope of Typology

Gaebelein never gave a technical definition of typology for his readers.[123] Nevertheless, an analysis of his practice in this area shows him to pursue the topic in much the same way as specified by Chafer. Chafer defined a type as "a divinely purposed anticipation which illustrates its antitype."[124] A type is a person, event, or thing in Scripture which usually points ahead to a person, event, or thing men-

---

next chapter speaks of the first resurrection. Taken in a strict chronological sense, the sequence is incompatible again with Gaebelein's view that the resurrection and rapture of Old Testament saints takes place before the tribulation. William E. Biederwolf, a contemporary of Gaebelein, gave a thorough analysis of the various views of that day mentioning Gaebelein (*The Millennium Bible* [Chicago: W. P. Blessing Co., 1924], 233-39).

[121] This particular interpretation indicates that Gaebelein's absolute distinction between Israel and the church is not so absolute after all. This is Dwight Pentecost's complaint about Gaebelein (*Things to Come* [Grand Rapids. MI: Zondervan Publishing House, 1958], 407-11).

[122] In addition to these examples, Gaebelein's use of dispensational-theological integration can be seen in his rejection of a Pentecostal interpretation of the reception of the Holy Spirit by the Samaritans in Acts 8:14-24 (*Acts*, 150) and in his general approach to the Book of Revelation (*Revelation*, 12).

[123] Gaebelein was a practitioner of theology more than a definer of systematics. Recall the absence of definition with respect to literal interpretation cited earlier.

[124] Chafer, *Systematic Theology*, 1:xxx. Compare this terse definition with the similar one given by Scofield, "A type is a divinely purposed illustration of some truth" (*The Scofield Reference Bible*, ed. C. I. Scofield [New York: Oxford University Press, 1909], 4 [hereafter cited as SRB]). In an alternate formulation, Chafer expanded on this basic idea. "A type is a divinely framed delineation which portrays its antitype. It is God's own illustration of His truth drawn by His own hand. The type and the antitype are related to each other by the fact that the connecting truth or principle is embodied in each" (*Systematic Theology*, 1:131).

tioned in later revelation.[125] The thing referred to is called the antitype. Types are usually viewed as elements in the Old Testament which refer to antitypes in the New Testament.[126] However, as the examples below will demonstrate, Gaebelein's exposition of types in the New Testament rivals, if it does not surpass, his understanding of types in the Old Testament.[127]

Chafer noted that "a true type is a prophecy of its antitype."[128] In fact, being saturated with "God's great pictures of truth" may lead a person to an increased measure of spirituality.[129] However, there is an element of subjectivity to Chafer's presentation in his smoothing over of the differences between types, allegories, and analogies.

> In answer to the question as to how a type can be distinguished from an allegory or analogy, some rules have been advanced. Among these it is declared that nothing is to be deemed typical which is not sustained as such in the New Testament. This statement is subject to two criticisms: (a) In the light of 1 Corinthians 10:11, there is no definiteness to the boundaries of the words "all these things"; yet, whatever is included is

---

[125] Gaebelein, on occasion, viewed typical elements with respect to past events. See Arno C. Gaebelein, *The Gospel of John: A Complete Analytical Exposition of the Gospel of John* (Wheaton, IL: Van Kampen Press, 1936). 98-100.

[126] This is the emphasis of Roy Zuck, *Basic Bible Interpretation* (Wheaton, IL: Victor Books, 1991), 169-84; Elliott E. Johnson, *Expository Hermeneutics: An Introduction* (Grand Rapids, MI: Zondervan Publishing House, 1990), 126, 208-9; and even Chafer, *Systematic Theology*, 1:xxix-xxxii, 1:31, 3:116-26.

[127] The extent to which Gaebelein used the New Testament with respect to typology is remarkable compared to most dispensational writers, Elmore's comment about Darby's breadth in the use of types notwithstanding (Floyd S. Elmore, "A Critical Examination of the Doctrine of the Two Peoples of God in John Nelson Darby" [Th.D. diss., Dallas Theological Seminary, 1990], 164). This writer's limited review of Darby finds nothing of detail, especially in the search for typological patterns, which can be found in Gaebelein. The typological patterns of historical events which are prevalent in Gaebelein's commentaries, especially in New Testament narrative, would be what Elmore categorized in Darby as historical analogies (184-86). For a dispensational writer who manifests widespread use of typology which rivals Gaebelein, and to whom Gaebelein appears to be dependent in many cases, see Frederick W. Grant, *The Numerical Bible* (New York: Loizeaux Brothers, 1904), 5:82, 102-5, 112-13.

[128] Chafer, *Systematic Theology*, 1:xxxi.

[129] Ibid., xxxii.

there said to be *typical*. (b) There are many easily recognized types which are not directly sanctioned as such by any specific New Testament Scripture. Like the problem of primary and secondary application of the Truth, the recognition of a type must be left, in any case, to the discernment of a Spirit-guided judgment.[130]

Gaebelein's use of typology conforms to this spirit of vagueness when discussing limits. In fact, with Gaebelein, the terms *correspondence, analogy, illustration, application, allegory, example, copy, resemblance, pattern*, and *foreshadowing* all appear to be valid when discussing an analysis of passages containing types.

Such thinking is not accepted by some modern dispensationalists. For example, Zuck is quite willing to keep typology as a formal and separate category. Illustrations, examples, parallels, and allegories have their place in Scripture, but must not be grouped under the heading of typology.[131] In light of such ground rules, Gaebelein could easily be classified as an abuser of typology.[132] However, Gaebelein attempted to address abuse in this area.

---

[130] Ibid., xxxi. Compare Darby's reliance upon the illumination of the Spirit when doing typology (Elmore, "A Critical Examination," 164).

[131] Zuck, *Interpretation*, 175-79. Zuck defined a type in terms of six qualifications: 1) the type and the antitype have a natural correspondence or resemblance, 2) the type has a historical reality, 3) the type is a prefigurement or foreshadowing of the antitype, 4) the type is fulfilled, completed, or heightened by the antitype, 5) the type is divinely designed, and 6) the type and the antitype are designated as such in the New Testament (172-179). All six criteria must be true for an item to be a type. It is easy to see that Gaebelein's category of types is broader and more flexible. Zuck apparently wants to see more than an analogy between two items before he will admit to any predictive tie between them. His qualifications generally rule out the use of types in New Testament exposition.

[132] George Adam Smith, a professor at Glasgow College in Scotland during the early years of Gaebelein's ministry, faulted the general theologies and pulpiteering which abused typology in his day (*Modern Criticism and the Preaching of the Old Testament* [New York: George H. Doran Co., 1901], 145-76). He objected that typology was taken beyond the boundaries set by the Apostles in the New Testament (145). He commented that "venturing beyond the furthest hint of the Apostolic writers, preachers have spun their allegories of Christ out of every plausible character and transaction in Old Testament history and poetry; or have assiduously polished each rite and institution of the Jewish Law in the attempt to make it a mirror of our Lord and His Sacrifice" (145-46). He viewed both medieval and Protestant styles of exegesis as infected with the desire to discover some type or prediction not seen by anyone else (146). Smith's diatribe can be aimed directly at Gaebelein although Gaebelein does his allegory in historical narrative and not generally in prophetic passages.

Before we follow this we wish to meet an objection which we have heard frequently and which is still used by many who do not care for prophecy. They object to the use of types. They look upon the use of them as revealing spiritual truths and things to come as capricious and arbitrary. They claim that almost anything can be read into the Bible by these typical applications.

We fully recognize the danger in this direction; there is such a thing as pressing types too far, especially when it concerns minor details.[133]

Nonetheless, in statement and practice, Gaebelein was anything but cautious in his use of types. He went on to argue:

But that there is a legitimate, a Biblical use of the types is fully authorized by the author of the Word of God, the Holy Spirit. We say more than that. The various types of men and women, of historical events, of certain divinely given institutions are one of the most interesting and striking evidences of the super-naturalness of the Bible, of the omniscience of the Spirit of God. The recorded sacred history in many events which happened of old foreshadow the great redemption truths of the New Testament and predict future events. Is this the case in profane history? And so we say again the types reveal the omniscience of God and are used in Scripture to make plain redemption truths and the future.[134]

Justification of this important role of typology in Bible interpretation is found in 1 Corinthians 10:6, 11 and Romans 5:14.[135] In the former, the events of the Old Testament are referred to as examples for present learning. In the latter Adam is viewed as a figure pointing to Christ. In practice, Gaebelein shows extended use of types by developing various foreshadowings in the Old Testament beyond the

---

[133] Gaebelein, "Wonders," 816. In Gaebelein's commentary on Acts 27, he made the following remarks about the shipwreck of Paul: "Behind the historical account one may easily see the stormy voyage of the professing church; her adversities, tossing about and shipwreck. However, such an application needs caution. It is easy to step into fanciful and far-fetched allegorical teaching" (*Acts*, 410). Here the word *allegorical* carries the same basic idea as *typical*. In light of the discussion below, such words of caution on the part of Gaebelein appear hollow.

[134] Ibid.

[135] Ibid., 816-17.

New Testament statement of them[136] and by unfolding numerous types within the New Testament itself.

The basic motivation for Gaebelein's typology is a belief that all of biblical history is prophetic. He stated directly that "everything in Israel's history is prophetic."[137] The historical books of the Old Testament are sacred as opposed to profane history. Written by the Holy Spirit, they contain "spiritual and dispensational lessons."[138] The context of the statement makes it clear that types found in the history of the Old Testament predict future events. Gaebelein's routine use of types in the interpretation of New Testament historical passages shows that he believed that portion of the Bible to be prophetic as well.

It must be remembered that while the motivation for expecting typology in the text is the view of biblical history, the underlying current behind Gaebelein's choices in typology is the conviction that distinctions in the progress of revelation lead to dispensational truths.[139] In addition, the dispensational-typological integration is the most frequently applied interpretive principle in Gaebelein's writings. The examples to follow reveal to the reader only a sampling of Gaebelein's activity in this area.

---

[136] For example, see Gaebelein's extension of Adam as a figure of Christ ("Wonders," 817-20).

[137] Arno C. Gaebelein, *Types in Joshua* (New York: Publication Office "Our Hope," n.d.), 41. See also Saphir, "Christ," 287.

[138] Gaebelein, "Jehu," 219.

[139] Elliott Johnson recognized this undergirding principle of typology. He wrote: "This prophetic sense of reference in historical narrative is commonly recognized in the broad context of the progressive revelation of the canon. God's purposes and direction in redemptive rule are introduced early in God's promises ... Each person, institution, or event serves to genuinely though only partially fulfill his purposes and promises. In the sense that each agency fulfills his promise at least in part, that instance is at once a historical fulfillment and a historical anticipation of the ultimate Agent" (*Hermeneutics*, 208).

The Genesis Account of Creation

One prominent instance of Gaebelein's use of typology can be found in Genesis 1:1-2:3. Creation week is, for Gaebelein, a typical outline of two separate truths.[140] First, the days of Creation trace the "story of individual redemption."[141] Day one (light divided from darkness), given in Genesis 1:3-5, pictures the rebirth of an individual who comes to Christ in this age.[142] Separation from the world is presumably foreshadowed by the dividing of the waters from the waters on day two in Genesis 1:6-8.[143]

The third day (Gen. 1:9-13) also marks an important typical truth. The land which emerges out of the water is a type of resurrection. The application of this to the resurrection of Christ on the third day is not surprising.[144] However, Gaebelein went beyond this in his usage of the text to point to the individual's redemptive history. Advancement in the believer's sanctification was associated with the appearance of the vegetation: "And here is progressiveness, grass, herbs and fruit tree bearing fruit. But such fertility is impossible in the state of death in which man is by nature; it is as 'risen with Christ,' on resurrection ground, that this becomes possible."[145] In addition, the creation of heavenly bodies (sun, moon, stars) on the fourth day in Genesis 1:14-19 points toward the truth that "in God's

---

[140] One must be careful here not to accuse Gaebelein of taking a symbolic view of the Creation account in Genesis. He took the account literally (holding to the Gap Theory) as referring to six restoration days (*As It Was*, 11-21). He simply adds another level of interpretation, a spiritual or typical level, which contains two simultaneous interpretations of its own.

[141] Gaebelein, *As It Was*, 20-24. For this particular view, Gaebelein mentioned his dependence upon the work of F. W. Grant (*Annotated Bible*, 1:18).

[142] Gaebelein, *As It Was*, 21. The Spirit of God mentioned in verse two and the speaking of God in verse three (the Word) illustrate for Gaebelein the two agents for the new birth given in the New Testament.

[143] Ibid.

[144] Ibid.

[145] Ibid., 22.

redemption plan we are not only risen with Christ but 'seated together in heavenly places in Christ Jesus,' as is so fully revealed in the great Epistle of our redemption, the Epistle to the Ephesians."[146]

On day five (Gen. 1:20-23), the living creatures which come from the waters (fish) typify the experience of Christians during the general tribulations of life in an evil world.[147] The sixth day (Gen. 1:24-27) "points to the time of the completion of the new creation."[148] Relating to Christ as the second man, the Christian will ultimately receive his inheritance pictured imperfectly by the unfallen condition and circumstances of the first man, Adam.[149] The seventh day of rest (Gen. 2:1-3) foreshadows the eternal rest awaiting all redeemed sinners.[150] Gaebelein attempted to justify his typical outline by referring to New Testament passages which directly or indirectly made analogies between the truth under consideration and Creation week.[151]

The second way that Gaebelein used typology with respect to the Creation account involved the outline of the seven dispensations. The first day (Gen. 1:1-5) contains several typical elements. The primitive earth of Genesis 1:1 points to the time of innocence in the Garden of Eden before sin. The judgment of chaos and

---

[146] Ibid.

[147] Ibid. Gaebelein did not mention what the fowl of the air might refer to.

[148] Gaebelein, *Annotated Bible*, 1:19.

[149] Gaebelein, *As It Was*, 22.

[150] Ibid.

[151] For example, the reference to 2 Corinthians 4:6, "For God, who commanded the light to shine out of darkness hath shined in our hearts, to give the light of the knowledge of the glory of God in the face of Jesus Christ," justified the use of the first day as a type of the new birth. Gaebelein takes Paul's reference as more than a use of Old Testament imagery to make a point. God, in his view, intended to make the connections in the precise way that Gaebelein has laid them out. In similar fashion, Gaebelein used Romans 5:3-5 to make the connection to the fifth day, Romans 8:29 for the sixth day, and Hebrews 4:9 for the seventh day. See Gaebelein, *As It Was*, 20-22.

ruin given in Genesis 1:2 foreshadows Adam's fall into sin.[152] The light of the first day is symbolic of the first hope given in the promise of Genesis 3:15. The waters, which cover the whole earth on the first day with no land having appeared as yet, foreshadow the end of the first dispensation with Noah's Flood.[153]

The second day typifies the dispensation of human government or the age of Noah.[154] The emerging of the land from the water on day number three is a picture of the call of Abraham and the choosing of Israel from among the nations. This corresponds most closely with what is generally understood as the dispensation of the Law. The fourth day with its heavenly bodies foreshadows the Christian dispensation.[155] The fifth day typifies the day of Great Tribulation which will occur at the close of the Christian dispensation.[156] Day six with the perfect conditions of Eden foreshadows the millennial kingdom. The final day of rest speaks of eternity.[157] These tracings of the dispensations in Creation week, along with the correspondence to individual redemption studied above, Gaebelein called the "deeper lessons of the Creation."[158]

The Psalms

The subtitle to Gaebelein's commentary on the Psalms characterized itself as devotional and prophetic. The first term relates to the experiential application

[152] Gaebelein held to the Gap Theory which teaches that a cataclysmic judgment came upon the earth after Satan's original sin. The results of this judgment is supposedly described in Genesis 1:2.

[153] Gaebelein, *As It Was*, 24.

[154] Ibid. See also Gaebelein, *Annotated Bible*, 1:19.

[155] Gaebelein, *As It Was*, 24. In Gaebelein's approach, "Christ is the Sun; the moon is the type of the Church; the stars typify the heavenly seed." This typology corresponds precisely to that taught by Scofield (SRB, 4).

[156] Gaebelein, *As It Was*, 24-25.

[157] Ibid., 25. Gaebelein is not as clear on this point as he is on the others.

[158] Gaebelein, *Annotated Bible*, 1:18.

of the text to an individual's life. Gaebelein complained that the latter aspect of
the Psalms, the predictive element, was not studied as much as it should be.[159]
That predictive element many times can only be seen by using dispensational-
typological integration.

Gaebelein believed that the order of the Psalms, not just the content, was
inspired by the Holy Spirit of God.[160] In this light, he referred to the Psalms as
being linked in such a way that brings out a progressive revelation.[161] The arrangement "reveals a consecutive prophetic story."[162] Gaebelein illustrated this
with a discussion of the prophetic cluster found in Psalms 42-48. Concerning the
contents of this cluster, which he felt could be found in several places in the
Psalms, he noted that

> *the order never changeth.* (1) Literal Israel, suffering among the nations
> of the world, finally plunged into their greatest national calamity, the
> Great Tribulation. (2) The Coming of their Messiah-King in power and
> great glory dealing with Israel's enemies. (3) Their deliverance, their
> spiritual regeneration and national restoration follows. The King Himself
> reigns over Israel and the nations and the kingdom blessings of redemp-
> tion for all the world have come.[163]

Thus, Gaebelein expected to find this specific pattern repeated throughout the
Psalms.

Associated with Gaebelein's search for such patterns is the analogy he saw
between the five books of the Pentateuch and the five books or collections of
Psalms. Such an association he apparently learned from Jewish sources.[164] The

---

[159] Arno C. Gaebelein, "Notes on Prophecy and the Jews" *Our Hope* 9 (December 1902): 379.

[160] Gaebelein, *Millennium*, 48-50; *Annotated Bible*, 3:207; *Psalms*, 12.

[161] Gaebelein, *Psalms*, 12.

[162] Gaebelein, *Millennium*, 50.

[163] Ibid., 51.

[164] Gaebelein, *Psalms*, 12; "A Song of the Beloved" *Our Hope* 9 (January 1903): 401; *Annotated Bible*, 3:215. In connection with this analogy between the Pentateuch and the Psalms, Gae-

analogy consisted of more than simple numerical association. The character of Genesis, for example, was seen to be repeated in Psalms 1–41.[165] The significance of this analogy for Gaebelein's dispensational-typological integration is that it serves as the framework for his use of types throughout the Psalms.

> These brief remarks show that the Psalms are arranged in an orderly way and that they have a prophetic meaning. This latter fact has been altogether too much overlooked. Generally, one might say almost universally, the Psalms are read for devotional purposes. We believe to do so can only result in great good to our souls. May we be kept from saying as some have done, the Psalms are not for us, and therefore we have nothing to do with them. This is unscriptural. All in the Word is *for* us, though it may not be about us.[166]

Consequently, the order of the Psalms, including clusters of prophetic unfolding and the comparison to the arrangement of the Pentateuch, led Gaebelein to conclude that passages in the Psalms possessed a dual purpose.

The prophetic message of the Psalms consisted of three major topics: 1) the humiliation and exaltation of the Messiah, 2) the suffering of the nation Israel and its coming deliverance, and 3) the future glories to come for God's redeemed people, the nations of the earth, and creation.[167] With respect to these messages, Gaebelein noted that the "chosen instruments," the historical personages and events in the Psalms, actually experienced what is written, but on a prophetic plane they are pictures provided by the Holy Spirit.[168]

---

belein referenced an Aramaic Midrash on Psalm 1:1 (*Annotated Bible*, 3:215). However, one must also note that F. W. Grant, whom Gaebelein sometimes referenced, had taught the same thing (*Numerical Bible*, 3:10).

[165] The other associations are Exodus with Psalms 42–72, Leviticus with Psalms 73–89, Numbers with Psalms 90–106, and Deuteronomy with Psalms 107–150. See Gaebelein, *Annotated Bible*, 3:215-16 and *Psalms*, 12–14. The same division is found earlier in Grant, *Numerical Bible*, 3:10.

[166] Gaebelein, *Psalms*, 14.

[167] Gaebelein, *Annotated Bible*, 3:211-14.

[168] Ibid., 212.

180

Specific examples can be seen in the view that the wicked or deceitful man mentioned in Psalms 10–15, 37, 43, 52, 53, 55, 74, and 140 refers typically to the coming Antichrist.[169] Concerning his expectation to find the Antichrist throughout the Psalms, Gaebelein commented: "If the Psalms are applied in dispensational light, and the afflicted, persecuted, and driven ones are seen to mean the faithful remnant of the Jews at the close of the age, we shall have no difficulty to find the wicked one, the enemy, fully described in them."[170] The word *dispensational* is once again seen in the context of typology.

A second example is Gaebelein's perspective that Psalm 103 "stands dispensationally for the praise of restored Israel."[171] He also included Psalm 118 in this appraisal. The adverb *dispensationally* carries with it the connotation that the words of the passages in question must be comprehended with respect to a particular time in history, namely the future time of Israel's conversion and restoration. Gaebelein referred to Psalm 118:22–36 as a contextual marker which placed the entire Psalm into the future at the time of Christ's kingship in Israel.[172] However, Psalm 103 has no such marker and must be interpreted typically to use it in that same way. In similar ways, the dispensational standpoint of various Psalms can only be seen through "majestic and sublime pictures of the future."[173]

In a final example, Gaebelein demonstrates that some Psalms are capable of multiple meanings. In Psalm 1:1–3, there is certainly application to those godly believers who were alive at the time of the composition of the psalm. However,

---

[169] Gaebelein, *Harmony*, 80-81.

[170] Ibid., 79-80.

[171] Ibid., 134.

[172] Ibid., 134. The particular elements which forced the conclusion that a later time of Davidic fulfillment was in view are the statements in verse twenty-two, "the stone which the builders refused is become the head stone of the corner," and verse twenty-six, "blessed be he that cometh in the name of the Lord."

[173] Gaebelein, "Notes on Prophecy and the Jews" *Our Hope* 9 (December 1902): 379.

Gaebelein saw three prophetic interpretations of the passages as well.[174] First, there was a typical portrayal of the incarnate Lord in his sinlessness. Second, he found a description of the life of a true New Testament believer. Third, a "prophetic picture of what the God-fearing part, or remnant, of the people Israel, will be" during the coming Great Tribulation is painted.[175] In all three cases, the interpretations involve typology which moves the meaning of the passage to a different dispensation. The outcome is that Gaebelein used Psalm 1:1–3 in four different ways with four different resultant meanings.[176]

The Gospel of Matthew

The first book of the New Testament marks an interesting turn in the methodology of Gaebelein. It shows foremost that he did not limit his use of types to the Old Testament and that his New Testament typological interpretations were widespread in historical material. Furthermore, it establishes that types as used by Gaebelein are not always predictive in the most technical sense. Many of the expositions of Gaebelein involving New Testament typology use types to point backwards to the history of Israel. Finally, Gaebelein's use of typology in New Testament texts helps readers to see the overall connection in his mind between the progress of revelation, schemes of dispensations, and dispensational-typological integration.

Gaebelein's understanding of Matthew's Gospel allowed a few examples of types in which various persons are typical pointers to some group of future people. In this respect, the Magi of Matthew 2 are types of future Gentiles who

---

[174] Gaebelein, *Psalms*, 17-20.

[175] Ibid., 19

[176] Another example of multiple typological meanings in Gaebelein's approach to a text is his understanding that the story of Jonah shows him to be a type of Christ while at the same time being a type of the whole history of the nation of Israel. See Gaebelein, *Harmony*, 151; *Matthew*, 255.

182

would seek the Lord.[177] Also, the Jewish disciples who listened to the Olivet Discourse foreshadow the Jewish disciples who will suffer the events of the Great Tribulation at the end of the present age.[178] However, Gaebelein also saw an event throughout the entire book as consistently typical.

> We have learned before the typical meaning of healing by touch in this Gospel. Whenever the Lord heals by touch it has reference, dispensationally to His personal presence on the earth and His merciful dealing with Israel. When He heals by His Word, absent in person, as it is in the case of the Centurian's servant, and the Canaanitish woman, or if He is touched in faith, it refers to the time when He is absent from the earth, and Gentiles approaching Him in faith are healed by Him.[179]

Thus, the activity of healing has associated with it certain aspects, namely the recipients of the healing whether Jewish or Gentile, which help to define the typological meaning for the entire book. One can readily see in this example the emphasis upon distinctions between Jews and Gentiles with respect to a dispensational approach to passages.

However, the most prominent way that Gaebelein used typology in Matthew was in a search for patterns of events which outline, in some form, the history of the dispensations (in line with progress of revelation). In particular, the sequence of past, present, and future history as it relates to the nation of Israel has preeminence. The table below demonstrates this sequence with five examples from Gaebelein's commentary on Matthew.[180]

---

[177] Gaebelein, *Return*, 16.

[178] Gaebelein, *Last Words*, 25.

[179] Gaebelein, *Matthew*, 420.

[180] In this exposition of patterns, Gaebelein demonstrates a remarkable dependence upon the prior commentary of F. W. Grant. Although all details do not correspond, compare Gaebelein, *Matthew*, 127-28, 170-75, 194-96, 304-23 and 324-35 with Grant, *Numerical Bible*, 5:82, 102-5, 112-13, 156-59 and 160-64.

PASSAGE	TYPE	ANTITYPE SEQUENCE
5:25–26	the adversary	Christ as rejected by Israel
	cast into prison	national punishment, judicial blindness of Israel
	paid the uttermost farthing	Christ's acceptance of Israel
8:1–18	cleansing of leper	Jehovah among people Israel
	centurion's servant healed by His word	Gentile/present dispensation
	healing of Peter's mother-in-law	God's restoration of His relationship to Israel
	all demons cast out	Millennial blessings
9:18–26	death of ruler's daughter	rejection of Christ by Israel and the nation's death
	healing of woman with issue of blood	Gentile/present dispensation
	raising of ruler's daughter	Second Coming of Christ and restoration of Israel
14:1–36	martyrdom of John the Baptist by Herod	character of present age
	feeding of 5,000	God's preservation of His people
	storm on the sea while Jesus prays on mountain	character of present age while Jesus is with the Father
	Jesus comes down from mountain and walks on water	Second Coming of Christ
15:1–39	Rebuke of Pharisees	Apostasy of Israel and the setting aside of the nation
	Canaanite woman's daughter healed	Call of salvation to Gentiles
	healing of multitudes and feeding of 4,000	Millennial blessings

Some salient points emerge from an examination of these sequences as given by Gaebelein. First, he is comfortable looking for historical sequences in didactic portions of the New Testament as well as in narrative accounts. The last four passages give historical proceedings. However, Matthew 5:25–26, from the Sermon on the Mount, yields doctrinal material. Gaebelein finds the historical sequence of the rejection of Christ by Israel, the resulting national and judicial blindness of the nation, and the filling up of that judgment with complete payment at the Second Coming of Christ.

Second, all examples except one emphasize the historical sequence with respect to Israel. Only Matthew 14 accentuates the present church age. Yet, a thorough investigation of Gaebelein's comments reveals that even in the details of the text, Israel has a prominent place.[181]

Finally, a basic sequence can be determined with the following elements: 1) Jehovah among His people Israel through the incarnate Christ, 2) the rejection of Christ by Israel, 3) the resultant death of Israel in the form of judicial blindness, 4) the parenthetical church age during which Gentiles come to Christ and a time of great persecution for both Israel and the church, 5) the Second Coming of Christ, 6) the restoration of Israel and 7) millennial blessings. This sequence fits the overall scheme of dispensations which Gaebelein outlined. In the Gospel of Matthew he sought through the narrative to find a deeper, typical meaning which pointed to this dispensational progression. All elements of the series are not present in the chosen narratives but the important point to be made for Gaebelein's theological method is that the chronological order or pattern of events had to be maintained.

The Gospel of John

Gaebelein did not limit the application of his dispensational-typological integration to the Jewish and dispensational Gospel of Matthew.[182] He approached

---

[181] This section of Gaebelein's work is extremely difficult to follow. Typology with respect to the church age and that which is based on the nation of Israel are somewhat mixed or overlapping. It is not clear, for example, if the preservation of God's people during the period refers to New Testament believers or to the Jewish nation during the absence of Christ from earth. See Gaebelein, *Matthew*, 304-23.

[182] Many dispensationalists have emphasized the Gospel of Matthew because of the perceived Jewish character and the ease with which it fits into dispensational schemes. See Gaebelein, *Matthew*, 5-6; W. H. Griffith Thomas, *Outline Studies in the Gospel of Matthew* (Grand Rapids, MI: William B. Eerdmans Publishing Co., 1961), 14-20; William L. Pettingill, *The Gospel of the Kingdom: Simple Studies in Matthew* (Findlay, OH: Dunham Publishing Co., n.d.), 7-11 and Frank

the text of John's Gospel with a search for types in much the same way. Several specific types are seen throughout. Gaebelein acknowledged Jesus' comparison of the serpent in the wilderness to his own death on the Cross (John 3:14-15) as an example of typology.[183] The cleansing of the temple in John 2:13-25, according to Gaebelein, "has a striking dispensational, prophetic meaning. It foreshadows that cleansing which will take place when He comes again."[184] The impotent man in John 5:1-15 is for Gaebelein a "picture of Israel's condition as under the Law" without remedy for sin.[185] As in Matthew's Gospel, the feeding of the 5,000 foreshadows the provision of the King in the millennium.[186]

One particular typological pattern seen in John, which reinforces how Gaebelein interpreted Matthew, involves the use of various chronological events to demonstrate historical sequences within the scheme of dispensations. Three separate series of events are presented by Gaebelein as foreshadowing events on the prophetic calendar.[187] The first series consists of the following: 1) the statements of John the Baptist given on the "next day" of John 1:29 concerning the coming Messiah and the baptism of the Holy Spirit, 2) the coming of the disciples, especially Nathanael, to Christ on the "next day" of John 1:35, and 3) the wedding of Cana on the third day beginning in John 2:1. These three days taken

E. Gaebelein, Preface to *Studies in the Gospel According to Matthew*, by E. Schuyler English (New York: Our Hope Publications, 1935), 9-10.

[183] Gaebelein, *John*, 68-69.

[184] Ibid., 52. Notice that once again the close association of the word *dispensational* with typology is displayed.

[185] Ibid., 100. Gaebelein carried this particular type over into the book of Acts with his understanding of the lame man in Acts 3:1-11 (*Acts*, 71).

[186] Gaebelein, *John*, 118-19.

[187] Once again Gaebelein in this exposition shows a remarkable dependence upon the prior commentary of F. W. Grant. Compare Gaebelein, *John*, 37, 95-97, and 400-6 with Grant, *Numerical Bible*, 5:480-87, 499-506, and 619-20.

as a series are types of 1) the present church age, 2) the national restoration of Israel after Christ comes, and 3) the millennial blessings.

The third series is exactly parallel to this first sequence. The three resurrection appearances of Christ to his disciples are directed to the same three time periods and events. The first appearance to the disciples (John 20:19-23), without Thomas, points toward the rejection of Christ by the Jews and their continuing unbelief during the present age (Thomas is a type of the Jews in unbelief). The second resurrection appearance, with Thomas present and coming to faith (John 20:24-29), is typical of the national restoration of the Jews after they accept Jesus as Messiah at the Second coming. The final resurrection appearance (John 21:3-14) involving the catch of fish (provision from the Lord) foreshadows the provision of millennial blessings.

The second series overlaps, but is not identical to, the other two sequences. Jesus leaves Judea in John 4:3. This action is a type of the rejection of Christ by the Jews and the subsequent setting aside of the nation. Then, His coming to Samaria in John 4:4-42 pictures the present age when the Gentiles come to the Lord. Finally, the healing of the nobleman's son by Christ in Galilee (John 4:43-54) foreshadows the healing and restoration of the nation of Israel when Christ comes a second time. By this sequence, in conjunction with the others above, Gaebelein demonstrates that typology is more than analogy between individual persons or events and some future antitypes. Historical sequences or patterns are placed in the text by the Holy Spirit so that the plan of the ages can be discerned by the spiritual believer.[188]

Dispensational-Applicatory Integration

The third aspect of Gaebelein's dispensational integration can be characterized as dispensational-applicatory. It has already been noted that he rarely de-

---

[188] The Book of Acts is another New Testament writing which can be explored to demonstrate Gaebelein's widespread use of typology in historical passages.

fined terms or discussed various nuances within the topic of methodology. The same is true of the word *application*. His use of the term would broadly cover the three areas of meaning, application, and significance as understood by Elliott Johnson.[189]

Gaebelein's dispensational-applicatory integration can perhaps best be comprehended in light of previous discussions. The overall scheme of dispensations seen in view of the progress of revelation highlights distinctions between various elements in the revelation (Jews, Gentiles, church). These distinctions must be kept in mind at three levels. First, the primary or direct application of a text cannot be violated by a distortion of these distinctions (dispensational-theological). Second, a secondary or indirect application or meaning can be obtained by observation of types within the primary application of the text (dispensational-typological). Third, a secondary or indirect application or meaning can be obtained without observation of types within the primary application of the text if the primary application is not violated by doing so (dispensational-applicatory).

In addition, the discussion of the applicatory aspect always has as its focus the use of the text for the reader. This distinguishes the applicatory from the typological element because the latter often has as its focus the application of a text for future persons unrelated to the reader. Since in all three cases the primary meaning is not to be undone, the dispensational distinctions which are vital to the basic understanding of this primary meaning form an important backdrop for all three approaches to a text.

One can best see the operation of dispensational-applicatory integration in Gaebelein's exposition of the Sermon on the Mount. In this respect, he cited F. W. Grant's general approach.

---

[189] Elliott Johnson defined meaning in terms of the "author's point of view in the textual composition" (*Hermeneutics*, 227). Definitions and clarifications are based upon the word in the text. Application is the activity of relating the author's message (found in the text) to the reader. Significance is not part of textual interpretation at all, but involves the integration of textual messages into a world view (238).

In the sermon on the mount we have, then, the principles of the Kingdom of heaven, with very plain references to the millennial earth ... Yet let it not be thought that this takes from us the application to ourselves which Christians seek in it. The fuller revelation only completes the partial one; the higher blessing but transcends the lower. Through all dispensations God is the same God, and we are 'blessed with all spiritual blessings in heavenly places in Christ Jesus.' Of many things we can only argue, indeed a more perfect (or at least a fuller application) to ourselves than to them. To take from Israel what is hers is only to diminish her and not enrich ourselves.[190]

Applications of the sermon to the church can be found. In fact, any valid application to the church has a superior quality over the direct meaning associated with the future millennial kingdom. In this way, primary application cannot be automatically construed as the most important aspect of the passage in question.

Previous analysis of Gaebelein's dispensational-theological integration demonstrated that there were some passages in the Sermon on the Mount which had no application whatsoever to the church. Gaebelein essentially interprets such texts with only a primary meaning for the Jews in the coming kingdom. All other passages are then available for secondary applications. In short, Gaebelein de-Judaizes the text; that is, he removes all passages which are for the Jews only and then considers the rest for application to the church. In this way, the result of doing dispensational-theological integration becomes the starting point for use of dispensational-applicatory integration.

Several examples of this application can be found while keeping in mind the primary application brought about by understanding dispensational distinctives. First, with respect to the beatitudes in Matthew 5:3-12 Gaebelein commented on its relevance to the church in the present age. "But while all this is a true application or rather a faint outline of that which is so richly told out here, we must not forget that there is also a direct application to the believing remnant of Israel. This remnant of Israel will pass through the great tribulation through which

---

[190] Grant, *Numerical Bible*, 70. Gaebelein referred to these words in *Matthew*, 110-11.

the Church (which of course can never be put into the first part of Matthew) will never pass."[191] Later in the same chapter, Gaebelein affirmed that Matthew 5:23-24 (reconciling with a brother before bringing a gift to the altar) refers "primarily to Israel" but "in principle" applies during the Christian age.[192]

As was shown before, the Lord's Prayer in Matthew 6:9-13 was rejected by Gaebelein for Christian application. However, in the latter portion of the chapter, he changed emphases.

> In the second half of the sixth chapter we are taken upon another ground. The heirs of the kingdom are seen in this section as in the world, subject to the cares and temptations of the wilderness. We must not lose sight here of its Jewish application ... To this remnant going through the tribulation the exhortations have a special application. However, we pass this by and apply it to ourselves as believers, for all which our Lord speaks in this section is for every member of the body of the Lord Jesus Christ, as such, who are in the earth, pilgrims and strangers, waiting for the coming of the Lord.[193]

After proceeding with a stimulating exhortation to Christians based upon this chapter, he remarked, "and all this is applicable to even the *smallest* matters of the daily life [of Christians]."[194]

Similarly in Matthew 7, Gaebelein belabored the point that the dispensational truth of the sermon's direct application to the future of the nation of Israel must be maintained. Concerning Matthew 7:21-23 ("Not every one that saith unto me, Lord, Lord, shall enter into the kingdom of heaven"), Gaebelein firmly noted "that this has no reference to the Church is evident."[195] The verses also do not ap-

---

[191] Gaebelein, *Matthew*, 116.

[192] Ibid., 127. The next verse (Matt. 5:25) was discussed in the section on typology. It is surprising to see Gaebelein sometimes come to a literary unit like this and cut out one or two verses for typological application when the rest of the unit is applied differently.

[193] Ibid., 144-45.

[194] Ibid., 149.

[195] Ibid., 163.

190

ply, in Gaebelein's view, to the great white throne judgment after the millennium. The judgment brought about immediately by Christ's coming at the beginning of the millennium is meant. Then he added, "From this dispensational aspect, we may well look to our times."[196] Application is then made to false professors during the Christian era.

In another example outside of the Sermon on the Mount, Gaebelein gave some insight into his thinking along these lines. The remark by Jesus that the least in the kingdom of heaven is greater than John the Baptist (Matt. 11:11) provoked the following response to the meaning of the term *kingdom of heaven*:

> Its common application is generally the thought that our Lord speaks here of the church age, and that the least in this present dispensation is greater than John in the old dispensation, to which he fully belonged. That such is the case no one doubts. We as Christian believers are higher in our standing than the Old Testament saints. However, the primary meaning of the passage is a different one.[197]

He went on to discuss the kingdom of heaven as the earthly kingdom to be established when Christ returns. The point to be made is that before the differing primary and secondary applications could be made, some understanding of dispensational distinctives must be comprehended.

Conclusion

Dispensational integration used by Gaebelein has been seen as the use of passages based upon an understanding of distinctions existing in the framework of the Bible (e.g., dispensations) which can only be comprehended by the proper application of the analogy of faith in light of the progress of revelation. Its use was verified in the three areas of theology, typology, and application. Such an approach has some dangers as well as some major strengths.

---

[196] Ibid.

[197] Ibid., 224.

A reflection on possible dangers yields four areas to be mentioned. First, Gaebelein did not spell out precise rules for using the analogy of faith or interpreting Scripture by Scripture. Hints were given which noted that the correct basis was to be found in the concept of the progress of revelation. However, some of Gaebelein's searches for patterns do not always reflect a commitment to this basis.[198]

Second, one must be cautious not to beg the question concerning the theological argument based upon the distinction between Israel and the church. For Gaebelein, it was usually an absolute distinction although at times this was not followed exactly. One example is his interpretative scheme for the Olivet Discourse which followed the pattern of distinctions in this order: Israel, the church, and the nations. However, careful exegesis would just as easily lead to the conclusion that the church is not involved in the passage at all. Was it incorporated into the passage as part of a prior commitment to distinctions? There is also the equal danger when interpretation excludes a particular people.

Third, Gaebelein's use of typology was well beyond what most interpreters would be willing to accept. He appears to overuse analogies. Analogies in Scripture, by themselves, do not prove typical connections any more than similarities in species suggest evolution. In addition, his typological commentary overpowers the historical-grammatical aspect of his interpretation which he still maintains. Consequently, the pursuit of themes, sequences, and patterns through types in Gaebelein's writings makes one wonder if he is finding what he wants to see rather than letting the text speak for itself. This would especially be true of his use of New Testament passages for typological sequences.

Fourth, the de-Judaizing of some texts before establishing application possibilities, while honoring legitimate distinctions between Old and New Testament truth, actually prevents the Christian from applying the whole Bible. This would

---

[198] For example, recall Gaebelein's interpretation of Genesis 5.

be wrong in the light of Paul's universal statement in 2 Timothy 3:16-17. For example, Gaebelein does not allow the prayer, "Thy kingdom come," in the Sermon on the Mount for the New Testament believer because the earthly kingdom in the prayer is not for him. But could not the New Testament believer still pray for his Jewish counterparts and their desire to see the earthly kingdom? This is but one way to apply that passage for Christians. Although some passages would be difficult, it is likely that, with principles drawn from the text, proper application could be made.

In spite of these complaints and possible dangers in Gaebelein's approach, his use of dispensational integration has much to commend it. First, it gives a proper recognition of the progress of revelation. Even though the entire Bible is taken into account, it is taken into account by acknowledging the forms through which God has acted in history and delivered the inspired Word. This is an added corrective to mindless prooftexting in systematics which ignores the larger context of Scripture.

Second, the identification of the need to interpret literally the Old Testament promises to Israel and the uniqueness of the church in Ephesians captures two highly significant concepts which do provide a context for a large portion of the biblical revelation. Gaebelein's exegesis on these points is acceptable. The synthesis of these two truths, namely, the distinction between Israel and the church, is of immense value. Theological interpretation cannot be avoided. The concepts involved must truly yield a way to view the Bible comprehensively. The Israel-church distinction provides such a frame work. In Gaebelein's approach this will be confirmed when the central interpretive motif is established in the next chapter.

Third, Gaebelein's acknowledgment of the synthesis of passages through types and application helps avoid a strict literalism which would make the Bible a sometimes unusable book. Types are mentioned in the New Testament itself and cannot be eliminated from theology altogether. Application is universal as seen above. One consequence of this strength is a greater appreciation for who God is as His Word becomes a living force in life's applications. In addition, the action of God in history, causing that history to take forms which could serve as revelational types of later truths, manifests the integrity and inspiration of the Bible.

tASK

GENERAL CONTENT SURVEY

ANALYSIS OF MAJOR CANDIDATES.

PRESENTATION OF MOTIF
        EXPRESSIONS
        CHARACTERISTICS

CHAPTER 6
THE CENTRAL INTERPRETIVE MOTIF

While the last two chapters have examined the two basic aspects of Gaebelein's approach to the Bible, the present chapter will focus on the theological
themes which he emphasized. Specifically, the one central interpretive motif will
be identified from among those themes. Millard Erickson has cogently argued for
the need for any theologian to provide an integrating motif with which to view the
data of theology while at the same time making sure that such a motif does not
interject itself into passages where it does not belong.[1] With Gaebelein, such a
central theme is relatively easy to identify.

Yet the student of Gaebelein needs to understand the central interpretive
motif from the perspective of the general character of all of his theology and the
stratification of connecting issues.[2] Consequently, the study below will begin with
a brief survey of the general content of Gaebelein's theology followed by an
analysis of major candidates for the central interpretive motif. Finally, a presentation of the central integrating theme with its various expressions and characteristics will be made.

---

[1] Millard J. Erickson, *Christian Theology* (Grand Rapids, MI: Baker Book House, 1983), 1:77-
78.

[2] Ibid., 78-79. Stratification is the word Erickson used to express the prioritizing of one's outline of theological truths.

The Evangelical Character of Gaebelein's Theology

There is no question that Gaebelein falls within the purview of the American evangelical movement.[3] The essence of evangelicalism has been outlined by several different writers.[4] Doctrinally, it has been associated with a bevy of concerns which usually includes an acceptance of biblical authority, a belief in the sinful nature of man and the need for individual conversion and regeneration through the gospel of Christ, an emphasis on missions and evangelism as the main work of the church, and concurrence with basic Bible teaching.[5] On all counts, an analysis of Gaebelein's life, ministry, and writings classifies him as a thoroughgoing evangelical.

---

[3] This writer strongly rejects the notion presented by John H. Gerstner that dispensationalism is dubious evangelicalism with a distorted view of salvation (*Wrongly Dividing the Word of Truth* [Brentwood, TN: Wolgemuth & Hyatt, Publishers, 1991], 150-69). In fact, Gerstner suggested that dispensationalism is "a cult and not a branch of the Christian church" (150). The narrowness of his own presentation of Reformed doctrine is not conducive to dialogue and understanding. Other writers see dispensationalism as a part of the evangelical movement. See Mark Ellingsen, *The Evangelical Movement: Growth, Impact, Controversy, Dialog* (Minneapolis, MN: Augsburg Publishing House, 1988), 153-55.

[4] Ellingsen, *Evangelical Movement*, 295-300; David L. Edwards, *Evangelical Essentials: A Liberal-Evangelical Dialogue*, with a Response from John Stott (Downers Grove, IL: InterVarsity Press, 1988), 22-31; "The Evangelical Affirmations," in *Evangelical Affirmations*, eds. Kenneth S. Kantzer and Carl F. H. Henry (Grand Rapids, MI: Zondervan Publishing House, 1990), 27-38; Leonard I. Sweet, "The Evangelical Tradition in America," in *The Evangelical Tradition in America*, ed. Leonard I. Sweet (Macon, GA: Mercer University Press, 1984), 1-86; Perry Miller, *The Life of the Mind in America: From the Revolution to the Civil War* (New York: Harcourt, Brace & World, 1965), 3-95.

[5] Robert P. Lightner, *Evangelical Theology: A Survey and Review* (Grand Rapids, MI: Baker Book House, 1986), 1-2; with respect to concurrence with basic Bible teaching, the summary statement on evangelicalism sponsored by the National Association of Evangelicals and Trinity Evangelical Divinity School noted that "evangelicals are also to be identified by what is sometimes called the material or content principle of evangelicalism. They hold to all of the most basic doctrines of the Bible: for example, the triuneness of God the Father, God the Son, and God the Holy Spirit; the pre-existence, incarnation, full deity and humanity of Christ united in one person; his sinless life, his authoritative teaching; his substitutionary atonement; his bodily resurrection from the dead, his second coming to judge the living and the dead; the necessity of holy living; the imperative of witnessing to others about the gospel; the necessity of a life of service to God and human kind; and the hope in a life to come. These doctrines emerge from the Bible and are summarized in the Apostles' Creed and the historic confessions of evangelical churches" ("Evangelical Affirmations," 37).

Biblical Authority

It has already been observed that Gaebelein withdrew from his Methodist denomination largely on the grounds that it had abandoned faith in the integrity of Scripture.[6] He fully endorsed the divine inspiration of the Bible and believed it to be without error.[7] His devotion to the Scriptures is demonstrated by the numerous instances where he defended the Bible. In this area, Gaebelein's writings take on perhaps the strongest polemical tone. For this reason, his view of the inspiration of the Bible will be discussed later as a possible candidate for the central interpretative motif.

The Need and Provision of Salvation

Gaebelein commented on several aspects of the evangelical doctrine of salvation. For a starting point, he addressed the human need. He accepted the fact of original sin.[8] Individual men are born in a state of depravity which can be described as spiritual death. They are, apart from God, encompassed by a condition of death, ruin, and the wrath of God.[9] Under such conditions, salvation cannot be based on character, but only on the intervention of God.[10]

In addition, Gaebelein underscored both the objective and subjective side of the atonement. Concerning the former, Gaebelein spoke of the "poverty of the Cross" which meant the physical sufferings of Christ and the making of the Sav-

---

[6] Arno C. Gaebelein, *Half a Century: The Autobiography of a Servant* (New York: Publication Office "Our Hope," 1930), 79-82.

[7] Arno C. Gaebelein, *The Prophet Daniel: A Key to the Visions and Prophecies of the Book of Daniel* (New York: Publication Office "Our Hope," 1911), 39.

[8] Arno C. Gaebelein, *The Gospel of John: A Complete Analytical Exposition of the Gospel of John* (Wheaton, IL: Van Kampen Press, 1936), 323; *The Annotated Bible* (New York: Publication Office "Our Hope," 1913-22[?]), 7:34-35.

[9] Arno C. Gaebelein, *God's Masterpiece: An Analytical Exposition of Ephesians I-III* (New York: Publication Office "Our Hope," 1913), 61-67.

[10] Gaebelein, *Annotated Bible*, 7:205.

198

ior into sin for the human race.[11] Jesus came to do more than "bring the right philosophy of life" as expounded by modernists.[12] It was his death on the cross which was a vicarious suffering for sinners.[13] His rejection of a limited view of atonement demonstrated that he believed the provision of this death extended to all men.[14]

An interesting part of Gaebelein's theological position with respect to the objective side of the atonement concerns his attitude about the doctrine of election which he only infrequently discussed.

> Who then will come unto Him? He gives the answer. "All that the Father giveth Me shall come unto Me; and him that cometh unto Me I will in nowise cast out." Blessed and most precious as these words are they have occasioned a great deal of controversy. What is known as "Calvinism" has made much of the first clause, while the system called "Arminianism" has used the second part of the statement of our Lord ... There is an elect body, and of this body our Lord speaks, that it is given to Him and that each member of that elect body will come to Him. This is a blessed and most comforting truth for God's people. They are the gift of the Father to the Son, a gift He made when there was no world and no human being ... Of course here are mysteries which our poor finite minds cannot solve nor fully understand. We believe the plain statements of Scripture as to election, but we believe that the Gospel message is for all and knows nothing of election.[15]

[11] Arno C. Gaebelein, *His Riches—Our Riches: A Gospel Message* (New York: Gospel Publishing House, n.d.), 32-34.

[12] Arno C. Gaebelein, *The Church in the House* (New York: Publication Office "Our Hope," n.d.), 52.

[13] Gaebelein, *John*, 132; Gaebelein considered 2 Corinthians 5:21, "For he hath made him, who knew no sin, to be sin for us, that we might be made the righteousness of God in him," to be the key verse for explaining the substitutionary death on the cross. For an admirable discussion of this work, see *Church*, 52-55, 71.

[14] Arno C. Gaebelein, *Listen! – God Speaks* (New York: Publication Office "Our Hope," 1936), 149. See also Gaebelein, *John*, 72-75, 314.

[15] Gaebelein, *John*, 126-27.

Gaebelein attempted to find a middle ground for the tension between God's sovereign choice in election and man's responsibility to believe the gospel.[16] In doing so, he dismissed any form of hyper-Calvinism in which God predestinates the eternal damnation of unbelievers.[17] However, he intimated that all Methodists should be more like John Wesley in being acquainted with Christ as seen through Calvinistic teaching.[18] Therefore, it is best to view Gaebelein as a moderate Calvinist in terms of his theology of salvation.

The subjective side of salvation in Gaebelein's eyes is viewed primarily through the necessity of faith on the part of a believer as the only condition for salvation.[19] Gaebelein plainly rejected any salvation based on good works.[20] Rather, the new birth is received "by believing the Word of God, and through the Holy Spirit as the agent of life and power."[21] The believer simply accepts the free gift of life offered by God on the basis of the finished work of Christ on the cross.[22]

---

[16] Gaebelein did, however, hold that faith itself was a gift of God as was the entire scope of salvation (*God's Masterpiece*, 84).

[17] Ibid., 128.

[18] Arno C. Gaebelein, "A Lesson For Modern Methodists," *Our Hope* 8 (August 1901): 72. Such a comparison between Wesley and Calvin may give some insight into the Niagara Conference's influence upon Gaebelein as he withdrew from involvement in his Methodist denomination.

[19] Gaebelein, *Listen*, 161; *Annotated Bible*, 7:199, 211-12; *Church*, 140-41.

[20] Gaebelein, *God's Masterpiece*, 85. Gaebelein remarked that "man has no works. We are by nature positively and negatively bad. We have done no good thing. If righteousness and with it salvation were by the law, then Christ would be dead in vain. And how strange that some say that they believe salvation is not of works, but by Grace, and then assert, that if they are saved and wish to remain saved, they must work!" See also Gaebelein, *John*, 61-62. There he singles out baptismal regeneration as a dangerous doctrine.

[21] Gaebelein, *John*, 62.

[22] Gaebelein, *Annotated Bible*, 7:199.

In connection with Gaebelein's discussion of faith, it must be noted that he viewed faith as inseparably connected to repentance.[23] Repentance was generally defined as admission to God of guilt with respect to sin.[24] However, Gaebelein believed that repentance was emphasized for the nation of Israel whereas faith was stressed as the transition was made to the new dispensation of grace.[25]

On another related point, the dispensationalist Gaebelein did not admit to two different ways of salvation, one for the Old Testament (works) and another for the New Testament age of grace (grace through faith).[26] Concerning the salvation of those in the Old Testament, Gaebelein taught that "no condition is mentioned; for their salvation as well as ours, is 'not of works' but of Grace alone."[27] This continuity extends into the kingdom dispensation when the new birth is "the one unalterable condition for Jew and Gentile."[28]

Another aspect of salvation which Gaebelein frequently addressed was eternal security. The eternal life which a believer obtains at the moment of conversion is a permanent possession which can never be lost.[29] This truth is the basis

---

[23] Arno C. Gaebelein, *The Acts of the Apostles: An Exposition* (New York: Publication Office "Our Hope," 1912; reprint, Neptune, NJ: Loizeaux Brothers, 1961), 62.

[24] Ibid.

[25] Ibid, 62, 242. Gaebelein's language is somewhat stronger as to the distinction between the Jewish concept of repentance and the Christian concept of faith in his commentary on Matthew (*Matthew*, 64-70).

[26] This has been a charge leveled at dispensationalism. One of the most recent presentations of the claim can be found in Gerstner, *Wrongly Dividing*, 160-67. Gaebelein did not appear to leave himself open to this complaint. For the fine points in dispensational theology on this issue, see Ryrie, *Dispensationalism Today* (Chicago: Moody Press, 1965), 110-31.

[27] Arno C. Gaebelein, *The Book of Exodus: A Complete Analysis of Exodus with Annotations* (New York: Our Hope Publication Office, n.d.), 21.

[28] Gaebelein, *John*, 58-59. It must be admitted here that Gaebelein's discussion may not refer to Old Testament saints but to the Jewish remnant which accepts Christ upon his return. The future of Old Testament saints is somewhat of a mystery in Gaebelein's writings.

[29] Gaebelein, *John*, 107-8, 188-89, 296; see also Arno C. Gaebelein, "Editorial Notes," *Our Hope* 9 (January 1903): 389-90.

for assurance of salvation.[30] It is also defined in terms of perseverance of the saints. While discussing the assurance and eternal security aspects of John 10:27–29, Gaebelein commented:

> To thrust in, as some enemies of perseverance do, the qualifying clause, 'they shall never perish *so long as they continue My sheep,*' is adding to Scripture, and taking unwarrantable liberties with the words of Christ. But let us also note that only 'His sheep' shall never perish. The man who boasts that he shall never perish, while he is living in sin, is a miserable self-deceiver. It is the perseverance of the *Saints,* and not of sinners and wicked people, that is promised here.[31]

Apparently, Gaebelein could not conceive of the case where a person would accept Christ as Savior and not demonstrate outwardly some measure of appropriate Christian behavior.

Concerning the matter of ongoing aspects of salvation, or progressive sanctification, several elements of Gaebelein's theology can be outlined. In spite of the strong expectation to see Christian behavior in genuine believers in this age, he allowed for carnality to exist in the life of a believer. He described the addressees of the letter to the Ephesians with the following words:

> All believers are constituted saints, "separated ones." But a Saint may not be faithful. Many who are saved by Grace and called Saints are unfaithful in their walk and testimony. The believers addressed are such, who live in faithfulness in Christ Jesus, manifesting in practical holiness their calling as Saints. And to such the Holy Spirit can give the highest and the best...[32]

---

[30] Gaebelein, *John*, 107-8.

[31] Ibid., 188-89. The extent to which Gaebelein had apparently left his Methodist roots on this matter can be illustrated by the comment of a pastor of a Methodist church in Buffalo, New York, who reportedly commented after a week of meetings with Gaebelein, "After all this Calvinistic perseverance of the Saints and premillennial talk I think my pulpit ought to be fumigated" (Gaebelein, *Autobiography*, 120).

[32] Gaebelein, *Masterpiece*, 18. See also Gaebelein, *John*, 324. Gaebelein accepted the three classifications of the natural man (unbeliever), carnal man (unholy believer), and the spiritual man (holy believer) as outlined in 1 Corinthians 2:14-3:9 (*Annotated Bible*, 7:97-98).

202

Gaebelein taught that a believer has two natures, one fallen, the other a divine nature received at the moment of conversion.[33] Out of the fallen nature comes sinful deeds, while from the divine nature issues forth holiness.[34] The two natures are at war with each other in the individual believer.[35] He affirmed that "only the power of the Spirit of God can deliver from the outworking of this fallen nature, the flesh, which is still in the believer."[36] Furthermore, this power is not available to the individual unless he is submissive to the Spirit.[37] Thus, Gaebelein strongly encouraged holy living on the part of the saint and believed the mark of such living, which was generally absent in his day, was the hostility of the world (unbelievers).[38]

One final note on sanctification involves Gaebelein's dispensational distinction between law and grace.[39] In general, the law cannot give righteousness, deliver blessings for man, or annul the grace covenant of promise made with

---

[33] Gaebelein, *John*, 323-24.

[34] Ibid.

[35] Gaebelein, *Annotated Bible*, 7:44-45, 227.

[36] Ibid.

[37] Ibid.

[38] Gaebelein, *John*, 323-25.

[39] Gaebelein, perhaps surprisingly, never entered into a lengthy description of the important dichotomy between law and grace as did his colleague Lewis Sperry Chafer in *Grace* (Chicago: Bible Institute Colportage Association, 1922; reprint, Grand Rapids, MI: Zondervan Publishing House, 1976). Gaebelein addressed the issue mostly in his commentary on Romans and Galatians as given in the *Annotated Bible* (7:40-55, 214-30). It may be that the emphasis of this distinction involved a comparison with the past and present dispensations while his primary interests were elsewhere. He wrote a book to compare the pre-flood dispensation with the present dispensation (*As It Was—So Shall It Be, Sunset and Sunrise: A Study of the First Age and Our Present Age* [New York: Publication Office "Our Hope," 1937]). Even this had a futuristic thrust to it. The numerous books by Gaebelein tended to view the Old Testament mostly in terms of its predictions, direct and typical, about the future rather than in light of the instructions for how the Israelites were to live in their day.

Abraham.[40] Its primary function was to pronounce a curse upon man.[41] Not only did the law not have a place in procuring salvation for the sinner, the believer cannot use the law to produce obedience.[42] Such submission can only be brought about by the Holy Spirit which empowers believers in the present dispensation.[43] Consequently, the greatest distinction between the dispensation of law and the present age is that, for today, "the law, as a rule, for the believer's life is, therefore, not needed."[44] The believer possesses liberty from the bondage of the commandments, which liberty is to be used for personal holiness and not an occasion to sin.[45]

Missions and Evangelism

Gaebelein shared the evangelical concern to propagate the gospel to the entire world. His early longings to be a foreign missionary and his New York mission work to the Jewish people demonstrated that concern in a practical way.[46] He expressed genuine gratitude that the "Lord blessed the preaching of the Gospel in the salvation of not a few" during one of his pastorates.[47] In addition, one of his works, *His Riches—Our Riches*, was designed to be a witnessing tool for the spread of the gospel.[48] Wilbur Smith described him as a man who had a "consum-

---

[40] Gaebelein, *Annotated Bible*, 7:216-17.

[41] Ibid.

[42] Ibid., 214-16.

[43] Ibid., 226.

[44] Ibid.

[45] Ibid., 224.

[46] Gaebelein, *Autobiography*, 10-11, 17-38.

[47] Ibid., 11.

[48] The importance of such a work is highlighted by the fact that Gaebelein's main ministry after the turn of the century was a teaching ministry to the church.

ing passion to get the Gospel and the Truth into the hearts of men and women."[49] In this way, Gaebelein viewed theology as something to be lived out, not just theoretically maintained.

Basic Bible Doctrine

Gaebelein also shared the evangelical affirmation of the fundamental doctrines of the Christian faith in addition to what has already been stated. The pages of *Our Hope* were filled with lamentations about the apostate church's rejection of basic Bible truths.

> Matters are not only drifting about us, but they are rushing on towards an awful ending. Where are we coming to has often been asked in letters by our readers who watch closely. We do not speak of matters of the world, of political or social signs of unrest and confusion, but of the conditions prevailing in the professing "church." Such confusion and falling away from the faith, *never* has been before in this present age. Infidelity in Christendom ripens at a terrible rate. Every article of the faith once delivered to the saints is attacked, belittled, set aside and dishonored. His Word, forever settled in the Heavens, is treated by worse enemies in the beginning of the XX century, than it was treated at the beginning of the XIX.[50]

In a book chapter entitled "God Has Spoken and Still Speaks in His Word," Gaebelein outlined what he believed to be basic Bible doctrine which must be accepted.[51] His list included Creation as detailed in Genesis, the Fall of man into sin and the resulting alienation from God, and the fact of the uniqueness of the Bible as the direct, written revelation from God.[52] He acknowledged the orthodox doctrine of the Trinity along with the divine attributes such as omnipotence and omniscience.[53] The miraculous and supernatural events mentioned in the Bible were

---

[49] Wilbur M. Smith, *Arno C. Gaebelein: A Memoir* (New York: Our Hope Press, 1946), 17.

[50] Arno C. Gaebelein, "Editorial Notes," *Our Hope* 9 (April 1903): 552-53.

[51] Gaebelein, *Listen*, 58-94.

[52] Ibid., 58-60.

[53] Ibid., 69-73.

not to be discarded.[54] The miraculous nature of prophecy with respect to Christ and the nation Israel were especially noteworthy.[55] Gaebelein accepted without reservation the orthodox view of the Incarnation including the deity of Christ and His virgin birth, the atonement of the Cross, the physical resurrection of Jesus, and Christ's literal Second Coming.[56] Such doctrines were revealed in "the one, outstanding, unique Book in possession of the entire human race."[57]

From among this representative litany of basic Bible doctrines, some particular truths are highlighted. First, the person and work of Christ maintains a high profile in virtually all of Gaebelein's writings. For this cause, Christological assertions must be examined for a possible candidate for central interpretive motif. Similarly, the overwhelming futuristic tone of Gaebelein's writings necessitates a search for the central theme within the realm of his eschatology.

Other interesting emphases appear as well. Gaebelein frequently attacks the Pentecostal movement's teachings about the baptism of the Holy Spirit and the practice of faith healing.[58] Although Pneumatology is significant for Gaebelein, there is, however, insufficient evidence that it provides an integrating influence for his theology. The same could be said for ecclesiology in Gaebelein's thinking. The fact that he considered the church truth of Ephesians to be the highest revelation given by God might lead someone to consider the church in some way connected to the central interpretive motif. The main specifics in this area are the concept of the true church as the body of Christ (as opposed to the apostate

[54] Ibid., 73.

[55] Ibid., 74-81.

[56] Ibid., 76.

[57] Ibid., 60.

[58] For example, see Arno C. Gaebelein, *The Holy Spirit in the New Testament* (New York: Publication Office "Our Hope," n.d.), 13-14 and *The Healing Question: An Examination of the Claims of Faith-Healing and Divine Healing Systems in the Light of Scriptures and History* (New York: Publication Office "Our Hope," 1925).

church) and the Israel-church distinction. However, the church gains its greatest value in his theological scheme by how it relates to the overall plan of God. This plan moves toward a goal providing a futuristic concern for the church which once again highlights eschatology.[59]

Clearly the character of Gaebelein's theology is evangelical. From within this general framework, three possible candidates emerge for consideration as the central interpretive motif: 1) bibliology and inspiration of the Bible, 2) Christology and Messianic expectation, and 3) eschatology and prophetic hope.

Possible Candidates for the Central Interpretive Motif

When trying to establish the central interpretive motif of a given writer and speaker, one immediately encounters the problem of determining how to weigh various elements within the theological presentation. Several questions must be answered.

First, is finding the central theme a simple matter of statistical analysis of topics covered? The answer should be understood in the negative. Even the constant enumeration of a certain idea does not necessarily imply that the concept fundamentally ties the theological system together. The relationship of the possible candidate to the whole system of theology must be understood to be crucial in some organizational way. Basically, the central interpretive motif is truly an integrating theme giving unity to the whole.

Second, one must be careful to distinguish a devotional center from a theological one. For example, with respect to Gaebelein, it is possible to observe that "for a number of years the first pages of each issue of 'Our Hope' have been devoted to brief meditations on the Person and Glory of our adorable Lord Jesus

---

[59] In the interplay between ecclesiology and eschatology, eschatology predominated in Gaebelein's writings.

[handwritten:] WHAT I LEARNED.
① WHAT GABELEIN'S BASIC THEOLOGY IS.
② METHODOLOGY OF DETERMINING A WRITER'S
INTEGRATING THEME.

207

Christ."[60] He went on to cite reasons for emphasizing Christ in this way including Christ's worthiness, the great need for Christians to know Him better, and the denial of Christ by so many in his day.[61] Therefore, no one can read Gaebelein and question his loyalty and devotion to the person of Jesus Christ of Nazareth. However, the issue is not the devotional concerns of Gaebelein's life. Because theology and life overlap, Christology will certainly be examined in his case. Nevertheless, any aspect of the doctrine of Christ can only serve as a central interpretive motif if the theological system articulated by the writer is knit together by it.

Third, how broad is a central interpretive motif? Erickson commented,

> By basing our central motif upon the broadest possible range of biblical materials rather than upon selected passages, we can make sure the motif will not distort our theology. The result may be a somewhat broad and general motif, but we will be assured it is truly comprehensive.[62]

In other words, while searching for a central theme presented by another, what does one look for? Does one think in expansive terms like bibliology, Christology, and eschatology, or more definite themes like inspiration, Messianic expectations, and prophetic hope? The more narrow designations are preferred if detailed conclusions are possible which relate the terms to the entire sweep of theological concerns. It is best if the writer himself is the source of the categories. In this respect, the present study of Gaebelein will satisfy those concerns.

[handwritten margin note:] more NARROW Teans

---

[60] Arno C. Gaebelein, *The Lord of Glory* (New York: Publication Office "Our Hope," 1910), v. The articles in this book came from earlier editions of *Our Hope*. Later he published a second volume based on the same idea. See *The Christ We Know* (New York: Publication Office "Our Hope," 1927).

[61] Ibid.

[62] Erickson, *Christian Theology*, 1:78.

The Inspiration of the Bible

One of the most frequently mentioned and strongly defended doctrines in Gaebelein's writings was the divine inspiration of the Bible.[63] He believed in the concepts of verbal and plenary inspiration.[64] Any definition of inspiration which diminished the uniqueness of the human authors and their writings was to be rejected.[65] The source of the Scriptures was God and the ultimate authorship of the Holy Spirit was generally emphasized above the human instruments used to produce the words.[66]

One implication of this truth was an inerrant Bible. To underscore this high view of Scripture, Gaebelein often used the word *inerrant* as well as *inspiration* to describe the quality and source of the written Word.[67] The strength of Gaebelein's faith on this point can be seen in spirited language.

> Again and again the enemies of the Bible have charged the glorious book with errors, claiming that its historical records are untrustworthy, unconfirmed by ancient historians. Archeology is continuously answering these puerile inventions, confirming more and more the accuracy of the events of sacred history, and sounding a veritable death-knell to all schools of infidelity. The great institutions of learning, universities like the Chicago University, who deny the belief of Christians in an inerrant Bible, send forth their expeditions into Bible lands to excavate, to uncover the records of the past, written in clay tablets and cones. They are literally "digging

---

[63] Virtually all of Gaebelein's published works of book size contain some defense of the truth of the Bible.

[64] Gaebelein, *Matthew*, 18; *John*, 211.

[65] Gaebelein, *Church*, 17-18.

[66] Gaebelein, *Listen*, 62. Some statements on the part of Gaebelein attempted balance between the human and divine authors. In a comparison of the Bible as the written Word to Christ as the living Word, Gaebelein remarked: "The Holy Spirit came upon these chosen instruments, the power of the highest overshadowed them. The Lord put His own words into their mouths and pens. Therefore the Bible is the Book divine. But they were human beings. Their individuality was not ignored nor set aside. The human element is easily seen in this great Book also. It is the God-Man Book; the divine-human Book. But like the God-Man, the God-Man Book is also infallible" (*Church*, 18-19).

[67] Ibid., 61.

their own grave," the grave where ere long rationalistic modernism will be hopelessly buried, for their own archeological discoveries and decipher- ments prove the Bible true and prove its enemies nothing but brazen li- ars.[68]

The use of archeology as proof for the accuracy of the Bible raises the issue of Gaebelein's main reasons for acceptance of an inspired text. His approach to the topic generally falls into three broad categories.

First, there is an *a priori* commitment to the truth of the Bible based upon a subjective experience related to faith.

> It is a common question asked by all classes of people—*"How do we know that the Bible is really the Word and Revelation of God?"* The author re- members how in his early youth he had to battle with such thoughts, till finally, through the reading and study of the Bible, these questionings, un- doubtedly originating from the dark being, who on the threshold of human history injected the seeds of doubt and unbelief into the heart of man, *"Yea hath God said?"*, were dispelled, and for ever banished from mind and heart. And ever since we have recommended to those who are assailed by doubt, first the prayer, "Lord I believe, help Thou mine unbelief" and next the daily meditative reading of the Scriptures.[69]

These words imply more than the reasoned search for internal evidence in the Bible to demonstrate its trustworthiness. Faith in the integrity of Scripture is nec- essary before one can fully understand its divine source and inerrant words.[70]

Second, Gaebelein saw a doctrinal and practical necessity for an inerrant Bible. The fact of the Fall of man into sin, a position of separation from God, means that

---

[68] Ibid.

[69] Ibid., 62.

[70] It will become clear in the later discussions that Gaebelein believed that the Bible did not "violate man's reason, and does not demand of faith what is unbelievable" (*Listen*, 60). Gae- belein's faith in the Bible was also demonstrated by his statement that "we do not believe the Bible because its historical statements can be verified from profane history. We believe the Bible because its records are divinely inspired and therefore correct" (*The Prophet Daniel: A Key to the Visions and Prophecies of the Book of Daniel* [New York: Publication Office "Our Hope," 1911], 39).

A direct, written revelation became a necessity *for man,* for inasmuch as man cannot find out God by searching of his darkened mind, and is unable through sin to find his way back to God, God had to step in and reveal Himself and His eternal purposes to the human race.[71]

Without a written revelation as that found in the Bible, mankind would be without hope and salvation. Gaebelein found in the Scriptures the only truth which satisfied this need in man.[72]

Third, Gaebelein sought justification for his belief in the inspiration of the Bible by examining internal evidence. In particular, he saw in the harmony of the Scriptures and in the prophecy which was proclaimed conclusive evidence that the Bible was truth from God. The harmony or unity of the Scriptures was of paramount significance to Gaebelein. His example is instructive in light of Gerstner's recent rehashing of the old claim that dispensationalists were like higher critics in that they distorted the Bible by approaching it through divisions or distinctions.[73]

Gaebelein's most frequent criticisms were leveled at evolutionists, modernists, and especially, higher critics.[74] He affirmed that the Bible had no scientific errors in it whatsoever.[75] Modernists, those who emasculated the Bible by remov-

---

[71] Ibid., 60.

[72] Ibid., 59-60.

[73] Gerstner, *Wrongly Dividing*, 98-99. Gerstner raised the same issue that had been voiced by Oswald T. Allis over fifty years ago ("Modern Dispensationalism and the Doctrine of the Unity of the Scriptures," *Evangelical Quarterly* 8 [15 January 1936]: 23-24, 35).

[74] In *Our Hope*, one can find in almost every issue an attack upon higher criticism, usually in the editorial section. A survey of one volume demonstrates this. See Arno C. Gaebelein, "Editorial Notes," *Our Hope* 8 (October 1906): 235-36; "Editorial Notes," *Our Hope* 8 (December 1906): 365-66; "Editorial Notes," *Our Hope* 8 (January 1907): 440-43; "Editorial Notes," *Our Hope* 8 (February 1907): 508-10; "Editorial Notes," *Our Hope* 8 (April 1907): 632-33; "Editorial Notes," *Our Hope* 8 (June 1907): 765-69; "Notes on Prophecy and the Jews," *Our Hope* 8 (June 1907): 814; Walter Scott, "The Inspiration and Divine Authority of the Holy Scriptures," *Our Hope* 8 (September 1906): 174-79.

[75] Arno C. Gaebelein, *Annotated Bible*, 1:89; *The Angels of God* (New York: "Our Hope" Publication Office, 1924; reprint, Grand Rapids, MI: Baker Book House, 1969), 11.

ing any supernatural accounts, were compared to the unbelieving Sadducees who opposed Jesus.[76] Mosaic authorship of the Pentateuch was vigorously defended[77] while the authenticity of the Gospels was beyond question.[78]

The negative invectives which Gaebelein hurled at the critics were also joined by positive affirmations of the significance of biblical harmony.

> The harmony which exists throughout the Bible from Genesis to Revelation is one of the strongest arguments for the plenary inspiration of the Scriptures. The unity which we find here is superhuman, it is divine. The inspired writers of the Bible cover a period of almost two thousand years, living in so many different ages and under different circumstances, yet all agree perfectly, and there is no clash of opinions. This unity is a miracle. No human genius or human endeavor could produce it. There is nothing like it in all the literary products of men, and there will be nothing like it in the future. *God* spake at sundry times and in divers manners (Heb. i:1), and therefore all in this precious Book, God-breathed (2 Tim. iii:16), must be a perfect, infallible whole. What an awful sin to criticize the Bible, to deny its verbal inspiration, to put the Word of God which He has exalted above all His Name down to the level of profane literature. Yet this is the common drift of our times.[79]

The internal evidence of unity in the biblical writings demonstrated, for Gaebelein, beyond any doubt that the Bible as a whole was an inspired manuscript.

However, one paradoxical way in which this unity demonstrates inspiration is by the diversity which it allows. For example, Gaebelein strongly resisted any effort to harmonize the four Gospels.

> There has been and is still a great deal of wrestling, so to speak, with these events as they are recorded in the different Gospels, to arrange them in a perfect chronological order, or, as it is said, to harmonize the Gospel records. The infidels of all ages have made the most of it to prove contradic-

---

[76] Arno C. Gaebelein, *Gabriel and Michael, the Archangel* (Wheaton, IL: Van Kampen Press, 1945), 4-5.

[77] Gaebelein, *Annotated Bible*, 1:2-6; *Exodus*, 2-3; *Hopeless—Yet There is Hope: A Study in World Conditions and Their Solution* (New York: Publication Office "Our Hope," 1935), 160-61.

[78] Gaebelein, *John*, 210-13.

[79] Gaebelein, "Harmony," 130-31. A similar presentation is given in *Harmony*, 207.

212

tions, and the rationalistic preachers and professors in the camp of Christendom have generally founded their accusations of numerous contradictions in the New Testament upon these apparent discrepancies, which they think exist in the different statements concerning the public ministry of our Lord. The Holy Spirit could have written a perfect account of the earthly life of our Lord Jesus Christ and arrange a biography of Him accounting for every detail, but He has not done this ... In each Gospel the Holy Spirit makes prominent the events which are calculated to impress the specific teachings of the respective Gospels, and He has always arranged the events in such an order to suit Himself. Every Gospel is therefore to be studied and read separately from the others.[80]

In short, the Holy Spirit is an editor or redactor who led the human writers of Scripture to order the accounts, on occasion, in a non-chronological way.

One specific illustration of this can be found in Gaebelein's handling of the accounts in Matthew 8:1-18. Previously, the typology of the passage was explored. The events, which historically may have occurred out of sequence, are placed together in a theological pattern pointing to the dispensational outlines of the history of Israel. Gaebelein viewed this diversity from other Gospel accounts of the same events as evidence that the Bible was divinely inspired.

Now that which moved the infidel and the preacher tainted with higher criticism to ridicule the divinity and infallibility of the written Word, moves the believer and diligent searcher of the Scriptures to praise, for the very argument which the denier of a verbal inspiration uses to build his infidel fabric on, is to the believer the most positive evidence of the divinity of the Bible and its verbal inspiration.[81]

Consequently, distinctions in the Bible did not always bother Gaebelein. Alleged discrepancies could sometimes be interpreted as divinely intended differences.[82]

---

[80] Gaebelein, *Matthew*, 97.

[81] Ibid., 169.

[82] Of course, Gaebelein did not handle all alleged discrepancies in this way. For example, he appealed to details within grammar and context to answer supposed contradictions in the three accounts of Paul's conversion in Acts (*Prophet Paul*, 44-46).

Another example of diversity in unity was Gaebelein's approach to the imprecatory Psalms.[83] Critics who belittle the Bible because of the supposed contradiction between Christian love for enemies (Matt. 5:43-48) and prayers for their destruction given in the Psalms (e.g., Psalms 43 and 56) fail to realize that those Psalms are dispensationally targeted for Israel to pray during the future Great Tribulation on the earth.[84] Thus, the discrepancy disappears when one understands that the imprecatory Psalms are not for the Christian dispensation. In this way, distinctions in the overall scheme of the Bible help to maintain the inerrancy of the text.

The second aspect of internal evidence, one related to harmony, which proved to Gaebelein that the Bible was inspired by God, was found in prophecy. Especially enlightening was the existence in the Bible of progressive prophecies such as the one concerning the coming of Christ which begins in Genesis 3:15, continues throughout the Bible, and ends with fulfillment in Galatians 4:4.[85] Such harmonious unfoldings over lengthy periods of time point irrefutably, in Gaebelein's estimation, to the supernatural character of the Scriptures.[86]

However, the greatest way that prophecy has proven inspiration is through those examples for which fulfillment is known in detail.[87] Gaebelein's article in *The Fundamentals* was entitled "Fulfilled Prophecy, a Potent Argument for the

---

[83] The imprecatory Psalms were approached in the previous chapter from the perspective of dispensational integration. The point to be made here is that divisions in Scripture over applicability of the text did not eliminate the unity of the Bible in Gaebelein's mind.

[84] Gaebelein, *Harmony*, 46.

[85] Arno C. Gaebelein, "The Wonders of Progressive Prophecy," *Our Hope* 46 (May 1940): 740-47.

[86] Ibid., 747.

[87] Gaebelein, *Listen*, 74-77. Included in the discussion is prophetic history or typology as well as direct prophecies.

214

Bible."⁸⁸ He pointed to prophecies concerning the first coming of Christ, the nation of Israel, and other nations. Primary focus was on Israel. In a brief commentary on Deuteronomy 28, Gaebelein noted that

> Here thousands of years ago the Spirit of God through Moses outlined the history of the scattered nation, all their suffering and tribulation, as it has been for well nigh two millenniums and as it is still. Here are arguments for the Divine, the supernatural origin of this book which no infidel has ever been able to answer; nor will there ever be found an answer.⁸⁹

The supreme example of fulfilled prophecy was cited as Daniel 9:24-27 (the seventy weeks) in which the precise number of years, even days, from the command to rebuild and restore Jerusalem until the coming of the Messiah was given.⁹⁰

Also, at length, Gaebelein outlined the detailed fulfillment of the predictions in Daniel 11 which he found in the history of the Ptolemaic and Seleucid dynasties.⁹¹ Such detailed fulfillments gave hope of the literal fulfillment of prophecies yet unfulfilled. However, more than that, they pointed to the divine inspiration of the Holy Bible.

In summary, Gaebelein held to the inerrancy of the Bible because of an *a priori* faith in its integrity, the necessity of an inerrant Word due to man's sin, and the internal evidences of progressive harmony and prophetic fulfillment which graced its pages. The regular appeals to this doctrine, along with the forceful manner in which he addressed it, establish the significance a proper bibliology possessed in Gaebelein's theology.

However, is there any way in which the inspiration of the Bible integrates the whole theological system for Gaebelein? Several implications of the discus-

---

⁸⁸ Arno C. Gaebelein, "Fulfilled Prophecy, a Potent Argument for the Bible," in *The Fundamentals* ed. Reuben A. Torrey (Chicago: Testimony Publishing Co., 1910), 11:55-86.

⁸⁹ Ibid., 62-63.

⁹⁰ Ibid., 76-77. The coming of the Messiah here refers to the first coming of Christ, not the second.

⁹¹ Ibid., 78-86.

sions above can be mentioned to address this issue. First, the inerrancy of the Bible was creatively associated with dispensational distinctions. Second, the harmony which aided recognition of the divine origin of Scripture was described as progressive. The written revelation in the Bible was a gradual unfolding of unified truth. Therefore, inerrancy must be observed within the framework of the progress of revelation. Third, the major doctrines related directly to bibliology and inspiration were found to be the depravity of man, which necessitated the need for an inerrant revelation, and eschatology as seen in the prominent role which prophecy played as an argument for inerrancy. Most of the discussion of these areas involved hermeneutics. This points in the direction that Gaebelein's acceptance of an inerrant Bible is the hermeneutical ground or foundation of his theology.[92] However, although prominent, it does not seem to integrate the theological content of his system.

The Centrality of Christ

Gaebelein showed the important role of Christ in his preaching ministry by limiting his preaching on the Lord's Day to the subject of Jesus and His accomplishments on the Cross.[93] By doing so he refrained from spending a lot of time on prophetic details which could detract from the Lord on Sundays. In addition, he published three books about Christ. Two books, *The Lord of Glory* and *The Christ We Know*, consist of collections of the short meditations which for years introduced each issue of *Our Hope*. However, only one book, *The Work of*

---

[92] Gaebelein, speaking of Satanic opposition to truth, noted that "inasmuch as the true faith revealed in the infallible, inerrant Word of God, is the foundation upon which everything rests, Satan aims at that first of all" (*The Return of the Lord* [New York: Publication Office "Our Hope," 1925], 77).

[93] See Gaebelein, *Autobiography*, 101, 191, 232; David A. Rausch, *Arno C. Gaebelein 1861-1945: Irenic Fundamentalist and Scholar* (New York: Edwin Mellen Press, 1983), 230. One must remember that the sermons of Gaebelein were not essentially different from his writings.

Christ, was a theological treatise outlining the past, present, and future work of Christ.[94]

As one reviews the writings of Gaebelein, it is easy to find references to Jesus Christ as the central theme of theology. In particular, the person and work of Christ can be seen as the focus of the theological truths about revelation, redemption, and prophecy. With respect to the revelation (by which Gaebelein meant written revelation in the Bible), he gave the following remarks concerning Messianic prophecies in the Old Testament:

> The Old Testament contains a most wonderful chain of prophecies concerning the person, the life and work of our Lord. As He is the center of the whole revelation of God, the One upon whom all rests, we turn first of all to a few of the prophecies which speak of Him.[95]

Gaebelein encouraged Christians by stating, "whenever we take our Bibles in hand to read the Word of God, the foremost thought should be 'We would see Jesus.'"[96] In addition, in Christ are "hid all the treasures of the wisdom and knowledge of God."[97] Therefore, Gaebelein apparently viewed the Bible as a Christocentric document. He expected to find evidence throughout of Christ, "the key to the Scriptures," even in the Old Testament.[98]

In addition to Christ as the center of biblical revelation, Gaebelein often focused on Jesus as the centerpiece of God's redemptive purpose. He declared that the purpose of prophecy, in general, was to reveal the "final solution of sin and its curse" and to lead us "close to the heart of God."[99] After this experience-

---

[94] Arno C. Gaebelein, *The Word of Christ* (London: Alfred Holness, n.d.).

[95] Gaebelein, "Fulfilled Prophecy," 58.

[96] Gaebelein, *Church*, 48.

[97] Ibid., 49.

[98] Gaebelein, *Listen*, 75.

[99] Gaebelein, "Wonders," 665.

oriented expression, he offered a more detailed theological, yet practical, description.

> Needless to say that the eternal redemption purpose centers in the Son of God—"according to the eternal purpose which He purposed in Christ Jesus our Lord" (Eph. 3:11). It should then be the supremest joy and occupation for a true believer to listen to Prophecy and follow its unfoldings from Genesis to Revelation. How rich then our lives would be! How through this study we should be lifted above earthly circumstances, delivered from fear and filled with the hope of glory which redeemed sinners, saved by grace, will possess throughout all eternity. The neglect of Prophecy is disastrous. It robs us of the true knowledge of Him and His redemption work who is the one theme of all prophecy.[100]

The many types in the Old Testament, such as the sacrificial system and the tabernacle, reinforce the centrality of Christ in the redemptive plan of God given in the Bible.[101] In particular, the work of Christ on the Cross for the redemption of men is to be considered as the "one great message" magnified above all else.[102] In this sense, the contribution of Christ to the doctrine of redemption is considered the most important theme of the Bible.

The connection between Christocentric redemption and prophecy was seen above in the statement which concluded that Christ was "the one theme of prophecy."[103] The adjective *one* should be taken in the sense of priority and breadth rather than exclusion of other topics. Gaebelein highlighted the centrality of Christ with respect to prophecy more than any other theme. The significance of the content of prophecy as taught in 1 Peter 1:10-13 was summarized by Gaebelein as following:

> This makes it very clear that the prophetic Word contains two great sections—the sufferings and the glories, and the center, Christ, for it is Christ

---

[100] Ibid.

[101] Gaebelein, *Exodus*, 4-5.

[102] Ibid., 65.

[103] Gaebelein, "Wonders," 665.

218

who suffered and Christ and His glories and all that is connected with them. How truly He said Himself then concerning the Scriptures, "They testify of Me." They testify of the cross and the crown, the first coming and the second coming, the humiliation and the exaltation.[104]

In these words, Christ appears to be the center of everything which His work touches. This leaves little else to compete with His predominance in prophecy. Consequently, Gaebelein could repeat the sentiment with assertions that Christ is the "great theme of progressive prophecy"[105] and "the crown of all Bible prophecy is what is written concerning the Messiah."[106] In addition, concerning the dispensations, the "Lord Jesus Christ is the framer, the centre, the object in every age."[107]

Prophecy by its very nature has a tendency to force one to look forward. This tendency can be seen in a futuristic emphasis of Gaebelein's Christology. He noted that prophecy cannot be understood at all without recognizing the specific feature of the Lord's return.[108] In his autobiography, Gaebelein described such a theological trend in his own messages.

While my messages covered all phases of His glory and all phases of His precious work, I have been led to stress His future glory, which will be His in the day of His personal and visible return.[109]

This future glory was to Gaebelein the only hope for the world.[110]

---

[104] Gaebelein, "Harmony," 132.

[105] Gaebelein, "Wonders," 740-41.

[106] Gaebelein, *Church*, 177. The context of Gaebelein's assertion is the biblical predictions about the Messiah for Israel.

[107] Arno C. Gaebelein, "The Dispensations," *Our Hope* 37 (December 1930): 343.

[108] Arno C. Gaebelein, *Meat in Due Seasons: Sermons, Discourses, and Expositions of the Word of Prophecy* (New York: Arno C. Gaebelein, Inc., n.d.), 13. Gaebelein also included in this analysis the need to understand the character of the present age and the events following the Second Coming, primarily the millennium, before biblical prophecy could be comprehended.

[109] Gaebelein, *Autobiography*, 234; Smith, *Memoir*, 12.

[110] Arno C. Gaebelein, *Hopeless, Yet There is Hope: A Study in World Conditions and Their Solution*, (New York: Publication Office "Our Hope," 1935), 179.

In summary, Jesus Christ was seen, in Gaebelein's own words and emphases, to be the center of revelation, redemption, and prophecy. In the last instance, a futuristic tendency was ascertained when the coming glory of Christ was stressed above the other works of Messiah. Unlike the doctrine of the inspiration of the Bible, which became a hermeneutical basis for Gaebelein's theological exercises, the Christological arena has shown more likelihood of finding a central interpretive theme which relates the content of his theology. The emphasis on future Christological hope suggests that this central motif may be found in the intersection of Gaebelein's Christology and eschatology.

Eschatology and Prophetic Hope

A survey of the published books written by Gaebelein shows that over twenty of them are devoted to the theological area of eschatology. More than five others can be added if an emphasis on eschatology through typological interpretation is included. The result is that a majority of the books written by Gaebelein (almost thirty) focus on eschatology. Added to this are the thousands of pages in *Our Hope*, written by Gaebelein and others, which deal with eschatological issues in biblical interpretation, current events as signs of the times, and Jewish expectations in Zionism. In spite of the previous affirmations of the centrality of Christological issues, the immediate impact of the weight of this evidence forces one to include eschatological overtones to the central interpretive motif of Gaebelein's theology.

To begin the exploration of this important field, several basic teachings of Gaebelein will be presented. A few words about dispensations and the biblical covenants will be followed by an analysis of his views of the kingdom of God. An examination of the significance of the nation of Israel will also prove useful. In this way, the reader will be prepared for a precise definition of the central interpretive motif.

The Dispensations and Biblical History

It has already been observed that Gaebelein emphasized the three dispensations that correspond to law, grace, and kingdom. In the light of the progress of revelation, the kingdom age, called the Age of Consummation, becomes the focus of the greatest hope. It is the "promised morn, when the shadows flee away."[111] The kingdom dispensation "means the age of righteousness, peace and glory; the age which brings the restitution of all things."[112] In short, the scheme of dispensations demonstrates, for Gaebelein, that history has a goal. All believers can look forward with optimistic anticipation.

This optimistic view of the end of history is also suggested by Gaebelein's view that all of biblical history is prophetic. Given the fact that direct prophecy looked forward, mostly to consummation, the added typological nature of historical narratives yields a Bible that is almost entirely prophetic. Therefore, in one sense, the supreme interest of the Bible is prophetic hope looking toward the day of consummation. This overall view of where history is heading is also supported by Gaebelein's understanding of the biblical covenants.

The Biblical Covenants

There is little trace of the theological covenants of works and grace, which are delineated in much Reformed thinking, in Gaebelein's theology.[113] He simply did not think in those categories. On the other hand, he saw extreme importance in the biblical covenants which God made to various individuals and people groups (Noah, Abraham, David, Israel) in biblical history. The emphasis on these cove-

---

[111] Gaebelein, "Dispensations," 346.

[112] Arno C. Gaebelein, *Our Age and Its End* (New York: Our Hope Publications, 1940[?]), iii. The millennial kingdom will receive more thorough treatment in the section below on the kingdom of God.

[113] For discussions of these theological covenants see Louis Berkhof, *Systematic Theology*, rev. ed. (Grand Rapids, MI: William B. Eerdmans Publishing Co., 1941), 211-18, 262-304 and Charles Hodge, *Systematic Theology* (New York: Charles Scribner's Sons, 1891), 2:117-22; 354-76.

nants in Gaebelein's eschatology does not rival the basic role which they play in the writings of Ryrie and Pentecost.[114] However, the basic teaching about the covenants appears to be the same.

The Abrahamic Covenant

The first major covenant which Gaebelein saw in biblical history was the one made with Abraham beginning in Genesis 12.[115] Gaebelein believed that "these and similar promises made to Abraham, Isaac, and Jacob are the germs of all which the prophetic Word has to say of Israel's future restoration."[116] Israel's place in God's plans "goes back to Genesis (Chapter 12). Here is God's starting point."[117] A starting point implies a progression which could be traced through the "ever-increasing expansion of the promises made to the fathers of the nation."[118] Such was evidence of a God active in human history and a demonstration of the progressive revelation of the Bible.[119]

Gaebelein identified several characteristics of this covenant. First, it was an unconditional pledge from God not dependent upon future human faith or obedience.[120] Simply described, it was a divine promise. This unconditionally was rooted in two theological truths, God's sovereign grace and His faithfulness. Gae-

---

[114] Charles C. Ryrie, *The Basis of the Primillennial Faith* (Neptune, NJ: Loizeaux Brothers, 1953), 48-125 and J. Dwight Pentecost, *Things to Come* (Grand Rapids, MI: Zondervan Publishing House, 1958), 65-128.

[115] Gaebelein did not mention an Edenic or Adamic covenant. The earliest covenant in his thinking appears to be the Noahic covenant which he passed over lightly in *The Annotated Bible* (1:37). He viewed the Noahic covenant as valid for all men, including Gentiles, even in the church age (*Acts*, 269).

[116] Gaebelein, *Harmony*, 125.

[117] Gaebelein, *Millennium*, 38.

[118] Gaebelein, *Harmony*, 126.

[119] Gaebelein, *Prophet Paul*, 11-12.

[120] Gaebelein, *Harmony*, 125; *Church*, 164. Here Gaebelein actually used the words *unconditional* or *unconditionally* to describe the action of God giving the covenant to Abraham.

belein conveyed the former by noting that "God's sovereign grace had called Abraham and He established a relationship of grace."[121] He ascribed this relationship to Isaac, Jacob, and the nation of Israel as well. Furthermore, the basis of the covenant on the faithfulness of God was couched in comparative terms with respect to the law covenant made with Moses and Israel.

> God did not reveal Himself in His glory and a mediator was needed, that is, Moses. The statement "a mediator is not of one" (Gal. 3:19) means that mediatorship necessitate two parties. So there were God and Israel, Moses between as the mediator. But in the promise, the covenant made with Abraham and his seed, God was the only One who spoke. Its fulfillment is not (as in the law-covenant) dependent upon a faithful God and Israel's obedience, but on God's faithfulness alone; all depended upon God Himself.[122]

In short, there were no human actions which could abrogate the promise of the Abrahamic Covenant.

Second, Gaebelein expected a literal fulfillment of the covenant. Focusing on the promise of a curse for those who cursed Abraham and his seed (Gen. 12:2–3), Gaebelein remarked:

> And all God promised to Abram He hath kept. Every word has been literally fulfilled. Nations upon nations who hated Abraham's seed, his natural descendants, have found to their great sorrow how true Abraham's God is. These promises still hold good. To the seed of Abraham belong still the promises (Rom. ix.4). The nations of the earth, all the families are unconsciously waiting to be blessed by Abraham's seed. Salvation is still of the Jews.[123]

Apparently, Gaebelein viewed the covenant as having past, present, and future fulfillment. He expected the terms to be fulfilled in a literal sense, especially as it related to the literal, physical descendants of Abraham in the Jewish nation.

---

[121] Gaebelein, *Church*, 164.

[122] Gaebelein, *Annotated Bible*, 7:218.

[123] Ibid., 1:43.

Third, in spite of the emphasis above on the physical descendants of Abraham, Gaebelein taught that Gentiles through faith would partake of the Abrahamic Covenant. Commenting on Paul's understanding of the Christian's relationship to Abraham, he noted:

> Paul writes … that, as believers, they are without the works of the law and circumcision, the children of Abraham. "Know ye, therefore, that they which are of faith, the same are the children of Abraham." And the Scriptures, the Word of God, had anticipated this. The Word of God foresaw that, ultimately in God's gracious purpose, the Gentiles were to be justified by faith. The Word of God had, so to speak, preached the gospel unto Abraham, the very gospel Paul was heralding among the Gentiles. This gospel-message, preached by the Scriptures, is the announcement, "In thee shall all nations be blessed." The logical conclusion, therefore, is "they which be of faith are blessed with believing Abraham."[124]

Just how participation by the Gentiles in the biblical covenants was to be fully understood should become clearer as the remaining covenants are studied. For now, the truth that identification of a Christian believer through faith in Christ, who was a physical descendant of Abraham, is one way in which Gentiles can participate in the fulfillment of the promises to Abraham.

Finally, the ultimate fulfillment of the covenant is placed in the future. While previous statements showed past fulfillment, Gaebelein observed that "very little of what God promised unconditionally to Abraham has been fulfilled. He never possessed the land, nor did his seed possess it in the dimensions as promised to Abraham."[125] The rest of the prophetic Scriptures could be seen as outlining Israel's future as the promises of the Abrahamic Covenant unfolded in fulfillment. God's faithfulness, once again, confirmed that these prophetic promises were the "word of Hope for Israel."[126]

---

[124] Ibid., 7:216.

[125] Gaebelein, *Harmony*, 125.

[126] Ibid., 126.

224

The Davidic Covenant

In similar fashion, Gaebelein described the biblical covenant made with David in 2 Samuel 7:8-17 and reaffirmed in Psalm 89. While more discussion of this covenant will occur when the concept of the kingdom of God is taken up, basic elements of Gaebelein's thoughts about the Davidic Covenant can be outlined here. Specifically, the same four characteristics of the Abrahamic covenant apply.

First, the Davidic Covenant is unconditional. This was approached from several angles. The covenant was rooted in the sovereign grace and faithfulness of God.[127]

> The Lord asked nothing of David, and the words of sovereign grace, "I will," are prominent in the covenant. The covenant is assured through Jehovah's faithfulness. Though centuries may come and go and millennia pass, during which David's throne is unoccupied and all seems to have failed, yet the time is surely coming when verse 27 of this Psalm (89) will find its blessed accomplishment in Him, the glorified Son of Man.[128]

This highlighted what Gaebelein referred to as the "unratified covenant and its seeming failure."[129] In spite of human failure, however, the provisions would eventually come to pass. The oath of God was emphasized in this connection along with the words from God, "I will not lie," found in Psalm 89:34-35.[130] Consequently, the Davidic Covenant should be considered a permanent divine promise.

Second, the Davidic Covenant was interpreted in literal terms. "When God made a covenant with David He did not promise him a spiritual throne in heaven,

---

[127] Arno C. Gaebelein, *The Book of Psalms: A Devotional and Prophetic Commentary* (New York: Our Hope Press, 1939), 336-37. Gaebelein equated the Old Testament attribute of the loving-kindness of God with the New Testament emphasis on the grace of God (337).

[128] Ibid., 337.

[129] Ibid., 339.

[130] Ibid., 336. See also Gaebelein, *Annotated Bible*, 2:204.

nor a spiritual kingdom, but an earthly throne and an earthly kingdom."[131] Any attempts to understand the promises to David in a nonliteral way without a national, earthly application was absurd. The covenant was to be understood in the way that David would have received the words. This meant that the enthronement of Christ at the right hand of the Father (Acts 2:30-36) could in no wise be considered a fulfillment of the Davidic Covenant.

Associated with this discussion was Gaebelein's distinction between two thrones, the Father's throne and Christ's throne called the throne of His glory.[132]

> Christ some day will receive as a gift from His Father's hands the Throne of His father David and the House of Jacob and a great world wide kingdom will be his domain. But it cannot be till His return.
> And here we call attention at once to the fact that our Lord differentiated between *His Father's Throne* and *His own Throne*, which He calls *the Throne of His Glory*. But that Throne He does not occupy till His Second Coming and when He receives it He will not be Judge alone and end the history of mankind by a universal judgment, but He will reign over the earth, He will be King of Righteousness and King of Peace and will reign till all things are put under His feet. Let the reader keep this distinction clearly in mind, the difference between the Throne of God and the Throne of Christ, which He calls My Throne, and the fogs of perverted prophetic assumptions will soon clear away.[133]

The throne to be shared with the Apostles at the end of the age where the tribes of Israel are judged (Matt. 19:28) was cited to reinforce the fact that the throne associated with the Davidic Covenant is a literal, earthly one.

Third, as in the Abrahamic covenant, there is an affirmation that Gentiles are in some way partakers of the Davidic Covenant. Gaebelein believed that the "heavens" were mentioned in the promise of the Davidic Covenant (Ps. 89:29) for the express purpose of connecting the heavenly people to the covenant. The pre-

---

[131] Gaebelein, *Return*, 31-32. See also Arno C. Gaebelein, "Editorial Notes," *Our Hope* 8 (June 1902): 618 and "Editorial Notes," *Our Hope* 44 (November 1937): 294-98.

[132] Gaebelein, *Millennium*, 61-62.

[133] Ibid., 61.

226

vious two verses describe Christ, not David. Consequently, the promise of being raised above the kings of the earth (Ps. 89:27-28) refers to Christ and the next verse of promise to the seed applies to the seed of Christ, which can only be taken as those who have put faith in him. This group, of course, includes believing Gentiles as well as believing Jews from this age. However, in no way should this interpretation by Gaebelein be taken to mean that he approved of a present-day application of the Davidic Covenant to the church. The reference, in his mind, pointed to the future coronation of Jesus as the King on David's throne.[134]

This leads to the fourth characteristic of the Davidic Covenant as outlined by Gaebelein. The ultimate fulfillment was future. Gaebelein plainly stated that the Davidic kingdom promised in the covenant had not yet been received.[135] Christ alone can fulfill the promises through His second coming.[136] Again, the conclusion can be drawn that the Davidic Covenant, according to Gaebelein, was not being fulfilled in any form in the present church age.

The New Covenant

Proportionate to the Abrahamic and Davidic Covenants, Gaebelein's commentary on the New Covenant is limited. His words on Jeremiah 31:27-34 give the best source of information of his thinking on this matter.

> This covenant is not made with Gentiles, nor even with the church as so often erroneously stated. It is the new covenant to be made with the house of Israel and the house of Judah. This is fully confirmed in the Epistle to Hebrews (Hebrews viii:8–13). The old covenant is the law-covenant, which the Lord did not make with the Gentiles, but with Israel exclusively. The new covenant is of grace. The ground of this new covenant is the sacrificial death of the Lord Jesus Christ, His blood, as we learn from His own words when He instituted the supper. He died for that nation, and therefore all Israel will yet receive the promised blessing of this new

[134] Gaebelein, *Psalms*, 337. See also Gaebelein, *Annotated Bible*, 2:204-5.

[135] Gaebelein, *Annotated Bible*, 2:204.

[136] Ibid. Also see Gaebelein, *Millennium*, 70; *Psalms*, 338.

covenant. This prophecy is therefore still unfulfilled, for Israel does not enjoy this new covenant now.[137]

He went on to say that Gentiles who put faith in Christ, presumably in the church age, "possess the blessings of this new covenant to the full."[138] This appears to conflict with the previous words emphasizing that the New Covenant was exclusively for the nation of Israel. What is probably meant is that there is a difference between actually being a partaker of the covenant and possessing blessings which take the same form as those which the covenant will produce in the future for Israel. With that understanding, Gaebelein's view is that there is one New Covenant which is targeted only for the nation of Israel. His strong wording about the interpretation of Hebrews 8:8-13 confirms this.[139]

Conclusion

The three divine covenants, Abrahamic, Davidic, and New, were all seen by Gaebelein as relating primarily to the nation of Israel although in some ways participation of Gentiles was acknowledged. In each case, fulfillment was seen ultimately through the person of Christ and the time of the covenant's realization was future. In this way, the biblical covenants point toward the idea of prophetic hope coupled with the agency of Christ as the central theme of Gaebelein's theology.

---

[137] Gaebelein, *Annotated Bible*, 4:228.

[138] Ibid.

[139] In the Synoptic Gospels, Gaebelein, though not clearly, treated the disciples as Jewish rather than church disciples. However, the New Covenant was basically ignored with respect to the institution of the Lord's Supper (*Annotated Bible*, 6:53-56, 101, 168-69). In the letters to the Corinthians, he also ignored the New Covenant in commentary on 1 Corinthians 11:25 and used it as a synonym for the gospel in 2 Corinthians 3:1-18 (*Annotated Bible*, 7:121-22, 160-64). Gaebelein inadequately handled the passages in question.

228

The Kingdom of God

Distinctions in the Concept of Kingdom

For Gaebelein, the kingdom of God is a scriptural expression which simply means "whatever God rules over."[140] He qualified this maxim by limiting it to those who "are willingly subject to the rule of God."[141] The kingdom of God is an inclusive term which "takes in the whole sphere where God rules."[142]

Gaebelein distinguished this general concept of the kingdom of God from the more specific term, the *kingdom of heaven*.[143]

> ...it refers to this period which we have come to call the millennium ... The "kingdom of heaven" is the establishment, through Christ, of God's righteous reign on the earth; it is always limited to the earth, that is its sphere—though glorified saints of this and past ages are concerned with it.[144]

The full manifestation of this kingdom of heaven can be found in the future millennium. This is supported by Gaebelein's understanding of the term in the Gospel of Matthew:

> In one word, the kingdom of the heavens is the *literal* fulfillment of all the prophecies and promises contained in the Old Testament, which the Lord gave to the seed of Abraham, and the blessings of the nations of the earth to come after this kingdom is set up.[145]

Thus, this kingdom concept looked forward to the time when God's rule would be established on the earth in conjunction with the national restoration of Israel. In essence, this kingdom is the answer to the prayer in the Sermon on the Mount,

---

[140] Arno C. Gaebelein, "The Millennium," *Our Hope* 9 (November 1902): 294.

[141] Ibid.

[142] Ibid. See also Gaebelein, *Acts*, 327.

[143] Gaebelein preferred the plural form of heaven in his commentary on Matthew.

[144] Ibid., 294.

[145] Gaebelein, *Matthew*, 60.

"Thy kingdom come. Thy will be done in earth, as it is in heaven" (Matt. 6:10). It is an earthly millennial kingdom which on one occasion was called the "theocratic" kingdom by Gaebelein.[146]

The kingdom of heaven, in this view, is part of the kingdom of God, but is not identical to it.[147] In no way is the kingdom of heaven to be equated with the church during this age. However, the church is associated with the kingdom of heaven in the sense that it is "a body of royal priests called out" during the present age for the purpose of being "co-rulers with the King over the millennial earth during a period of 1,000 years and to be forever with Him after that period is ended."[148]

The church is also related to, but not identical to, the kingdom of heaven in a second use of that term by Gaebelein. In light of the rejection of Christ by Jewish leaders cited in Matthew 12, Gaebelein viewed Matthew 13, with its parables of the mystery of the kingdom, as introducing a new aspect of the kingdom of heaven. The new meaning was summed up in the word *Christendom*.[149] Anyone who claims to have a relationship with Christ is to be included in this sphere.[150]

The Offer, Rejection, and Postponement of the Kingdom

Another common element in the concept of the kingdom in Gaebelein's writings involved the sequence, observed in the Gospels and Acts, of Israel's rejection of the kingdom offered by Christ, the absence of the King during an inter-

---

[146] Gaebelein, *Harmony*, 159-86. Here, Gaebelein presented an entire chapter discussing the future millennial kingdom with the chapter titled "The Theocratic Kingdom."

[147] Gaebelein, "Millennium," 295.

[148] Ibid.

[149] Gaebelein, *Matthew*, 262.

[150] Gaebelein held this view even though he interpreted one element in the kingdom of heaven to be the earthly people Israel—the field with a treasure which was bought in Matthew 13:44 (*Matthew*, 297-98). Israel certainly would not be a part of professing Christianity.

advent period, and the final acceptance of the King and the national restoration of Israel.

Gaebelein saw two basic offers of the kingdom. The first offer came through the preaching of John the Baptist and Christ in the Gospels. This offer was expressed in passages like Matthew 3:2 and 4:17 in which the proclamation was, "Repent, for the kingdom of heaven is at hand." There can be no mistaking the identification of this kingdom or its rejection in Gaebelein's opinion.

> Now the question is, What kingdom was it which our Lord offered to Israel? It was the kingdom which He promised to Israel in the Old Testament, a literal kingdom, which has for its seat Jerusalem; the throne of David established in it and upon this throne, ruling, a son of David. This kingdom is promised to extend from Jerusalem over the whole earth. This kingdom the Lord offered to Israel, and He Himself is the King and the rightful heir to the throne of David. This kingdom and their own King the Jewish people rejected.[151]

The existence of a second offer is based on a rather literal application of the parable in Matthew 22:1-10.[152] There, two invitations to the wedding of the king's son are issued and rejected. The second invitation was associated with Peter's sermons in Acts two and three. While there is some response, the continuing rejection of the message by Jewish leadership constituted the repudiation of the kingdom by the nation.[153]

This rejection of Christ by Israel and the return of Jesus to heaven led to the understanding that the present inter-advent age was a parenthesis in God's dealing with respect to the Davidic kingdom.[154] In addition to this terminology, language about the postponement of the kingdom was used.

---

[151] Gaebelein, *Harmony*, 160.

[152] Gaebelein, *Prophet Paul*, 19.

[153] Gaebelein, *Acts*, 33, 69-81.

[154] Gaebelein, *Our Age*, iii. Gaebelein viewed the present age as having a Jewish beginning and a Jewish ending. In between, Jewish history was formally put on hold (ii-iii.).

> The kingdom promised to Israel and their King was then rejected by the nation; however, this does not alter the fact that our Lord *is* the King of Israel, heir to the throne of David, and that this promised kingdom is His and will yet come in power and glory. It has not been abandoned by Israel's unbelief, but only *postponed*. Its coming is connected with the return of our Lord as Son of Man in glory.[155]

The motivation for use of the word *postponement* is the necessity to explain the delay in the establishment of the literal, earthly kingdom of David. Gaebelein wanted to affirm that God's plan for Israel would still take place in the future precisely as the Old Testament had predicted.

Premillennialism

David Rausch argued that premillennialism, the view that Jesus would return before the establishment of an earthly millennial kingdom, dominated the theology of Gaebelein.[156] There can be no question that much of Gaebelein's writings centered on the debate between premillennialism and its two principle rivals, amillennialism and postmillennialism, the latter being prominent. He castigated both opposing perspectives as being negative in their presentation and challenged the proponents to make a clear enunciation of the views based on Scripture with a justification for the spiritualizing hermeneutic applied to the kingdom-hope of Israel.[157]

He targeted postmillennialism's optimistic view of the church as the advancing kingdom with especially harsh words.[158] Such a scheme ignores the dispensational aspects of the Bible and is a deluded dream.[159] The answer to the

---

[155] Gaebelein, *Harmony*, 161.

[156] David A. Rausch, *Irenic Fundamentalist*, 87.

[157] Arno C. Gaebelein, "Editorial Notes," *Our Hope* 45 (April 1939): 663-64.

[158] Arno C. Gaebelein, "The False Idea of the Kingdom," *Our Hope* 38 (October 1931): 214-19.

[159] Gaebelein, "Editorial Notes," *Our Hope* 8 (June 1902): 617-19.

world's problems is the Second Coming of Christ, not the successful ministry of the church.

Only a portion of Gaebelein's overwhelming antagonism to this system is revealed in statements like the following:

> Postmillennialism makes time and history end with the end of this present age. It creates an irreconcilable antagonism between Daniel and John, and between Christ and both, as to the first resurrection. It interprets "the world to come" to mean the disembodied state of the soul, after death, in a super-earthly sphere. It identifies the throne of David with the throne of God the Father in heaven. It obliterates the distinction between Israel and the Church. It is responsible for the most deplorable condition of the professing Church of our times. It is part of the predicted apostasy.[160]

The superiority of the premillennial position was established in passages like Acts 15:14–17 which demonstrated that the Second Coming of Christ was a prerequisite for the establishment of the Davidic kingdom.[161] In Gaebelein's estimation, "the fulfillment of Old Testament prophecies as to the future, all these kingdom blessings, depended wholly on His Second Coming."[162] In this way, the premillennial faith was a basis for prophetic hope.[163]

The Prominence of the Nation of Israel

Much of what has been outlined from Gaebelein's eschatology thus far has revolved around the ethnic and political reality of Israel, not the church. This raises the serious question of whether national Israel in some form can serve as an integrating theme for Gaebelein's theology. At one point in the study of Gae-

---

[160] Gaebelein, *Meat*, 37.

[161] Gaebelein, *Millennium*, 68-70.

[162] Ibid., 45.

[163] Associated with Gaebelein's premillennialism was the acceptance of the pretribulational rapture of the church at least seven years before the actual coming of Christ to the earth to set up His kingdom. This aspect of his eschatology will receive more attention below.

belein, this writer felt that national Israel was the central theme.[164] Gaebelein occasionally hinted at this crucial role for Israel.

> All God's redemption purposes center in Israel, the seed of Abraham, the
> descendants of the twelve sons of Jacob; all His purposes are linked with
> that nation. The land He bestowed upon them, called "the Holy land," also
> "Immanuel's Land," became the theatre of God's manifestations. It was so
> in the past and it will be so again in the not very distant future. Yet the
> greater part of Christendom, by far the greatest, gives no heed to this im-
> portant fact, and knows nothing of the place which Israel holds in the re-
> demption plans and purpose of God.[165]

As the last chapter showed, even the typological interpretations of the Gospels
focused on the historically predicted events of the Old Testament which were
centered in the nation of Israel.

However, in spite of this prominence for Israel, the discussion to follow
will demonstrate that Gaebelein's theological thinking traveled in broader territory. To be sure, Israel appears to be the key to the prophetic calendar. Nonetheless, when all theological elements are accounted for, the nation is just one element related to the unifying theme.

Identification of the Central Interpretive Motif

The Statement of the Central Interpretive Motif

In light of Gaebelein's overall evangelical theology with its emphases on
Bible inspiration, the centrality of Christ, and eschatological issues, one can determine with more precision a statement of the central interpretive motif. Bible
inspiration was ruled out because it did not integrate the content of Gaebelein's
theology (although it did provide a hermeneutical basis). The centrality of Christ

---

[164] Rausch also highlighted the Jewish people as central to Gaebelein's theological assertions
(*Irenic Fundamentalist*, 63). During the Jewish outreach ministry in the 1890s this may have been
true.

[165] Gaebelein, *Millennium*, 36.

is clearly stated. However, the sheer weight of discussion of eschatology with its various focuses, speaks as forcefully as many direct statements.

Nonetheless, it is possible to merge the theological statements about the centrality of Christ with eschatology to produce one statement clarifying the integrating theme of Gaebelein's theology. This can be done through the concept of prophetic hope which finds its fulfillment in the Second Coming of Christ. Thus, the central interpretive motif of Gaebelein's theological formulations can be stated as *prophetic hope centered in the personal Second Coming of Jesus Christ*. That this theme truly integrates Gaebelein's theological system will be seen by an examination of the several expressions of prophetic hope which he outlined. One must always keep in mind in each case that this hope can *only* be fully realized when Jesus comes again.

The Expressions of Prophetic Hope

There are five major ways in which Gaebelein discussed the idea of prophetic hope. The method of presentation will adhere to the chronological order in which each element of hope is realized in his dispensational scheme.

The Hopelessness of the Present Age

The first area, while not technically a matter of positive hope, serves as an introduction to the four manifestations of hope which Gaebelein believed would take place in the future. The fact that hope exists implies that in the present there must be conditions which need to be changed. For Gaebelein, the present church age was characterized by such an unwanted environment.

In a series of five books beginning in the turbulent times of the 1930s, Gaebelein outlined for his readers a dark picture for the world. In *Conflict of the Ages* (1933), he portrayed the historic development of the mystery of lawlessness which was, in his mind, close to pushing the world to the precipice. His work, *World Prospects* (1934), held out final hope for Israel, the Gentiles, and the church, but not until a time of great darkness and difficulty.

Over half of the pages in the next book of the sequence, *Hopeless, Yet There is Hope* (1935), were devoted to a description of the bleak condition of the Twentieth Century due to war, financial chaos, and the rise of communism. *As It Was—So Shall it Be* (1937) compared the time before Noah's Flood to the present hour. Finally, the optimistic book, *The Hope of the Ages* (1938), described the present absence of kingdom-hope and noted that only by the Second Coming of Christ can this void be filled with lasting hope. A small booklet, *What Will Become of Europe* (1940), during the beginning days of World War II, observed that "there is no nation which does not tremble."[166] All that appeared from a human perspective on the horizon was darkness, distress, and destruction.[167]

For Gaebelein, the problem with the human race could always be identified with the existence of sin.[168] Specifically, two major areas of concern are emphasized. First, the present age is characterized by an increasing persecution of the Jews. After the destruction of Jerusalem in A.D. 70 and the subsequent scattering of the Jews throughout the nations, Gaebelein observed that "the fires of persecution burned fiercely in almost every century."[169] This persecution would culminate one day in the Great Tribulation or time of Jacob's trouble when the nation would go through its darkest hour.[170]

The second major characteristic of the present age was the increasing moral and religious declension.

---

[166] Arno C. Gaebelein, *What Will Become of Europe? World Darkness and Divine Light* (New York: Our Hope Publications, 1940), 9.

[167] Ibid., 10.

[168] Arno C. Gaebelein, *The Conflict of the Ages, the Mystery of Lawlessness: Its Origin, Historic Development and Coming Defeat* (New York: Publication Office "Our Hope," 1933), 23.

[169] Arno C. Gaebelein, *World Prospects, How is it All Going to End? A Study in Sacred Prophecy and Present Day World Conditions* (New York: Publication Office, "Our Hope," 1934), 46.

[170] Ibid., 49-59.

Morally the world sinks lower and lower. Christendom is turning more and more away from the supernatural, the foundation of true Christianity, turning from the spiritual to the material, giving up the message of power for social improvements ... The faith as revealed in God's infallible Book is abandoned; apostasy is seen everywhere. World conversion, the world accepting Christianity? *What mockery!* The nations of the world were never as far away from accepting Christ as Saviour and recognize Him as Lord as in 1938.[171]

Both apostasy within Christendom, associated with moral decline, and the persecution of the Jews were understood by Gaebelein as a fulfillment of prophecy. Both called for a cry of hope, the former from the genuine Christian and the latter from the Jewish people. It has already been noted that the divine line of revelation, for Gaebelein, began with creation, continued with God's work with the nations, took a turn with God's choosing of Israel, and culminated in the highest revelation of the church.[172] The fulfillment of hope for each takes place progressively in reverse order so that the first manifestation of hope is found in the church.

The Blessed Hope and the Rapture of the Church

Gaebelein believed strongly that the first manifestation in history of the fulfillment of prophetic hope would be the rapture of the church. This was the "blessed hope" of Titus 2:13 which was to be looked for expectantly by true Christians. It was a common topic in the pages of *Our Hope*, especially the aspect of pretribulational timing, with more outside writers invited to address it than perhaps any other single issue.[173] This hope was the catching up of New Testament

[171] Arno C. Gaebelein, *The Hope of the Ages* (New York: Publication Office "Our Hope," 1938), 170–71. One wonders what Gaebelein's analysis would have been had he seen the fifty or so years since he made that statement.

[172] Gaebelein, *Meat*, 19-20.

[173] Some examples would be Arno C. Gaebelein, "Opening Address," *Our Hope* 8 (September 1901): 93-96; "Notes on Prophecy and the Jews," *Our Hope* 8 (November 1901): 294-95; "The Patient Waiting for Christ," *Our Hope* 8 (January 1902): 345-46; "Editorial Notes," *Our Hope* 8 (February 1902): 394-95; "Who Will Be Caught Up When the Lord Comes," *Our Hope* 8 (Febru-

believers to be with. It included both those who had died in Christ and believers alive at the moment of the rapture.

One aspect of the rapture which often received attention was its imminency. Gaebelein defined imminency with these words:

> Now the word *imminency* or *imminent* means that an event is impending, the matter in question is liable to occur at any moment. When we speak of the imminency of the coming of the Lord we understand by it that the Lord *may* come at any moment. This is the meaning of imminent.[174]

In light of the fact that Jesus could come for the church at any moment, no signs were expected to herald His coming in advance.[175] The significance of this doctrine for Gaebelein is clear when he warned that to do away with it was to rob the rapture of its "glory and power."[176]

The second aspect of the rapture of the church is its pretribulational timing. Another way of describing this doctrine is to note that the church would not go through the Great Tribulation. The coming of Christ in the air to receive the church is a separate event from His coming to the earth to set up His kingdom seven years later.

Gaebelein gave several reasons for his view with the discussions at times being extremely tedious. However, the following arguments appear to be the ma-

---

ary 1902): 408-17; "Editorial Notes," *Our Hope* 9 (August 1902): 116-21; "Editorial Notes," *Our Hope* 9 (October 1902): 225-27; "Will There be a Partial Rapture?" *Our Hope* 44 (August 1937): 100-4; John Nelson Darby, "What Saints Will Be in the Tribulation?" *Our Hope* 8 (May 1902): 597-605; Charles Campbell, "The Interval Between the Lord's Coming For Us, and His Coming With Us," *Our Hope* 9 (August 1902): 81-92; G. L. Alrich, "The Imminency of the Coming of Our Lord Jesus," *Our Hope* 9 (August 1902): 167-74; and I. M. Haldeman, "The Two Distinct Stages of the Coming of the Lord," *Our Hope* 9 (January 1903): 418-19. Many others can be cited. Most of the articles here appeared during the height of the controversy with Robert Cameron which was discussed in an earlier chapter.

[174] Arno C. Gaebelein, "Editorial Notes," *Our Hope* 9 (October 1902): 225. See also Arno C. Gaebelein, "Editorial Notes," *Our Hope* 39 (August 1932): 76-77.

[175] Arno C. Gaebelein, "Notes on Prophecy and the Jews," *Our Hope* 8 (November 1901): 295.

[176] Gaebelein, "The Patient Waiting for Christ," 345. See also Gaebelein, "Opening Address," 96.

jor support for a pretribulational rapture as taught by Gaebelein. First, he argued that the rapture had to come before the start of the Great Tribulation because the coming of the Lord for the church was imminent.[177] Second, there were exegetical reasons for pretribulationalism. In 1 Thessalonians 5:9 ("For God hath not appointed us to wrath but to obtain salvation by our Lord Jesus Christ"), there is a promise from God that church believers will not suffer the wrath of God during the Great Tribulation. The context of the book indicated to Gaebelein that the start of the day of the Lord or tribulation period is in mind.[178] Another passage (Rev. 3:10) promised that the church would be kept from the "hour of temptation" which was interpreted to be the Great Tribulation of the latter days.[179]

Third, the most frequent argument used by Gaebelein in the rapture debate was the fact that the Great Tribulation or time of Jacob's trouble, was exactly that, a period designated for Jacob's offspring, the Jews. Here the absolute distinction between Israel and the church prohibits the involvement of the church in a Jewish event. Gaebelein, in a representative remark, noted:

> All passages which have to do with the great tribulation prove that it is Israel's time of sorrow (Jer. xxx; Mark xiii:14-22; Rev. vii:1-14; Dan. xii:1; Matt. xxiv). "Jacob's trouble," not the Church's trouble. Christ saved us from wrath to come and will deliver us from that hour of trial that shall try

---

[177] Arno C. Gaebelein, "The Attempted Revival of an Unscriptural Theory," *Our Hope* 41 (July 1934): 24-25. This argument stems from an understanding that watching for the coming of Christ, as Scripture exhorts, would be meaningless without imminency. Gaebelein commented: "Looking for that blessed Hope [Titus 2:13] can mean only one thing, that daily we should look for Him and for His promised coming, not for death, but for Himself. But how is this daily looking possible if He cannot come at any moment?" (24).

[178] Arno C. Gaebelein, *The First and Second Epistles to the Thessalonians* (New York: Our Hope Publications, n.d.), 116-19. For a more recent approach with similar argumentation, see Zane C. Hodges, "The Rapture in 1 Thessalonians 5:1-11," in *Walvoord: A Tribute*, ed. Donald K. Campbell (Chicago: Moody Press, 1982), 67-79.

[179] Gaebelein, *Return*, 101. For perhaps the best description of how this passage plays a role in the rapture debate, see W. Robert Cook, *The Theology of John* (Chicago: Moody Press, 1979), 168-72. The exegetical arguments of Gaebelein with respect to 1 Thessalonians 5 and Revelation 3:10 appear to be the strongest and are based, in large measure, on grammatical-historical interpretation.

them that dwell on the earth. When this takes place the Church will be far above the storm (John iii:36; 1 Thess. v:9; Rev. iii:10).[180]

The third aspect of the rapture of the church was found in the blessings which constituted the realization of the hope. First, the blessed hope pointed toward the resurrection of all saints who have died and the glorification of the bodies of those saints alive at the time of the rapture.[181] Second, the church will receive rewards at the judgment seat of Christ in heaven during the earthly Great Tribulation.[182] Third, the church saints will become rulers with Christ during the millennial kingdom. While living in heaven, they will be priests and kings who will reign and judge the world and angels.[183] Thus, the blessed hope of the rapture of the church is summed up in the encompassing truth that "the Church's glorious prospect is the eternal fellowship with the Son of God."[184]

The Hope of the National Restoration of Israel

It has already been observed that Gaebelein's use of the literal hermeneutic concentrated on that portion of the Scriptures which prophesied the national restoration of Israel in the millennium. This literal promise provided hope for the

---

[180] Arno C. Gaebelein, "The True Church: Its Translation Before the End," *Our Hope* 38 (September 1931): 184. See also "Editorial Notes," *Our Hope* 39 (August 1932): 78. This method of arguing is a use of dispensational-theological integration. The distinction between Israel and the church becomes the switch which helps to determine an interpretation. There are two problems with using this argument which Gaebelein was not careful to address. First, as seen earlier, he included the Old Testament saints in the rapture of the church. An alert nondispensationalist might ask if the heavenly people can be mixed, what keeps the earthly people from being mixed in the tribulation? That is one reason that contemporary dispensationalists have come to view the resurrection of Old Testament saints at the end of the tribulation. Second, Gaebelein included the Gentiles in the tribulation (*Revelation,* 59). Since distinctions between Israel and the nations are made, why not between Israel and the church? This shows that the particular distinction between Israel and the church had priority for Gaebelein over all other distinctions.

[181] Gaebelein, "True Church," 184-85.

[182] Gaebelein, "Unscriptural Theory," 24. This aspect of the blessed hope was considered by Gaebelein the greatest incentive for holy living (*Return,* 118).

[183] Gaebelein, *Return,* 118.

[184] Gaebelein, *World Prospects,* 166.

240

nation, a hope that was a living hope.[185] One of the greatest evidences of that hope was the desire, stated during Passover ceremonies, to be in Jerusalem the next year.

> And this has been going on generation after generation, century after century, during the darkest ages, during the times when satanic powers attempted their complete extermination. "This year here—next year in Jerusalem." The Jewish Hope is a never dying Hope. Israel is *the nation of Hope*.[186]

In addition, this hope was not known by other nations.[187]

According to Gaebelein, the basis for this national hope was clearly outlined in prophetic Scripture.

> The foundations of the hope of Israel, that never dying Hope, are the two promises; the promise of the Messiah and the promise of the land in the dimensions as given ... in the [Abrahamic] covenant.[188]

In this way, the future restoration of Israel is tied to the coming of Messiah, which from a Christian perspective, meant the Second Coming of Jesus Christ.

Although the focus of this hope is on the unique relationship between God and the Jewish people, it is also the basis of hope for other nations. Gaebelein observed:

> And the people Israel have been thus preserved because the other great promise of Hope and Glory, the promise of the land, their national restoration, spiritual regeneration, and the promise of future blessing to "all the families of the earth" will have to be fulfilled. Such is Israel's Hope, and, when it is reached, it will mean *the Hope and blessing for all the world*.[189]

---

[185] Gaebelein, *Hopeless*, 156.

[186] Ibid., 157.

[187] Ibid., 160.

[188] Ibid., 162.

[189] Ibid., 165.

The realization of the national restoration of Israel with its overflowing blessings upon other nations awaits fulfillment when Jesus, Israel's Messiah comes again.

The Hope of the Nations

Hope for the nations of the world was seen above as a side effect of the restoration of Israel. Gaebelein outlined the history of God's dealings with the Gentile nations beginning with Israel's own apostasy and resultant judgment via the Babylonian captivity.[190] The setting aside of "Israel as a nation in government and dominion" started with Nebuchadnezzar.[191] The book of Daniel yields the prophetic account of the history of the dominion of the Gentiles during a period known as the times of the Gentiles.[192]

However, this period of Gentile supremacy was only temporary. Again, following closely the prophecies in Daniel (especially chapters two and seven), Gaebelein noted the future defeat of Gentile domination culminating in the setting up of the kingdom of God on earth.[193] This was preceded by the seven-year time of Jacob's trouble which also included the wrath of God poured out on Gentiles. However, during this time many Gentiles will come to know the Lord, mainly due to the witness of the Jewish remnant which also follows Him.[194] However, this is not the great hope of the Gentiles. At the coming of Christ at the end of the tribulation, the conversion of the world will take place.

> But there are other nations; though missionaries went and brought them the message of salvation, as nations they were hardly touched by the Gospel. Millions upon millions never heard it. Humanly speaking, as conditions are today they would never hear that Gospel of Grace. There is not the remotest chance of the conversion of these great nations of Asia, Af-

---

[190] Gaebelein, *World Prospects*, 101-8.

[191] Ibid., 108.

[192] Ibid., 109-23.

[193] Ibid., 124-42.

[194] Ibid., 151.

rica and other parts of the world.

Now these nations, such as China, Japan and the millions of India and the millions living in Africa, will heed this Gospel of the Kingdom, they believe, and then turning away from their idols and their false system will learn righteousness. The great revival comes to the unevangelized masses of the heathen world. Out of them comes the great multitude; though they suffer in the great tribulation, they come out of it victoriously and enter as saved nations the earthly Kingdom of our Lord.[195]

Gaebelein associated this conversion with the judgment of the nations found in his interpretation of Matthew 25:31.[196] As with the national hope of Israel, the ultimate realization of this hope of the nations occurs when Jesus returns to earth.

The Hope for Renewal of Creation

Gaebelein marveled at the wonder of God's creation. However, the existence of sin in the universe led to another less beautiful facet of nature.

What about the other side? Cyclones and tornadoes sweep over God's fair creation, working a terrible destruction. Earthquakes devastate many regions of different continents; volcanoes emit their streams of hot lava inflicting sufferings on man, beast, and vegetation. There are droughts and dust storms which turn the most fruitful lands into a hopeless wilderness. Ferocious animals attack man, poisonous snakes and insects claim many thousands of human victims ... There is a terrible blight upon all creation. Did a kind and loving Creator create such things for His own pleasure and glory?[197]

As in the case of the church, Israel, and the nations, only the intervention of God could correct the situation and give cause for hope.

Gaebelein expected a reversal of the fortunes of creation in a literal fashion. Two key passages were Isaiah 11:6-9 and Romans 8:19-22. The first passage predicted a time when wolves would dwell in peace with sheep and, among other changes, children would be able to play with and around what used to be danger-

---

[195] Ibid., 153-54.

[196] Ibid., 154.

[197] Gaebelein, *Hope of the Ages*, 68.

ous animals. Gaebelein's literal interpretation is indicated by his rhetorical question: "Who authorizes the expositor to say that these words have not a literal meaning but they must be understood allegorically and given a spiritual interpretation."[198]

Gaebelein believed that "the hope of Creation" was evinced in the second passage (Rom. 8:19-22). There, the Pauline picture is one of the entire creation groaning and longing for the day when the sons of God (believers) will be manifested.[199] The theme of hope dominates the context of this passage and takes in not only creation, but the church (Romans 8) and the hope of Israel and the Gentiles (Romans 9–11).

When will the hope of a renewed creation be realized? In the context of a commentary on the crown of thorns, Gaebelein highlighted the answer.

> That crown of thorns is emblematic of creation's curse. Not science with its inventions and discoveries can arrest or even ameliorate the curse of sin. Only One can remove it. He is Creation's Lord who paid the price of redemption and whose redemption power can alone deliver groaning creation. But it will never come till He comes again, no longer wearing the crown of mockery, but crowned with many diadems.[200]

Renewal of creation will then be the last hope to come to fruition when Jesus comes again.

---

[198] Ibid., 69. This literalism with respect to the restoration of creation is also evident in passages such as Zechariah 14:1-4. There the topographical changes in the Mount of Olives are taken literally in Gaebelein's exposition (*Studies in Zechariah*, 8th ed. [New York: Publication Office "Our Hope," 1911], 140-46). However, he is not consistent throughout the passage. Later in verse eight, living waters flow out of Jerusalem into the Mediterranean and Dead Seas (149-50). The association is made with the pouring out of the Holy Spirit as mentioned in the description of John 7:38-39.

[199] Gaebelein, *Hope of the Ages*, 69-71.

[200] Ibid., 75.

244

The Christological Focus of Hope

The theme of prophetic hope expressed, in spite of the hopelessness of the present age, to the church, Israel, the Gentile nations, and creation is the thread that unites the theological system of Gaebelein.[201] It is not surprising then to find the name of his Jewish outreach ministry to be *The Hope of Israel Movement* or to note that the highly significant expository magazine which he edited for over half a century was named *Our Hope*.

However, this thread has a Christological focus. While the evangelical character of Gaebelein's theology shows that the benefits of God for the human race are grounded in the work of Christ on the cross, the Christological spotlight falls on the doctrine of the Second Coming.[202] In a chapter entitled "Hundreds of Questions But Only One Answer,"[203] the message is unblurred,

> There is but one answer to all these questions concerning the promised hope for Israel, for the nations of the earth and for all creation. That answer is:
>
> ### The Lord Jesus Christ.
>
> He alone is the only answer, the completest answer, the never-failing answer to all our questions. But what do we mean when we give His ever blessed and adorable Name, the Name above every other name, as the only answer? We do not mean that the answer is a practical application of the principles of righteousness declared by the infallible teacher in the sermon on the mount. We do not mean the practice of what has been termed the golden rule. We do not mean a leadership of Jesus. We do not mean that

---

[201] The consistency of Gaebelein's theology over the years can be seen by comparing the books mentioned above from the 1930s to an earlier article in *Our Hope*. See Arno C. Gaebelein, "The Coming of the Lord, the Hope of Israel, and the Hope of the Nations and Creation," *Our Hope* 8 (September 1901): 194-99. This article was actually the publication of an address given at the first Sea Cliff Bible conference.

[202] Gaebelein viewed the atonement on the cross by Christ as the greatest event in the human history while the Second Coming of Christ was the second greatest event (*Hope of the Ages*, 76). Yet the Second Coming is "the great hope, the only hope, for all the earth ... All waits for that coming event" (76). It is the work of Christ in the Second Coming, rather than the first advent, which serves as the focus of the unifying theme of hope.

[203] Gaebelein, *Hope of the Ages*, 54-76.

these questions will be answered by future spiritual revivals, nor do we mean that a blasted Western civilization, misnamed Christian, will influence heathen nations to accept Christianity and turn to God from their idols. The sorrowful fact is that what military Christendom has done and is doing, and the shameful failures of Western civilization, has been a curse to heathen nations.

What we mean, the only answer, the completest and never-failing answer to all our questions, is

The Glorious Reappearing of the Lord Jesus Christ.

This future event will answer every question, solve every problem which humanity faces today, and all the existing chaotic conditions, and bring about that golden age of which heathen poets dreamed, which the Bible promises is in store for the earth.[204]

In light of such an emphasis, it is no wonder that for many years the cover of *Our Hope* magazine had on it the words "The Lord Jesus Christ, Who is Our Hope." The central interpretive motif, prophetic hope through the Second Coming, was best captured in a prayer which closed Gaebelein's volume, *Hopeless, Yet There is Hope,*

Even so Come, Thou Hope of the hopeless, Thou Hope of Israel, Thou Hope of the World, all Nations and Creation. Even so, Come Lord Jesus.

---

[204] Ibid., 71-72.

CHAPTER 7
SUMMARY AND CONCLUSION

Summary of the Study

The study of Arno C. Gaebelein's theological method has been fruitful in many respects. In chapter two, a survey of his life and ministry, while revealing many details about his strong Christian character and ministry, showed, most of all, that his theological method or approach to the Bible was impacted by three specific sources: 1) Émile Guers, the Genevan pastor, 2) Orthodox Judaism with which he came in contact during his Jewish missionary endeavors in New York City, and 3) the Niagara Bible Conference movement.

A more detailed look at these influences in chapter three demonstrated, first of all, that Émile Guers brought to Gaebelein through his writing the importance of methodology in approaching the Bible. Added to this was the fact that this methodology and the resulting doctrinal conclusions were essentially the same as that of John Nelson Darby who had strategically impacted Guers and the Genevan Brethren.

In like manner, it was discovered that the major influence of the Niagara Bible Conference upon Gaebelein came through contacts with the Plymouth Brethren who introduced him to many Brethren writings and teachings. Thus, two sources, Guers and the Brethren of the Niagara Conference impacted Gaebelein with Darbyite views.

A special study of Gaebelein's interest in the hope of Zionism reinforced the notion that he was heavily influenced by the orthodox Jews he was attempting to impact with the Gospel. They, along with Guers, prompted him to endorse the doctrine of premillennialism. It remained for the Niagara circle to invigorate his premillennialism with the Darbyite view of the pretribualtional rapture.

In addition to these influences upon Gaebelein, the study of historical factors in Gaebelein's theological development exhibited a strong reaction on his part to communism and the rise of anti-Semitism. This reaction, while in the context of a complex relationship between Gaebelein and the Jews (communistic, atheistic, or orthodox), proved that the charge that he was anti-Semitic was to be rejected entirely.

With these presuppositional tracks fully explored, Gaebelein's theological method was studied by identifying the major methodological rules used to develop doctrines from various texts and by determining the central interpretive motif around which his theological system was organized. Literal interpretation in the sense of grammatical-historical interpretation was found to operate primarily in two areas. First, Gaebelein explicitly taught that literal interpretation of prophecy about Israel's future national restoration was the only acceptable approach. Second, he emphasized also the literal interpretation of the church as a new entity unrevealed in the Old Testament, but clearly outlined in the book of Ephesians. The synthesis of the two led to a distinction between Israel and the church which Gaebelein usually described in absolute terms.

The second rule of interpretation used by Gaebelein was called, in this work, dispensational integration. His concept of dispensations (three major ones: law, grace, kingdom), the analogy of faith, and the progress of revelation combined to provide a way of looking at passages that went beyond the grammatical-historical interpretation of an individual text. Passages were to be interpreted in light of unfolding patterns or themes within the progress of revelation given in the entire canon of Scripture.

Within this general outlook, three specific approaches to integration were identified. First, dispensational-theological integration operated when the distinction between Israel and the church was used as a switch to decide the meaning of a passage. Second, dispensational-typological integration was used to allow a prophetic secondary meaning for the text (usually narrative) in light of the distinction between Israel and the church. Third, dispensational-applicatory integration allowed application of a secondary meaning for a text without typology in the light of the same distinction. The implication of these approaches leads one to the conclusion that Gaebelein interpreted texts in the light of grammatical, historical, and theological concerns although each factor was not necessarily considered in each passage.

The analytical study of Gaebelein's central interpretive motif identified his unifying theme as prophetic hope centered in the personal Second Coming of Jesus Christ. This hope was couched within a thoroughly evangelical theology and was expressed with respect to the four areas of the church, Israel, the nations, and creation. In doing so, this motif encompassed, for Gaebelein, the entire breadth of the theological message of Scripture. In addition, the expectations of hope in each case stood in stark contrast to the dark hopelessness of the present age.

The Significance of Gaebelein

The important role of Gaebelein and his theological approach can be measured with respect to the history of both fundamentalism and dispensationalism. However, in the primary area of theological method, this study culminates in an attempt to define dispensationalism by referring to major features in the dispensational understanding and use of Scripture as found in Gaebelein's example.

The History of Fundamentalism

Sandeen theorized that the tradition of millenarianism was the primary force driving the formulation of American fundamentalism in the late nineteenth

250

and early twentieth centuries.[1] Marsden objected that such a view of fundamentalism, while matching closely the state of affairs in more recent times, does not give
proper weight to cultural roots of fundamentalism.[2] Gaebelein's example illustrates the validity of both millenarian and cultural tracks in the development of
fundamentalism.

Marsden highlighted Gaebelein's ambivalence toward World War I as one
example of a "shared interest in the cultural question" in which American civilization was eyed "with a mixture of hopeful loyalty and increasing alarm."[3] Indeed,
the central interpretive motif for Gaebelein's theology highlighted future hope in
light of the cultural decay of the present age. Gaebelein's constant appeal to current events which heralded moral decline demonstrates that much of his thinking
was impacted by cultural reaction.

Yet the millennialism which caught Sandeen's interest was near the core
of Gaebelein's theology. The reaction to present cultural decadence was coupled
with the future hope of the Lord's return to set up His kingdom. In this way, Gaebelein would stand in the stream of fundamentalism which captured most of Sandeen's attention.[4]

On one other point, it must be observed that Gaebelein's example also
speaks against the old view that fundamentalism was "a manifestation of cultural

---

[1] Ernest R. Sandeen, *The Roots of Fundamentalism: British and American Millenarianism
1800-1930* (Chicago: University of Chicago Press, 1970).

[2] George M. Marsden, *Fundamentalism and American Culture: The Shaping of Twentieth-
Century Evangelicalism, 1870-1925* (New York: Oxford University Press, 1980), 5. Marsden's
view is broader, but encompasses the aspect of millenarianism as seen by Sandeen. In light of the
significance of such American fundamentalists who did not hold to premillennialism (for example,
William Jennings Bryan), Marsden's thesis is probably best (132-35).

[3] Marsden, *Fundamentalism*, 149-50, 53.

[4] Ibid., 5. Recall that this writer adopted the view that fundamentalism in Gaebelein's time represented a kind of orthodox Protestantism or evangelicalism. The present discussion simply ampli-
fies various emphases within that overall view.

lag that time and education eventually would eliminate."[5] He was a northerner who was considered a well-educated man even though he was self taught. His ministry centered in the large metropolitan area of New York City. In no way could he be considered "backwards" except by those who were his theological opponents.

The History of Dispensationalism

This study of Gaebelein surfaced some contact points for his theological and ministerial development which reveal an impact on the history of dispensationalism. First, the nationwide itinerant ministry including teaching at several schools, the numerous books, and the publication of *Our Hope*, gave a type of stability and growth to dispensationalism in America. The footnotes in the *Scofield Reference Bible* provide only a glimpse of dispensational theology. Gaebelein's writings serve as one of the most reliable sources, along with Chafer's *Systematic Theology*, of codified Scofieldism. Yet Chafer did not write numerous commentaries like his colleague from New York. It is doubtful that dispensationalism would have had the popularity it had, if the Scofield Reference Bible and its teachings had not had a spokesman of Gaebelein's caliber representing it in the churches and schools across the land.[6]

Also, the study of Gaebelein brought to light the influence of the Geneva connection to American dispensationalism. At least some of Guer's works had circulation in the United States so that another stream of Darbyite dispensationalism can be identified. In addition, the impact of the Niagara Bible Conference movement was confirmed in Gaebelein's example. Direct contact with Brookes, Scofield, and Plymouth Brethren associated with the conferences was well established.

---

[5] Ibid., 4. Marsden here also speaks against the older view of fundamentalism.

[6] H. A. Ironside could also be considered in the same light.

Finally, this study of Gaebelein highlighted the important truth that Orthodox Judaism has had an impact upon dispensational thinking, even to the point of influencing a prominent figure toward a premillennial theology. The existence of such a connection, in light of the overall interest of the Niagara men in Zionism, cannot be taken too lightly.

Theological Method

General Comments

The larger significance of this study relates to the primary focus on theological method. Several conclusions can be drawn about Gaebelein and the direction which his theological method takes. First, it is clear that he was a practitioner and disseminator of theology more than an innovator. Mark Bailey cited Gaebelein as one who contributed creatively to the definition of the kingdom of heaven as it used in the Gospel of Matthew.[7] As such he would be in the formulative period of dispensationalism. Some ingenuity is also seen in the way that Gaebelein incorporated Jewish writings in his messages. However, in spite of such marks of creativity, Gaebelein did little to formulate new directions in dispensational theology.

In fact, many aspects of his theology have had apparently insignificant impact in terms of any lasting change. For example, the broad use of typology is rarely seen today in dispensationalists' writings.[8] In Gaebelein's case, it was also discovered that he was dependent upon F. W. Grant's *The Numerical Bible*. In addition, the de-Judaizing of the text, especially in the Sermon on the Mount, before secondary application of the text is made, is not universally accepted in dis-

---

[7] Mark Bailey, "Dispensational Definitions of Kingdom," (Paper presented at the dispensational theology pre-meeting at the annual meeting of the Evangelical Theological Society, November 1988), 6.

[8] Roy B. Zuck, *Basic Bible Interpretation* (Wheaton, IL: Victor Books, 1991), 169-84. Zuck's example shows the toning down of modern usage of types.

pensational circles. A final example would be the apparent change within most of dispensationalism to a view that Old Testament saints are resurrected after the tribulation rather than before as in Gaebelein. Consequently, Gaebelein was no pacesetter in the sense of introducing new avenues of theology. He would have viewed himself as simply expositing the faith once delivered to the saints and joining the renewal of prophetic interests which began in the early nineteenth century.[9]

A second general way in which Gaebelein's work can be judged a contribution to theological method is its practical nature. For him theology was not theoretical or merely abstract. Doing theology was as much living it out as formulating it systematically. The beginning of his dispensational thinking was hammered out as he sought to relate to Jews he was trying to win to faith in Jesus. Although a student at heart and at ease in the preacher's study, theology was truth that related to the real world. Such thoughts are fortified by the watchful eye he kept on world events such as Zionism. He expected God to act out in history what theology from the Bible had taught. This aspect of Gaebelein's life, ministry, and theology in concert livens the sometimes stale academic arena of theology.

A third broad way in which Gaebelein's example informs theological method can be found in his emphasis upon the priority of text in interpretation. Although the historical context of his theological development has been clearly shown, he only appealed to that tradition in limited measure for justification of theological decisions. In like manner, human reason failed to emerge as a major factor in Gaebelein's theological formulation.[10] The conclusion is that both tradition and reason are subordinated to the text of the Bible itself in the development

---

[9] Arno C. Gaebelein, *The Hope of the Ages* (New York: Publication Office "Our Hope," 1938), 161-69.

[10] Reason is used here to refer to both philosophical argumentation and the opinions generated in various academic disciplines such as philosophy, psychology, and natural science.

of theology. Such a description of theological method may well specify the general theological approach in the movement of which Gaebelein was a part.

The Definition of Dispensationalism

Gaebelein's example also proves significant by using his theology and methods in an attempt to define dispensationalism. Blaising outlined a history of dispensationalism in America that starts with the premillennialism of the Niagara Conference and then moves to the time of codification of dispensationalism in Scofieldism.[11] This is followed by a period in which the essentials of the system were emphasized as the definition. Charles Ryrie's *sine qua non* given in 1965 is representative of this approach.[12] Blaising suggested that dispensationalism is moving to a new stage of doctrinal development for which an emerging definition is framed in terms of a list of vital concerns.[13]

However, the influence of the Darbyite Émile Guers upon Gaebelein, which was surfaced in this study, shows that Ryrie's notion of an essential set of methodological and theological concerns within the history of modern dispensationalism must be taken seriously. Over one hundred years before Ryrie, Guers was sharing the same crucial core to his methodology in the early days of the tradition. The two major thrusts along this line were literal interpretation and the distinction between Israel and the Church. This historical continuity may suggest some substance to an essentialist outlook of dispensationalism's self-consciousness as a historical movement. However, as will be shown below, there is also value to understanding in a descriptive way, the major doctrinal and meth-

---

[11] Craig A. Blaising, "The Kingdom of God in Progressive Dispensationalism," (Paper presented at the dispensational theology pre-meeting at the annual meeting of the Evangelical Theological Society, November 1991), 1.

[12] Charles C. Ryrie, *Dispensationalism Today* (Chicago: Moody Press, 1965), 43-47.

[13] Blaising, "Progressive Dispensationalism," 1.

odological concerns which Gaebelein brings to his understanding of dispensationalism and which may or may not exist in the movement generally.

Doctrinal Concerns

There are three doctrinal issues which form the core of Gaebelein's dispensationalism. First, one must take note of his belief in the inerrancy of the Scriptures. Dispensationalists have always been regarded as having a high view of the Bible even by their opponents.[14] Whatever else can be said of the theological system, there is a genuine attempt, and Gaebelein was no exception as his attacks on higher criticism attest, to present theology in such a way that the Bible is shown to have no errors.

A second doctrinal concern is the basic thrust of premillennialism. This relates directly to the Second Coming which, for Gaebelein, was crucial to his central interpretive motif. It is also correlated with a view of the present culture as essentially evil and in moral decline. The main solution, then, for dispensational thinkers, is the premillennial coming of Christ to earth. One should not necessarily look at this view of the present age as pessimistic. Realistic is a more descriptive term. The dispensational approach of Gaebelein was ultimately optimistic because it was grounded in God's sovereignty and possessed a healthy view of the depravity of man. This concern associated with the coming of Christ also highlights the Christological focus found in dispensationalism.

The third theme at the core of dispensational doctrine is pretribulationalism. The decline of the Niagara Conference, partly due to controversy over this issue, demonstrates the crucial nature of this belief. Through Gaebelein and Scofield, the pretribulational rapture became a cardinal doctrine for many premillennialists. Referenced as the blessed hope, it was, for Gaebelein, one of the manifestations of the unifying theme of hope.

---

[14] John H. Gerstner, *Wrongly Dividing the Word of Truth* (Brentwood, TN: Wolgemuth & Hyatt, 1991), 84.

Hermeneutical and Methodological Concerns

Besides the three areas of doctrinal concerns seen at the core of Gaebelein's dispensational theology, there are several hermeneutical and methodological questions that Gaebelein's example helps to explain. At the outset, the practice of literal interpretation in many areas and further interpretation via dispensational integration, show a remarkably flexible approach to theology. Second, Gaebelein's dispensationalism recognizes, in some sense, the priority of the Old Testament text. Ladd, a nondispensationalist, remarked that dispensational eschatology begins with a literal interpretation of the Old Testament.[15] Saucy concurred that the interpretation of the Old Testament was one of the significant issues dividing dispensational and nondispensational theologies.[16] When a dispensationalist speaks of the priority of the Old Testament text, he is referring to the priority of that text for its own interpretation. In short, there is a biblical theology of the Old Testament which is not dependent upon any New Testament interpretations of it. This is not to say that New Testament uses of the Old do not play a role in systematic interpretation. It is simply affirming that there is a body of truth which can be derived from the Old Testament without any references to the New.

Gaebelein repeatedly practiced this approach with respect to texts which predicted the national restoration of Israel. While he acknowledged that the New Testament shed light on this issue, the Old Testament teaching on the subject could stand alone. It could not be contradicted nor reinterpreted in a nonliteral way by the New Testament understanding. Enhancements were allowed but the basic meaning derived from the Old Testament text for itself could never be undone.

---

[15] George Eldon Ladd, "Historic Premillennialism," in *The Meaning of the Millennium: Four Views*, ed. Robert G. Clouse (Downers Grove, IL: InterVarsity Press, 1977), 27.

[16] Robert Saucy, "The Crucial Issue Between Dispensational and Nondispensational Systems," *Criswell Theological Review* 1 (Fall 1986): 155.

Third, in a corollary to the above discussion, Gaebelein's dispensationalism concerns itself with maintenance of the literal understanding of Old Testament prophecy, particularly the literal interpretation of those passages that deal with the history of the nation of Israel and its future. This does not mean that there are no other ways of approaching the Old Testament text for the dispensationalist. Gaebelein's example of typological and applicatory usage prevents that conclusion. However, the preservation of the literal interpretation of these texts at all points of doing theology has been featured in dispensational theology.

Ryrie's *sine qua non* can be addressed in this connection. Two of the three points in his essence of dispensationalism are not held by Gaebelein in the same way or to the same degree. Only the distinction between Israel and the church is shared explicitly by Ryrie and Gaebelein. However, the contrast may be misleading. The doxological center for the Bible in Ryrie is replaced by a redemptive center in Gaebelein's explicit statements about the purposes of revelation. On the other hand, it was noted that within the scope of Gaebelein's theology could be found the overall doxological outline of God's multi-faceted program which went beyond individual soteriology.

In addition, contra Ryrie, Gaebelein freely spiritualized historical texts to produce the same conclusions arrived at in literal interpretation of prophecy. Nonetheless, literal interpretation consistently applied without any recourse to a spiritualizing hermeneutic is clearly practiced by Gaebelein in those passages which directly speak of the future of Israel. In general, Gaebelein practiced literal interpretation of prophecy fairly consistently, especially in the Old Testament, which is the crux of the matter in the debate.

Fourth, the above discussion naturally leads into the dispensationalist concern that a distinction between Israel and the church be maintained. This has been the identifying feature of the dispensational system in the minds of a majority of

258

theologians, dispensational and nondispensational alike.[17] However, there is some disagreement, even among dispensationalists, over the nature and degree of the distinction and whether the dissimilarities continue into the millennium and eternity.[18]

Gaebelein usually spoke in terms of an absolute distinction while at times allowing some mixing of the two programs of God. The contribution this study makes to the issue of Israel versus the church is to show that, at least in Gaebelein's example, the distinction goes beyond doctrinal content. The distinction, though definitely the resultant content from a synthesis of Old Testament prophecy about Israel and Ephesians truth about the church, plays a methodological role in approaching the Bible. Simply put, many texts that are not part of the above synthesis are interpreted, in whole or in part, by this distinction between Israel and the church. Gaebelein's use of dispensational integration clarified this important aspect.

Fifth, Gaebelein's dispensationalism honors the crucial place which the progress of revelation has in hermeneutics and theological method. Allowing the Old Testament text to have meaning based upon its own words with enhancement by later New Testament revelation is an example of how the dispensationalist respects the progress of revelation as part of the context of interpretation. Refusing to read the New Testament back into the Old demonstrates the integrity of the scriptural unfoldings. It was shown that Gaebelein's concepts of dispensations and the unfolding of God's purposes were both interpreted in light of this context. Individual passages were often observed in the light of patterns existing within this structure. Interpretation done in this way was an application of the analogy of faith.

[17] Robert Lightner, *Evangelical Theology* (Grand Rapids, MI: Baker Book House, 1986), 273; Craig A. Blaising, "Development of Dispensationalism by Contemporary Dispensationalists," *Bibliotheca Sacra* 145 (July-September 1988), 273.

[18] Blaising, "Development," 273-79.

If there is a singular essence to dispensationalism, the way that progress of revelation is understood may prove to be the deciding factor. Saucy concluded that the crucial issue between dispensational and nondispensational systems was the "one basic and rather comprehensive issue, namely God's purpose and plan for biblical history."[19] Without using the terminology, his discussion centers around the unfolding of God's purposes as revealed in the progress of revelation. It would remain for a study of nondispensational views of the progress of revelation to determine if such a distinction is actual.

Sixth, Gaebelein's dispensationalism, contrary to many later dispensationalists, affirms that biblical texts can be used in more than one way. This concern was pronounced in Gaebelein's approach to the text especially in the arena of eschatology. Through dispensational integration, especially typological and applicatory aspects, several passages are viewed as having two simultaneous targets for interpretation. Unfortunately, for Gaebelein the typical approach to many texts dominated the discussion.[20]

By means of such dual usage, Gaebelein could attest to the applicability in some way of all of Scripture (2 Tim. 3:16-17). In addition, one other corollary follows. If passages in the Old Testament can be used in more than one way, then the New Testament cannot prescribe a single way to approach passages found there by its own interpretation of them. Another way to say this is that New Testament use of the Old does not define the limits of Old Testament interpretation.[21]

---

[19] Robert Saucy, "Crucial Issue," 155.

[20] This writer would have trouble accepting the broadness of Gaebelein's typology. The controls of Roy Zuck (*Interpretation*, 172-79) are preferred. This is especially true of the typological connections which Gaebelein makes of New Testament passages. Basically, any analogy was sufficient grounds (if it fit the overall theological scheme) for using typology. However, that typology is an appropriate way to look at some passages is clear from the New Testament's references to Old Testament types (e.g., 1 Cor. 5:7, "Christ our Passover").

[21] This hinders the nondispensationalist's use of the New Testament to prescribe his own approach to texts not used by the New Testament. The way Old Testament allusions and quotations are handled in the New Testament, while useful, would not allow, for example, an Old Testament text to be taken only in a nonliteral way because of a New Testament nonliteral interpretation.

This would reinforce the idea that the Old Testament can be viewed apart from New Testament interpretations while at the same time being enhanced by them.

In conclusion, one more remark must be made with respect to these hermeneutical and methodological concerns. The avenue of discussion above points to the possibility that dispensationalism can best be identified by the hermeneutical approach rather than any particular doctrinal confession. It may be that the hermeneutical concerns have led to a modicum of unity throughout the history of dispensationalism.

Proposed Avenues for Further Research

David Rausch initiated the detailed historical study of Gaebelein while the present work is the first major examination of his theological method. There is much more that can be researched than these works have been able to accomplish. First, there are two historical connections that need to be pursued. A preliminary comparison of Gaebelein's use of typology with the commentaries of other dispensationalists near his time period (e.g., William Kelly, H. A. Ironside, W. H. Griffith Thomas, William L. Pettingill, and E. Schuyler English) reveals that his practice in that area was generally not followed with the same intensity. Elmore wrote that Darby's application of typology was broadly based.[22] The present writer's review of Darby's *Synopsis* shows that Gaebelein's typology was even more expansive. In this connection, it was mentioned that there appeared to be

Consequently, Poythress' claim that an understanding of the use of the Old Testament in Hebrews provides a corrective to dispensational interpretation, especially in its classical form, would be invalidated (*Understanding Dispensationalists*, [Grand Rapids, MI: Zondervan Publishing House, 1987], 69-70, 118-25). The debate between dispensationalism and nondispensationalism is currently being waged in this area. Many nondispensationalists are comfortable with saying they have followed literal interpretation because they have simply done with the Old Testament text what the New Testament did with it (see John Feinberg, "Salvation in the Old Testament," in *Tradition and Testament: Essays in Honor of Charles Lee Feinberg* [Chicago: Moody Press, 1981], 45). For a helpful survey of various views of this issue, see Darrell L. Bock, "Evangelicals and the Use of the Old Testament in the New," *Bibliotheca Sacra* 142 (July-September 1985): 209-23.

[22] Floyd S. Elmore, "A Critical Examination of the Doctrine of the Two Peoples of God in John Nelson Darby" (Th.D. diss., Dallas Theological Seminary, 1990), 164.

some dependency of Gaebelein upon F. W. Grant's *The Numerical Bible*. The establishment of the historical roots of this line of typological usage would place the peculiar aspects of dispensational typology in proper historical context.

Another historical connection which should be explored is the impact which specific Jewish interpretation schemes, such as midrashic formulas, had on Gaebelein. His early contacts with Orthodox Judaism aided his conversion to premillennialism. Other possible influences on specific interpretation points were surfaced in the study. Consequently, Gaebelein may be a contact point with which a comparison can be made between orthodox Jewish interpretation of the Old Testament and dispensational methodological and doctrinal concerns.

Beyond these historical connections the deeper study of typology and nonliteral interpretation in general would prove helpful. Gaebelein used the word *literal* primarily with respect to Old Testament prophecy about Israel. A comparison of his use of symbols to other dispensational writers might yield a better understanding of the scope of literal interpretation which has been considered by dispensationalists to be a cornerstone.

However, this study has brought to mind research which could be done for dispensationalism as a whole as well as needed areas in Gaebelein's theology. First, the theological method in light of historical influences should be investigated for all major players in the development of dispensationalism. Further studies in Guers, Kelly, Grant, Scofield, Brookes, Chafer, and even, Darby, could use more in depth analysis as to the specifics of argumentation and approach to various texts. If enough studies emerge, a synthesis of them might produce a more historically exact list of primary concerns or essentials in dispensationalism. In this way, sweeping generalizations could be eliminated.

It would also be useful at this time to study various themes as they make their way through various dispensationalists, including Gaebelein. One such study is Mark Bailey's investigation of the concept of the kingdom of God throughout

262

the history of dispensationalism.[23] Some possible themes would be 1) the de-Judaizing of texts like the Sermon on the Mount,[24] 2) the day of the Lord, 3) the rapture of the church, 4) the biblical covenants, 5) use of words like *dispensational* or *application*, 5) use of current events to confirm interpretations, 6) the resurrection of Old Testament saints, 7) the Abrahamic, Davidic, and New Covenants, and 8) the inspiration and inerrancy of the Bible, among others.

Another significant study would be a comparison of recent Reformed views of the progress of revelation to the dispensational framework. Associated with this would be a study of the analogy of faith as it is used in both Reformed and dispensational theologies. The result could be a presentation of rules for its use and a further understanding of how the two systems mentioned above oppose one another.

A rather significant issue raised by the controversy over Gaebelein's alleged anti-Semitism is the precise definition of that word. In the tension that exists between the Jews and evangelicals, just what constitutes anti-Semitism? From the other side, what would an evangelical have to give up doctrinally before the Jewish community will consider him not to be anti-Semitic? Are the issues primarily religious or secular? A study of such questions would help the evangelical community at large to relate to a group of people who, at times, seem to have few friends outside their own circles.[25] In addition, the significance of dispensationalists as the friends of Israel points in the direction of establishing what importance

---

[23] Mark Bailey, "Dispensational Definitions of Kingdom," (Paper presented at the dispensational theology pre-meeting at the annual meeting of the Evangelical Theological Society, November 1988).

[24] John A. Martin has done this in a preliminary way ("Dispensational Approaches to the Sermon on the Mount," in *Essays in Honor of J. Dwight Pentecost*, ed. Stanley D. Toussaint and Charles H. Dyer [Chicago: Moody Press, 1986]).

[25] David A. Rausch has attempted to deal with this among others; see *Building Bridges* (Chicago: Moody Press, 1988).

theological friendship has in practical relationships between the two communities.[26]

Another area that needs clarification is the role of the pretribulational rapture in dispensationalism. After the debate between the Scofield-Gaebelein tandem and Robert Cameron was decided in favor of the pretribulational view, posttribulationalists were generally excluded from the purview of dispensational theology. Yet before that time American premillennialists had made little of the issue. The question should be asked and answered, "Is a pretribulational rapture an essential aspect of the overall framework of dispensationalism?"

Finally, the surfacing of the Genevan connection, especially in the Darbyite writings of Émile Guers, has opened up a new source of input into the development of dispensationalism. The methodology of Guers (and those associated with him if possible) should be studied more intensely and observed within a broader context of his role in the spread of dispensationalism in Europe and the United States.

Some Final Remarks

The impetus for this work has been the writer's desire to advance his own thinking about the definition or essence of dispensationalism. The choosing of a major dispensationalist like Gaebelein to aid in this purpose should further the dialog between dispensationalists and nondispensationalists. The hermeneutical and methodological emphasis of this study clears the way, along with other works, to a more detailed analysis of how both sides argue their points.

Is it possible that dispensationalism and covenant theology can move closer together? In the opinion of this writer, very few of the doctrinal and hermeneutical concerns cited earlier are negotiable without giving up the entire system.

---

[26] This writer's own relationship to Jews has usually been an extremely positive one. As an engineer, nine months was spent training Israeli soldiers with one month on site in Israel. It was remarkable that these Jewish people responded with such friendship when they found out that this writer possessed a theological belief that the nation of Israel had a future as expressed in the Bible.

Continued refinement of exegesis might still cause some motion toward the middle. This could be due to the fact that there is more common ground than previously realized. However, just like the graph of a hyperbola grows ever closer to its axis, it never reaches out to touch it. Hence, the final common ground of eschatology in evangelicalism may turn out to be a spirit of love in the heart when there is no agreement of mind. The only alternative is for one side to abandon some crucial concerns in its theological method. It is doubtful that the dogmatic Gaebelein would have ever considered surrendering.

BIBLIOGRAPHY

Primary Sources

Books

Gaebelein, Arno C. *The Acts of the Apostles: An Exposition.* New York: Publication Office "Our Hope," 1912; reprint, Neptune, NJ: Loizeaux Brothers, 1961.

_____. *The Angels of God.* New York: "Our Hope" Publication Office, 1924; reprint, Grand Rapids, MI: Baker Book House, 1969.

_____. *The Annotated Bible.* 9 Vols. New York: Publication Office "Our Hope," 1913-22[?].

_____. *As It Was—So Shall It Be, Sunset and Sunrise: A Study of the First Age and Our Present Age.* New York: Publication Office "Our Hope," 1937.

_____. *The Book of Exodus: A Complete Analysis of Exodus with Annotations.* New York: Our Hope Publication Office, 1912.

_____. *The Book of Psalms: A Devotional and Prophetic Commentary.* New York: Our Hope Press, 1939.

_____. *Buchmanism.* New York: Arno C. Gaebelein, Inc., n.d.

_____. *Christ and Glory.* New York: Publication Office "Our Hope," 1919.

_____. *The Christ We Know: Meditations on the Person and Glory of Our Lord Jesus Christ.* New York: Publication Office "Our Hope," 1927.

_____. *Christianity or Religion? A Study of the Origin and Growth of Religion and the Supernaturalism of Christianity.* New York: Publication Office "Our Hope," 1927.

_____. *The Church in the House.* New York: Publication Office "Our Hope," n.d.

_____. *The Conflict of the Ages, the Mystery of Lawlessness: Its Origin, Historic Development and Coming Defeat.* New York: Publication Office "Our Hope," 1933.

_____. *The Epistle to the Galatians: A Complete Analysis of Galatians with Annotations.* New York: Our Hope Publication Office, n.d.

_____. *The First and Second Epistles to the Thessalonians.* New York: Our Hope Publication Office, n.d.

266

_____. "Fulfilled Prophecy, a Potent Argument for the Bible." In *The Fundamentals: A Testimony to the Truth*, ed. Reuben A. Torrey, 11:55-86. Chicago: Testimony Publishing Co., 1910[?].

_____. *Gabriel and Michael, the Archangel*. Wheaton, IL: Van Kampen Press, 1945.

_____. *God's Masterpiece: An Analytical Exposition of Ephesians I-III*. New York: Publication Office "Our Hope," 1913.

_____. *The Gospel of Matthew: An Exposition*. New York: Publication Office Our Hope, 1910; reprint, Neptune, NJ: Loizeaux Brothers, 1961.

_____. *The Gospel of John: A Complete Analytical Exposition of the Gospel of John*. Wheaton, IL: Van Kampen Press, 1936.

_____. *Half a Century: The Autobiography of a Servant*. New York: Publication Office "Our Hope," 1930.

_____. *The Harmony of the Prophetic Word*. New York: Fleming H. Revell Co., 1907.

_____. *Hath God Cast Away His People?* New York: Gospel Publishing House, 1905.

_____. *The Healing Question: An Examination of the Claims of Faith Healing and Divine Healing Systems in the Light of the Scriptures and History*. New York: Publication Office "Our Hope," 1925.

_____. *The History of the Scofield Reference Bible*. New York: Our Hope Publications, 1943.

_____. *His Last Words: A Study of the Last Discourse of our Lord Known as the "Olivet Discourse."* New York: Publication Office "Our Hope," n.d.

_____. *His Riches—Our Riches*. New York: Gospel Publishing House, n.d.

_____. *The Holy Spirit in the New Testament*. New York: Publication Office "Our Hope," n.d.

_____. *The Hope of the Ages*. New York: Publication Office "Our Hope," 1938.

_____. *Hopeless, Yet There is Hope: A Study in World Conditions and Their Solution*. New York: Publication Office "Our Hope," 1935.

_____. *The Jewish Question*. New York: Publication Office "Our Hope," 1912[?].

_____. *Listen!—God Speaks*. New York: Publication Office "Our Hope," 1936.

_____. *The Lord of Glory: Meditations on the Person, the Work and Glory of Our Lord Jesus Christ*. New York: Publication Office "Our Hope," 1910.

_____. *Meat in Due Season: Sermons, Discourses and Expositions of the Word of Prophecy*. New York: Arno C. Gaebelein, Inc., n.d.

_____. *Moses—His First and Second Coming: The Exodus in the Light of Prophecy*. New York: Publication Office "Our Hope," 1940.

_____. *The Olivet Discourse: An Exposition of Matthew XXIV and XXV*. New York: Gospel Publishing House, 1906[?]; reprint, Grand Rapids, MI: Baker Book House, 1969.

_____. *Our Age and Its End*. New York: Our Hope Publications, 1940[?].

_____. *The Prophet Daniel: A Key to the Visions and Prophecies of the Book of Daniel*. New York: Publication Office "Our Hope," 1911.

_____. *The Prophet Ezekiel: An Analytical Exposition*. New York: Publication Office "Our Hope," 1918.

_____. *The Prophet Joel: An Exposition*. Foreward by C. I. Scofield. New York: Publication Office "Our Hope," 1909.

_____. *The Prophet St. Paul: The Eschatology of the Apostle to the Gentiles*. New York: Publication Office "Our Hope," 1939.

_____. *The Return of the Lord*. New York: Publication Office "Our Hope," 1925.

_____. *The Revelation: An Analysis and Exposition of the Last Book of the Bible*. New York: Our Hope Publications, n.d.

_____. *The Seven Parables*. New York: Publication Office "Our Hope," n.d.

_____. *Studies in Prophecy*. New York: Publication Office "Our Hope," 1918.

_____. *Studies in Zechariah*. 8th ed. New York: Publication Office "Our Hope," 1911.

_____. *Things to Come*. New York: "Our Hope" Publication Office, n.d.

268

_____. *Types in Joshua.* New York: Publication Office "Our Hope," n.d.

_____. *What Will Become of Europe?* New York: Our Hope Publications, 1940.

_____. *Will There Be A Millennium? When and How?: The Coming Reign of Christ in the Light of the Old and New Testaments.* New York: Publication Office "Our Hope," 1943.

_____. *The Work of Christ: Past—Present—Future.* London: Alfred Holness, n.d.

_____. *World Prospects, How is it All Going to End? A Study in Sacred Prophecy and Present Day World Conditions.* New York: Publication Office, "Our Hope," 1934.

Gaebelein, Arno C., ed. *Things New and Old: Old and New Testament Studies by Dr. C. I. Scofield.* New York: Publication Office "Our Hope," 1920.

Periodical Articles

Gaebelein, Arno C. "Arab Propaganda in America." *Our Hope* 37 (July 1930): 56.

_____. "Aspects of Jewish Power in the United States." *Our Hope* 29 (August 1922): 103.

_____. "The Beginning of Glory and the Beginning of Sorrows." *Our Hope* 9 (February 1903): 454-64.

_____. "Bible Study: Its Conditions and Results." *Our Hope* 9 (March 1903): 517-22.

_____. "The Biblical Logic of Premillennialism." *Our Hope* 36 (December 1929): 347-56.

_____. "The Coming of the Lord, the Hope of Israel, and the Hope of the Nations and Creation." *Our Hope* 8 (September 1901): 194-99.

_____. "Current Events." *Our Hope* 29 (August 1922): 97-103.

_____. "Current Events and Signs of the Times." *Our Hope* 27 (November 1920): 293-98.

_____. "Current Events in the Light of the Bible." *Our Hope* 27 (June 1921): 734-38.

_____. "Current Events in the Light of the Bible." *Our Hope* 36 (October 1929): 226-32.

_____. "Current Events in the Light of the Bible." *Our Hope* 37 (November 1930): 286-92.

_____. "Current Events in the Light of the Bible." *Our Hope* 38 (March 1932): 556-60.

_____. "Current Events in the Light of the Bible." *Our Hope* 39 (December 1932): 373-78.

_____. "Current Events in the Light of the Bible." *Our Hope* 39 (July 1932): 27-32.

_____. "Current Events in the Light of the Bible." *Our Hope* 39 (March 1933): 548-52.

_____. "Current Events in the Light of the Bible." *Our Hope* 39 (September 1932): 159.

_____. "Current Events in the Light of the Bible." *Our Hope* 40 (May 1934): 670-75.

_____. "The Dispensations." *Our Hope* 37 (December 1930): 341-46.

_____. "Editorial Notes." *Our Hope* 8 (August 1901): 49-51.

_____. "Editorial Notes." *Our Hope* 8 (December 1901): 297-300.

_____. "Editorial Notes." *Our Hope* 8 (February 1902): 393-97.

_____. "Editorial Notes." *Our Hope* 8 (January 1902): 345-49.

_____. "Editorial Notes." *Our Hope* 8 (July 1901):1-4.

_____. "Editorial Notes." *Our Hope* 8 (June 1902): 617-23.

_____. "Editorial Notes." *Our Hope* 8 (November 1901): 249-53.

_____. "Editorial Notes." *Our Hope* 8 (October 1901): 201-6.

_____. "Editorial Notes." *Our Hope* 9 (April 1903): 547-56.

_____. "Editorial Notes." *Our Hope* 9 (January 1903): 385-95.

270

_____. "Editorial Notes." *Our Hope* 9 (June 1902): 617-23.

_____. "Editorial Notes." *Our Hope* 9 (November 1902): 281-85.

_____. "Editorial Notes." *Our Hope* 9 (October 1902): 221-28.

_____. "Editorial Notes." *Our Hope* 9 (September 1902): 113-21.

_____. "Editorial Notes." *Our Hope* 12 (August 1905): 65-73.

_____. "Editorial Notes." *Our Hope* 14 (July 1907): 1-17.

_____. "Editorial Notes." *Our Hope* 17 (July 1910): 1-12.

_____. "Editorial Notes." *Our Hope* 19 (July 1912): 1-15.

_____. "Editorial Notes." *Our Hope* 28 (August 1921): 65-89.

_____. "Editorial Notes." *Our Hope* 28 (May 1922): 643-64.

_____. "Editorial Notes." *Our Hope* 29 (July 1922): 1-23.

_____. "Editorial Notes." *Our Hope* 37 (April 1931): 577-93.

_____. "Editorial Notes." *Our Hope* 37 (December 1930): 321-40.

_____. "Editorial Notes." *Our Hope* 38 (October 1931): 193-211.

_____. "Editorial Notes." *Our Hope* 39 (August 1932): 65-83.

_____. "Editorial Notes." *Our Hope* 41 (January 1935): 385-99.

_____. "Editorial Notes." *Our Hope* 41 (September 1934): 129-46.

_____. "Editorial Notes." *Our Hope* 43 (July 1936): 1-15.

_____. "Editorial Notes." *Our Hope* 44 (July 1937): 1-17.

_____. "Editorial Notes." *Our Hope* 44 (November 1937): 289-306.

_____. "Editorial Notes." O*ur Hope* 44 (October 1937): 217-35.

_____. "Editorial Notes." *Our Hope* 44 (September 1937): 145-64.

_____. "Editorial Notes." *Our Hope* 45 (April 1939): 647-65.

_____. "The Epistle to the Philippians." *Our Hope* 9 (September 1902): 148-64.

_____. "The False Idea of the Kingdom." *Our Hope* 38 (October 1931): 214-19.

_____. "The Fifth Chapter of Genesis." *Our Hope* 9 (May 1903): 629-33.

_____. "The Gospel of Matthew: Chapter vi. 1-18." *Our Hope* 8 (July 1901): 5-12.

_____. "The Gospel of Matthew: Chapter vi. 19-34." *Our Hope* 8 (August 1901): 52-55.

_____. "The Gospel of Matthew: Chapter xi." *Our Hope* 9 (July 1902): 7-13.

_____. "The Gospel of Matthew: Chapter xii." *Our Hope* 9 (October 1902): 229-36.

_____. "The Gospel of Matthew: Chapter xiii." *Our Hope* 9 (January 1903): 395-401.

_____. "The Harmony of the Prophetic Word." *Our Hope* 9 (September 1902): 129-40.

_____. "The Hope of Israel Movement." *Our Hope* 4 (January 1898): 243-48.

_____. "The Imminency of the Coming of the Lord." *Our Hope* 9 (August 1902): 116-21.

_____. "Jehu, Jehoshaphat, Nimshi." *Our Hope* 8 (October 1901): 219-22.

_____. "Jewish Eschatology." *Our Hope* 5 (July 1898): 9-13.

_____. "Jewish Eschatology." *Our Hope* 5 (August & September 1898): 48-51.

_____. "Jewish Eschatology." *Our Hope* 5 (October 1898): 108-12.

_____. "Jewish Eschatology." *Our Hope* 5 (November 1898): 149-52.

_____. "Jewish Eschatology." *Our Hope* 5 (December 1898): 188-91.

_____. "Jewish Leadership in Russia." *Our Hope* 27 (June 1921): 734-35.

_____. "Jewish Massacres in the Holy Land." *Our Hope* 36 (October 1929): 230.

_____. "Jewish Notes." *Our Hope* 5 (December 1898): 287-88.

_____. "The Kingdom in the Old Testament." *Our Hope* 28 (July 1921): 36-55.

272

_____. "A Lesson For Modern Methodists." *Our Hope* 8 (August 1901): 72.

_____. "Material For the Temple Ordered." *Our Hope* 4 (January 1898): 242.

_____. "The Millennium." *Our Hope* 9 (November 1902): 293-306.

_____. "Misrepresenting 'Our Hope.'" *Our Hope* 46 (December 1939): 379-82.

_____. "The New Great World Crisis." *Our Hope* 49 (June 1943): 813-19.

_____. "The New Great World Crisis." *Our Hope* 50 (October 1943): 235-40.

_____. "Notes on Prophecy and the Jews." *Our Hope* 8 (July 1901): 39-47.

_____. "Notes on Prophecy and the Jews." *Our Hope* 8 (August 1901): 82-88.

_____. "Notes on Prophecy and the Jews." *Our Hope* 8 (November 1901): 291-96.

_____. "Notes on Prophecy and the Jews." *Our Hope* 8 (October 1901): 242-48.

_____. "Notes on Prophecy and the Jews." *Our Hope* 9 (August 1902): 104-11.

_____. "Notes on Prophecy and the Jews." *Our Hope* 9 (December 1902): 378-83.

_____. "Notes on Prophecy and the Jews." *Our Hope* 9 (February 1903): 486-90.

_____. "Notes on Prophecy and the Jews." *Our Hope* 9 (July 1902): 50-55.

_____. "Notes on Prophecy and the Jews." *Our Hope* 9 (March 1903): 532-38.

_____. "Notes on Prophecy and the Jews." *Our Hope* 9 (October 1902): 273-80.

_____. "Notes on Prophecy and the Jews." *Our Hope* 37 (January 1931): 427-31.

_____. "Notes on Prophecy and the Jews." *Our Hope* 38 (September 1931): 162-70.

_____. "Observations and Experiences." *Our Hope* 44 (January 1938): 460-65.

_____. "Opening Address." *Our Hope* 8 (September 1901): 93-96.

_____. "Our Blessed Hope." *Our Hope* 5 (November 1898): 156-62.

_____. "The Patient Waiting for Christ." *Our Hope* 8 (January 1902): 345-46.

_____. "The Post-Tribulation Theory." *Our Hope* 7 (February 1901): 261-70.

_____. "The Prayers of Orthodox Judaism." *Our Hope* 2 (August 1895): 37-40.

_____. "Program for Bible Conference in Sea Cliff." *Our Hope* 8 (July 1901): 3-4.

_____. "The Prophetic Teachings of Thessalonians." *Our Hope* 36 (April 1930): 611-16.

_____. "The Protocols of the Elders in Zion." *Our Hope* 27 (November 1920): 297-98.

_____. "A Short Review of Our Mission and the Principles of the Hope of Israel Movement." *Our Hope* 6 (September 1899): 67-73.

_____. "The Story of the Scofield Reference Bible." *Moody Monthly* 43 (October 1942): 65-66, 97; (November 1942): 128-29, 135; (December 1942): 202-3, 233; (January 1943): 277-79; (February 1943): 343-45; (March 1943): 400-1, 419.

_____. "A Song of the Beloved." *Our Hope* 9 (January 1903): 401-8.

_____. "Speculative Prophecy." *Our Hope* 51 (December 1944): 407-10.

_____. "The Twentieth Century New Testament." *Our Hope* 8 (August 1901): 55-62.

_____. "Unfulfilled Prophecies and the World Wide Preparations for Their Fulfillment." *Our Hope* 38 (December 1931): 336-50.

_____. "The Unutterable Name." *Our Hope* 44 (August 1937): 104-6.

_____. "Who Will Be Caught Up When the Lord Comes?" *Our Hope* 8 (February 1901): 408-17.

_____. "Whosoever." *Our Hope* 44 (November 1937): 317-20.

_____. "Will There Be a Partial Rapture?" *Our Hope* 38 (July 1931): 47-51.

_____. "Will There Be a Partial Rapture?" *Our Hope* 44 (August 1937): 100-4.

_____. "The Wonders of Progressive Prophecy." *Our Hope* 46 (April 1940): 663-67.

274

_____. "The Wonders of Progressive Prophecy." *Our Hope* 46 (June 1940): 815-20.

_____. "The Wonders of Progressive Prophecy." *Our Hope* 46 (May 1940): 740-47.

_____. "The Wonders of Progressive Prophecy." *Our Hope* 47 (August 1940): 91-97.

_____. "The Wonders of Progressive Prophecy." *Our Hope* 47 (December 1940): 380-85.

_____. "The Wonders of Progressive Prophecy." *Our Hope* 47 (January 1941): 449-53.

_____. "The Wonders of Progressive Prophecy." *Our Hope* 47 (July 1940): 21-27.

_____. "The Wonders of Progressive Prophecy." *Our Hope* 47 (March 1941): 591-94.

_____. "The Wonders of Progressive Prophecy." *Our Hope* 47 (November 1940): 305-10.

_____. "The Wonders of Progressive Prophecy." *Our Hope* 47 (October 1940): 235-41.

_____. "The Wonders of Progressive Prophecy." *Our Hope* 47 (September 1940): 161-67.

Unpublished Materials

Gaebelein, Arno C. Papers. Dallas Theological Seminary, Dallas, Texas.

Secondary Sources

Books

Allis, Oswald T. *Prophecy and the Church*. Phillipsburg, NJ: Presbyterian and Reformed Publishing Co., 1945.

Armerding, Carl Edwin. "The Meaning of Israel in Evangelical Thought.," In *Evangelicals and Jews in Conversation on Scripture, Theology, and History*, ed.

Marc H. Tanenbaum, Marvin R. Wilson, and A. James Rudin, 119-40. Grand Rapids, MI: Baker Book House, 1978.

Ariel, Yaakov S. *On Behalf of Israel: American Fundamentalist Attitudes Toward Jews, Judaism, and Zionism, 1865-1945.* Foreward by Martin E. Marty. Chicago Studies in the History of American Religion, no. 1. Brooklyn, NY: Carlson Publishing, 1991.

Bateman, Herbert W., IV, gen. ed. *Three Central Issues in Contemporary Dispensationalism.* Grand Rapids, MI: Kregel, 1999.

Berkhof, Louis. *Systematic Theology.* Rev. ed. Grand Rapids, MI: William B. Eerdmans Publishing Co., 1941.

Biederwolf, William E. *The Millennium Bible.* Chicago: W. P. Blessing Co., 1924.

Blackstone, William. *Jesus is Coming.* Chicago: Fleming H. Revell Co., 1908.

Blaising, Craig A. and Darrell L. Bock, eds. *Dispensationalism, Israel and the Church.* Grand Rapids, MI: Zondervan Publishing House, 1992.

Blaising, Craig A. and Darrell L. Bock. *Progressive Dispensationalism.* Wheaton, IL: Victor Books, 1993.

Brookes, James. *God Spake All These Words.* St. Louis: J. T. Smith, 1895.

_____. *I Am Coming.* London: Pickering & Inglis, n.d.

_____. *Israel and the Church: The Terms Distinguished as Found in the Word of God.* Chicago: Bible Institute Colportage Association, n.d.

_____. *Maranatha: or the Lord Cometh.* Chicago: Fleming H. Revell Co., 1889[?].

_____. *Till He Come.* Chicago: Gospel Publishing Co., 1891.

_____. *The Way Made Plain.* Philadelphia: American Sunday-School Union, n.d.

Bullinger, E. W. *Number in Scripture.* 4th ed. London: Eyre & Spottiswoode Ltd., 1921.

Buren, Paul M. van. *Discerning the Way: A Theology of the Jewish Christian Reality.* New York: The Seabury Press, 1980.

_____. *A Christian Theology of the People Israel: A Theology of the Jewish Christian Reality.* New York: Seabury Press, 1983.

Cameron, Robert. *The Doctrine of the Ages*. New York: Fleming H. Revell Co., 1896.

_____. *Scriptural Truth About the Lord's Return*. New York: Fleming H. Revell, 1922.

Canfield, Joseph M. *The Incredible Scofield and His Book*. Asheville, NC: By the Author, 1984.

Carpenter, Joel A. *Revive Us Again: The Reawakening of American Fundamentalism*. New York: Oxford University Press, 1997.

Chafer, Lewis Sperry. *Grace*. Chicago: Bible Institute Colportage Association, 1922; reprint, Grand Rapids, MI: Zondervan Publishing House, 1976.

_____. *Systematic Theology*. 8 vols. Dallas, TX: Dallas Seminary Press, 1947.

Chaponniere, Francis. *Pasteurs et Laïques de L'Éqlise de Genève au Dix-Neuvième Siècle*. Genève: n.p., 1889.

The Coming and Kingdom of Christ. Chicago: The Bible Institute Colportage Association, 1914.

Crutchfield, Larry V. *The Origins of Dispensationalism: The Darby Factor*. Foreward by John A. Witmer. Lanham, MD: University Press of America, 1992.

Darby, John Nelson. *Synopsis of the Books of the Bible*. 5 vols. New York: Loizeaux Brothers, n.d; reprint, Oak Park, IL: Bible Truth Publishers, 1970.

Davis, John. *Biblical Numerology*. Grand Rapids, MI: Baker Book House, 1968.

Dayton, Donald W., ed. *The Prophecy Conference Movement*. New York: Garland Publishing Co., 1988.

Eadie, John. *Commentary on the Epistle of Paul to the Colossians*. N.p.: Richard Griffin & Co., 1856; reprint, Minneapolis, MN: James and Klock Christian Publishing Co., 1977.

Edwards, David L. *Evangelical Essentials: A Liberal-Evangelical Dialogue*. Response from John Stott. Downers Grove, IL: InterVarsity Press, 1988.

Ellingsen, Mark. *The Evangelical Movement: Growth, Impact, Controversy, Dialog*. Minneapolis, MN: Augsburg Publishing House, 1988.

Erickson, Millard J. *Christian Theology*. 3 vols. Grand Rapids, MI: Baker Book House, 1983-85.

English, E. Schuyler. *Studies in the Gospel According to Matthew*. Preface by Frank E. Gaebelein. New York: Our Hope Publications, 1935.

"Evangelical Affirmations." In *Evangelical Affirmations*. eds. Kenneth S. Dantzer and Carl F. H. Henry, 27-38. Grand Rapids, MI: Zondervan Publishing House, 1990.

Fatio, Olivier, ed. *Genève Protestante en 1831*. Genève: Labor et Fides, 1983.

Feinberg, John S. "Salvation in the Old Testament." In *Tradition and Testaments: Essays in Honor of Charles Lee Feinberg*, ed. John S. Feinberg and Paul D. Feinberg, 39-77. Chicago: Moody Press, 1981.

Ford, Henry, Sr., ed. *The International Jew: The World's Foremost Problem*. Abridged by Gerald K. Smith. Los Angelos, CA: n.p., n.d.

Froom, Le Roy Edwin. *The Prophetic Faith of Our Fathers*. 4 Vols. Washington, DC: Review and Herald, 1946.

Fuller, Daniel P. *Gospel and Law: Contrast or Continuum?* Grand Rapids, MI: William B. Eerdmans Publishing Co., 1980.

Gadamer, Hans-Georg. *Philosophical Hermeneutics*. Edited and Translated by David E. Linge. Los Angeles, CA: University of California Press, 1976.

_____. *Truth and Method*. Translation revised by Joel Wensheimer and Donald G. Marshall. 2nd ed. New York: Crossroads Publishing Co., 1989.

Gaebelein, Frank E. Preface to *Dispensationalism Today*, by Charles C. Ryrie. Chicago: Moody Press, 1965.

_____. *The Story of the Scofield Reference Bible 1909-1959*. New York: Oxford University Press, 1959.

Gerstner, John H. *Wrongly Dividing the Word of Truth: A Critique of Dispensationalism*. Brentwood, TN: Wolgemuth & Hyatt Publishers, 1991.

Gileadi, Avraham, ed. *Israel's Apostasy and Restoration: Essays in Honor of Roland K. Harrison*. Grand Rapids, MI: Baker Book House, 1988.

Goltz, H. de. *Genève Religieuse au Dix-Neuvième Siècle*. Genève: Henri Georg, 1862.

Grant, Frederick W. *The Mysteries of the Kingdom of Heaven*. New York: Loizeaux Brothers, n.d.

278

_____. *The Numerical Bible*. 7 vols. New York: Loizeaux Brothers, 1891-1904.

_____. *The Numerical Structure of Scripture*. New York: Loizeaux Brothers, 1899.

Guers, Émile. *Le Camp et le Tabernacle du Désert, ou, Le Christ dans le Cuite Lévitique*. Genève: Chez MMes Beroud et Susan Guers, 1849.

_____. *Les Droits de la Papauté et le Devoir Actuel de la France*. Lyon: P.-N. Josserand, 1871.

_____. *Histoire Abrégée de l'Église de Jésus-Christ, Principalement Pendant Les Siècles du Moyen Age, Rattachee Aux Grands Traits de la Prophétie*. Genève: Madame Susan Guers, 1833.

_____. *L'Irvingisme et le Mormonisme Juges Par la Parole de Dieu*. Genève: E. Beroud, 1853.

_____. *Irvingism and Mormonisme Tested by the Scriptures*. London: James Nisbet and Co., 1854.

_____. *Israël aux Derniers Jours de L'Économie Actuelle ou Essai Sur La Restauration Prochaine de ce Peuple, Suivi D'Un Fragment sur le Millénarisme*. Genève: Émile Beroud, 1856.

_____. *Jonas Fils d'Amittai, ou, Méditations, Sur la Mission de ce Prophète*. Paris: Delay, 1846.

_____. *Notice Historique sur l'Église Évangélique Libre de Genève*. Genève: n.p., 1875.

_____. *Le Premier Réveil et la Première Église Indépendante à Genève*. Genève: Librairie Beroud and Kaufmann, 1871.

_____. *Les Prisonniers Français en Allemagne*. Lyon: J. Rossier, 1871.

_____. *Vie de Henri Pyt, Ministre de la Parole de Dieu*. Toulouse: Delhorbe, 1850.

Harris, R. Laird. "Prophecy, Illustration, and Typology." In *Interpretation and History*, ed. R. Laird Harris, Swee-Hwa Quek, and J. Robert Vannoy, 57-66. Singapore: Christian Life Publishers, 1986.

Hodge, Charles. *Systematic Theology*. 3 vols. New York: Charles Scribner's Sons, 1891.

The International Jew: The World's Foremost Problem. 4 vols. Dearborn, MI: Dearborn Independent, 1920-22.

Ironside, H. A. *Expository Notes on the Gospel of Matthew*. New York: Loizeaux Brothers, 1948.

_____. *A Historical Sketch of the Brethren Movement*. Grand Rapids, MI: Zondervan Publishing House, 1942; reprint, Neptune, NJ: Loizeaux Brothers, 1985.

_____. *Lectures on the Epistle to the Colossians*. Neptune, NJ: Loizeaux Brothers, 1929.

Jennings, Frederick C. *Studies in Isaiah*. New York: Loizeaux Brothers, Bible Truth Depot, 1930[?].

The Jew in History and Prophecy: Addresses Delivered at a Conference on Behalf of Israel. Foreward by Robert M. Russell. Chicago: Chicago Hebrew Mission, 1918.

Johnson, Elliott E. *Expository Hermeneutics: An Introduction*. Grand Rapids, MI: Zondervan Publishing House, 1990.

_____. "Hermeneutics and Dispensationalism." In *Walvoord: A Tribute*, ed. Donald K. Campbell, 240-54. Chicago: Moody Press, 1982.

Kelly, William. *Lectures on the Gospel of Matthew*. New York: Loizeaux Brothers, n.d.

Kelsy, David H. *The Uses of Scripture in Recent Theology*. Philadelphia: Fortress Press, 1975.

Ladd, George Eldon. "Historic Premillennialism." In *The Meaning of the Millennium: Four Views*, ed. Robert G. Clouse, 17-40. Downers Grove, IL: InterVarsity Press, 1977.

Lang, G. H. *The Local Assembly: Some Essential Differences Between Open and Exclusive Brethren Considered Scripturally and Historically*. Miami Springs, FL: Conley & Schoettle Publishing Co., 1985.

Lightner, Robert P. *Evangelical Theology: A Survey and Review*. Grand Rapids, MI: Baker Book House, 1986.

Malachy, Yona. *American Fundamentalism and Israel: The Relation of Fundamentalist Churches To Zionism and the State of Israel*. Jerusalem: The Hebrew University of Jerusalem, 1978.

Marsden, George M. *Fundamentalism and American Culture: The Shaping of Twentieth-Century Evangelicalism, 1870-1925*. New York: Oxford University Press, 1980.

Martin, John A. "Dispensational Approaches to the Sermon on the Mount." In *Essays in Honor of J. Dwight Pentecost*, ed. Stanley D. Toussaint and Charles H. Dyer, 35-48. Chicago: Moody Press, 1986.

Master, John and Wesley R. Willis, eds. *Issues in Dispensationalism*. Chicago: Moody Press, 1994.

Mauro, Philip. *The Hope of Israel: What Is It?* Boston, MA: Hamilton Books, 1929; reprint ed., Swengel, PA: Reiner Publications, n.d.

Midrash Rabbah. Edited by Harry Freedman and Maurice Simon. New York: Soncino Press, 1959.

Miller, Perry. *The Life of the Mind in America: From the Revolution to the Civil War*. New York: Harcourt, Brance, & World, 1965.

Noble, Paul R. *The Canonical Approach: A Critical Reconstruction of the Hermeneutics of Brevard S. Childs*. New York: E. J. Brill, 1995.

Noel, Napoleon. *The History of the Brethren*. 2 vols. Edited by William F. Knapp. Denver, CO: William F. Knapp, 1936.

Pentecost, J. Dwight. *Things to Come*. Grand Rapids, MI: Zondervan Publishing House, 1958.

Pettingill, William L. *The Gospel of the Kingdom: Simple Studies in Matthew*. Findlay, OH: Dunham Publishing Co., n.d.

Poythress, Vern S. *Understanding Dispensationalists*. Grand Rapids, MI: Zondervan Publishing House, 1987.

The Protocols and World Revolution. Boston: Small, Maynard, & Co., 1920.

Rabinowitz, Joseph. *Jesus of Nazareth, the King of the Jews*. Abridged and revised by Arno C. Gaebelein. New York: Hope of Israel, n.d.

Radmacher, Earl. "The Current Status of Dispensationalism and Its Eschatology." In *Perspectives on Evangelical Theology*, ed. Stanley N. Gundry and Kenneth S. Kantzer, 163-76. Grand Rapids, MI: Baker Book House, 1979.

Rausch, David A. *Arno C. Gaebelein 1861-1945: Irenic Fundamentalist and Scholar*. New York: Edwin Mellen Press, 1983.

_____. *Building Bridges*. Chicago: Moody Press, 1988.

_____. *Messianic Judaism: Its History, Theology, and Polity*. New York: Edwin Mellen Press, 1982.

_____. *Zionism Within Early American Fundamentalism 1878-1918*. New York: Edwin Mellen Press, 1979.

Richards, Jeffrey J. *The Promise of Dawn: The Eschatology of Lewis Sperry Chafer*. Lanham, MD: University Press of America, 1991.

Roy, Ralph Lord. *The Apostles of Discord*. Boston: Beacon Press, 1953.

Russell, C. Allyn. *Voices of American Fundamentalism: Seven Biographical Studies*. Philadelphia: Westminster Press, 1976.

Russell, D. S. *The Method and Message of Jewish Apocalyptic*. The Old Testament Library, edited by Peter Ackroyd, James Barr, Bernhard Anderson, and James Mays. Philadelphia: Westminster Press, 1964.

Ryrie, Charles C. *The Basis of the Premillennial Faith*. Neptune, NJ: Loizeaux Brothers, 1953.

_____. *Dispensationalism*. Chicago: Moody Press, 1995.

_____. *Dispensationalism Today*. Chicago: Moody Press, 1965.

Sandeen, Ernest R. *The Origins of Fundamentalism: Toward a Historical Interpretation*. Philadelphia: Fortress Press, 1968.

_____. *The Roots of Fundamentalism: British and American Millenarianism 1800-1930*. Chicago: University of Chicago Press, 1970.

Sanders, Carl E., III. *Premillennial Faith of James Brookes: Reexamining the Roots of American Fundamentalism*. Lanham, MD: University Press of America, 2001.

Saucy, Robert L. *The Case for Progressive Dispensationalism: The Interface Between Dispensational and Non-Dispensational Theology*. Grand Rapids, MI: Zondervan Publishing House, 1993.

Scofield, C. I. *Rightly Dividing the Word of Truth*. Findlay, OH: Fundamental Truth Publishers, n.d.

The Scofield Reference Bible. Edited by C. I. Scofield. New York: Oxford University Press, 1909.

Simon, Merrill Simon. *Jerry Falwell and the Jews.* Middle Village, NY: Jonathan David Publishers, 1984.

Smith, George Adam. *Modern Criticism and the Preaching of the Old Testament.* New York: George H. Doran Co., 1901.

Smith, Wilbur M. *Arno C. Gaebelein: A Memoir.* New York: Our Hope Press, 1946.

Stroeter, Ernst F. "Christ's Second Coming Premillennial." In *The Prophecy Conference Movement,* ed. Donald W. Dayton, 14-20. New York: Garland Publishing Co., 1988.

Sweet, Leonard I. "The Evangelical Tradition in America." In *The Evangelical Tradition.* ed. Leonard I. Sweet, 1-86. Macon, GA: Mercer University Press, 1984.

Thomas, W. H. Griffith. *Outline Studies in the Gospel of Matthew.* Grand Rapids, MI: William B. Eerdmans Publishing Co., 1961.

Toussaint, *Behold the King: A Study of Matthew.* Portland, OR: Multnomah Press, 1980.

Trumbull, Charles G. *The Life Story of C. I. Scofield.* New York: Oxford University Press, 1920.

_____. *Prophecy's Light on Today.* Introduction by Howard A. Kelly. New York: Fleming H. Revell Co., 1937.

Wallis, Wilber B. "Reflections on the History of Premillennial Thought." In *Interpretation and History,* ed. by R. Laird Harris, Swee-Hwa Quek, and J. Robert Vannoy, 225-51. Singapore: Christian Life Publishers, 1986.

Weber, Timothy. *Living in the Shadow of the Second Coming: American Premillennialism 1875-1925.* New York: Oxford University Press, 1979.

Who Was Who In America. 2 vols. Chicago: A. N. Marquis Co., 1950.

Wilson, Dwight. *Armageddon Now! The Premillennial Response to Russia and Israel Since 1917.* Grand Rapids, MI: Baker Book House, 1977.

We Hold These Truths: Statements on Anti-Semitism by 54 Leading American Writers, Statesmen, Educators, Clergymen and Trade-Unionists. New York: League of American Writers, 1939.

Zuck, Roy. *Basic Bible Interpretation.* Wheaton, IL: Victor Books, 1991.

Periodical Articles

Allis, Oswald T. "Modern Dispensationalism and the Doctrine of the Unity of the Scriptures." *The Evangelical Quarterly* 8 (15 January 1936): 23-35.

Alrich, G. L. "The Imminency of the Coming of our Lord Jesus." *Our Hope* 9 (September 1902): 167-74.

Baker, B. W. "Is There Modernism in the Scofield Bible? A Reply to L. S. Chafer." *Presbyterian of the South* 111 (18 March 1936): 1-4.

Barker, Kenneth L. "False Dichotomies Between the Testaments." *Journal of the Evangelical Theological Society* 25 (March 1982): 3-16.

BeVier, William. "C. I. Scofield: Dedicated and Determined." *Fundamentalist Journal* 2 (October 1983): 37-38.

Blaising, Craig A. "Development of Dispensationalism by Contemporary Dispensationalists." *Bibliotheca Sacra* 145 (July-September 1988): 254-80.

_____. Review of "Revelation and the Hermeneutics of Dispensationalism," by William H. Shephard. In *Bibliotheca Sacra* 147 (July-September 1990): 365-66.

Blocher, Henri. "The 'Analogy of Faith' in the Study of Scripture." *Scottish Bulletin of Evangelical Theology* 5 (Spring 1987): 17-38.

Bock, Darrell. "Evangelicals and the Use of the Old Testament in the New." *Bibliotheca Sacra* 142 (July-September 1985): 209-23.

_____. "Evangelicals and the Use of the Old Testament in the New." *Bibliotheca Sacra* 142 (October-December 1985): 306-19.

Brookes, James H. "Israel in the Gospels." *Our Hope* 50 (December 1943): 395-407.

_____. "Work Among the Jews." *The Truth* 20 (January 1984): 14-16.

Cameron, Robert. "Confusion on the Lord's Coming." *Watchword and Truth.* 23 (March 1901): 70-71.

_____. Review of *The Coming* One, by Albert B. Simpson. In *Watchword and Truth* 34 (September 1912): 271.

Campbell, Charles. "The Interval Between the Lord's Coming For Us, and His Coming With Us." *Our Hope* 9 (August 1902): 81-92.

284

Campbell, Henry. "The Translation of the Saints." *Our Hope* 36 (January 1930): 405-12.

_____. "The Translation of the Saints." *Our Hope* 36 (November 1929): 281-89.

_____. "The Translation of the Saints." *Our Hope* 36 (October 1929): 218-25.

_____. "The Translation of the Saints." *Our Hope* 36 (September 1929): 153-60.

"Christian Judaism." *Our Hope* 1 (July 1894): 8-12.

Darby, John Nelson. "What Saints Will Be in the Tribulation?" *Our Hope* 8 (May 1902): 597-605.

Dockery, David S. Review of *Arno C. Gaebelein, 1861-1945: Irenic Fundamentalist and Scholar*, by David A. Rausch. In *Grace Theological Journal* 7 (Spring 1986): 154-55.

Erdman, William J. "The Oral Teachings of St. Paul at Thessalonica." *Our Hope* 5 (July 1898): 17-19.

Fatio, Olivier. "Commémoration: Genève et le Refuge." *Bulletin de la Société de l'Histoire du Protestantisme Français* 133 (January-March 1987): 115-19.

_____. "Quelle Réformation? Les Commémorations Genevoises de la Réformation à Travers Les Siècles." *Revue de Théologie et de Philosophie* 118 (1986): 111-30.

Griswood, G. A. "The True Church: Its Translation Before the End." *Our Hope* 38 (August 1931): 114-21.

_____. "The True Church: Its Translation Before the End." *Our Hope* 38 (September 1931): 181-86.

Grogan, Geoffrey. "The Relationship Between Prophecy and Typology." *The Scottish Bulletin of Evangelical Theology* 4 (Spring 1986): 5-16.

Gundry, Stanley N. "Hermeneutics or *Zeitgeist* as the Determining Factor in the History of Eschatologies?" *The Journal of the Evangelical Theological Society* 20 (March 1977): 45-55.

Haldeman, I. M. "The Two Distinct Stages of the Coming of the Lord." *Our Hope* 9 (January 1903): 418-19.

Hall, Joseph H. "James Hall Brookes—New School, Old School, or No School." *Presbyterian: Covenant Seminary Review* 14 (Spring 1988): 35-54.

Hannah, John D. "A Review of *The Incredible Scofield and His Book.*" *Bibliotheca Sacra* 147 (July-September 1990): 351-64.

Hoch, Carl B., Jr., "The Significance of the *Syn*-Compounds for Jew-Gentile Relationships in the Body of Christ." *The Journal of the Evangelical Theological Society* 25 (June 1982): 175-83.

Jennings, Frederick C. "The Epistle to the Romans: Chapter i. to Chapter iii:20." *Our Hope* 8 (September 1901): 144-54.

Jennings, Frederick C. "Isaiah Chapter xix—(Continued)." *Our Hope* 27 (April 1921): 600-5.

Kaiser, Walter C. "Hermeneutics and the Theological Task." *Trinity Journal* 12 (Spring 1991): 3-14.

Kent, Homer A., Jr. "The New Covenant and the Church." *Grace Theological Journal* 6 (Fall 1985): 289-98.

"A Lesson for Modern Methodists." *Our Hope* 8 (August 1901): 72.

MacIntosh, C. H. "Diversity and Unity." *Our Hope* 8 (August 1901): 6871.

_____. "Our Standard and Our Hope." *Our Hope* 8 (July 1901): 23-26.

Marsden, George M. "Defining Fundamentalism." *Christian Scholar's Review* 1 (Winter 1971): 141-51.

_____. Review of *Arno C. Gaebelein, 1861-1945: Irenic Fundamentalist and Scholar*, by David A. Rausch. In *Church History* 54 (September 1985): 446.

Michaelson, Wes. "Evangelical Zionism." *Sojourners* 6 (March 1977): 3-5.

Mouly, Ruth and Robertson, Roland. "Zionism in American Premillenarian Fundamentalism." *American Journal of Theology and Philosophy* 4 (September 1983): 97-109.

"Must the Church Pass Through the Tribulation." *Our Hope* 8 (March 1902): 486-87.

Newton, J. W. "The Resurrection of the Just." *Our Hope* 9 (July 1902): 38-41.

"Principles of the Hope of Israel Movement." *Our Hope* 3 (November-December 1896): 149-50.

Rausch, David A. "Fundamentalism and the Jew: An Interpretive Essay." *Journal of the Evangelical Theological Society* 23 (June 1980): 105-12.

_____. "Our Hope: An American Fundamentalist Journal and the Holocaust, 1937-1945." *Fides et Historia* 12 (Spring 1980): 89-103.

_____. "A Rejoinder to Timothy Weber's Reply." *Journal of the Evangelical Theological Journal* 24 (March 1981): 73-77.

Roy, Ralph Lord. "Religion and Race." *Christian Century* 70 (April 22, 1953): 474-76.

Sailhamer, John H. "The Canonical Approach to the OT: Its Effect on Understanding Prophecy." *Journal of the Evangelical Theological Society* 30 (September 1987): 307-15.

Sandeen, Ernest F. "Towards a Historical Interpretation of the Origins of Fundamentalism." *Church History* 36 (March 1967): 66-83.

Saphir, Adolf. "Christ and the Scriptures." *Our Hope* 8 (July 1901): 27-34.

Saucy, Robert. "The Crucial Issue Between Dispensational and Nondispensational Systems." *Criswell Theological Review* 1 (Fall 1986): 149-65.

_____. "Dispensationalism and the Salvation of the Kingdom." *TSF Bulletin* 7 (May-June 1984): 6-7.

Scofield, C. I. "The Israel of God." *Our Hope* 8 (June 1902): 629-39.

_____. "Where Faith Sees Christ: Coming Again." *Our Hope* 8 (September 1901): 126-35.

_____. "Where Faith Sees Christ: In Glory." *Our Hope* 8 (September 1901): 107-15.

_____. "Where Faith Sees Christ: Indwelling the Believer." *Our Hope* 8 (September 1901): 115-25.

_____. "Where Faith Sees Christ: On the Cross." *Our Hope* 8 (September 1901): 97-107.

Scott, Walter. "The Inspiration and Divine Authority of the Holy Scriptures." *Our Hope* 8 (September 1906): 174-79.

Shepherd, William H., Jr. "Revelation and the Hermeneutics of Dispensationalism." *Anglican Theological Review* 71 (Summer 1989): 281-99.

Stallard, Mike. "Literal Interpretation, Theological Method, and the Essence of Dispensationalism." *The Journal of Ministry and Theology* 1 (Spring 1997): 5-36.

Stroeter, Ernst F. "Does the Jew, in Christ, Cease to be a Jew?" *Our Hope* 2 (January 1896): 148-54.

Stunt, Timothy. "Geneva and British Evangelicals in the Early Nineteenth Century." *Journal of Ecclesiastical History* 32 (January 1981): 35-46.

Thomas, Robert L. "A Hermeneutical Ambiguity of Eschatology: The Analogy of Faith." *Journal of the Evangelical Theological Society* 23 (March 1980): 45-53.

Turner, David L. "The Continuity of Scripture and Eschatology: Key Hermeneutical Issues." *Grace Theological Journal* 6 (Fall 1985): 275-87.

Van Gemeren, Willen. "Israel as the Hermeneutical Crux in the Interpretation of Prophecy." *Westminster Theological Journal* 45 (Spring 1983): 132-44.

Weber, Timothy P. "A Reply to David Rausch's 'Fundamentalism and the Jew.'" *Journal of the Evangelical Theological Society* 24 (March 1981): 67-71.

_____. "A Surrejoinder to David Rausch's Rejoinder." *Journal of the Evangelical Theological Society* 24 (March 1981): 79-82.

Wilson, Marvin R. "Zionism as Theology: An Evangelical Approach." *Journal of the Evangelical Theological Society* 22 (March 1979): 27-44.

Wuthnow, Robert. "Fundamentalism in the World." *The Christian Century* 109 (April 29, 1992): 456-58.

Unpublished Materials

Bailey, Mark. "Dispensational Definitions of Kingdom." Paper presented at the dispensational theology pre-meeting at the annual meeting of the Evangelical Theological Society, November 1988.

BeVier, William. "A Biographical Sketch of C. I. Scofield." M.A. thesis, Southern Methodist University, 1960.

Blaising, Craig A. "The Kingdom of God in Progressive Dispensationalism." Paper presented at the dispensational theology pre-meeting at the annual meeting of the Evangelical Theological Society, November 1991.

288

Bock, Darrell. "The Kingdom, Covenants, and Promise in Biblical Theology: A Progressive Dispensational Overview." Paper presented at the dispensational theology pre-meeting at the annual meeting of the Evangelical Theological Society, November 1991.

_____. "The Reign of the Lord Christ." Paper presented at the dispensational theology pre-meeting at the annual meeting of the Evangelical Theological Society, November 1987.

Chafer, Lewis Sperry. Letters. Dallas Theological Seminary, Dallas, Texas.

Elmore, Floyd S. "A Critical Examination of the Doctrine of the Two Peoples of God in John Nelson Darby." Th.D. diss., Dallas Theological Seminary, 1990.

Hannah, John D. "The Social and Intellectual History of the Origins of the Evangelical Theological College." Ph.D. diss., University of Texas at Dallas, 1988.

Herman, Douglas E. "Flooding the Kingdom: The Intellectual Development of Fundamentalism, 1930-1941." Ph.D. diss., Ohio University, 1980.

Hull, Gretchen. Personal telephone interview by author. 1 October 1990.

_____. Personal telephone interview by author. 6 April 1992.

Johnson, Dale Walden. "Millennial Thinking and its Implications for Social Reform: Premillennialism in Urban America 1865-1925.11 M.A. thesis, Florida Atlantic University, 1988.

Minutes of the Dispensational Theology Pre-Meeting of the Annual Meeting of the Evangelical Theological Society, Atlanta, GA, 20 November 1986.

Rausch, David A. Personal telephone interview by author. October 1990.

Thorsen, Donald A. D. "Theological Method in John Wesley." Ph.D. diss., Drew University, 1988.

Unger, Walter. "'Earnestly Contending for the Faith': The Role of the Niagara Bible Conference in the Emergence of American Fundamentalism, 1875-1900." Ph.D. diss., Simon Fraser University, 1981.

Walvoord, John F. Personal interview by author. Dallas Theological Seminary, Dallas, Texas, 17 July 1990.

162, 166, 168, 170, 182-184, 186-187,
200, 223, 226-228, 235, 239, 241-242,
244
German, 18, 27, 29, 58, 63, 87, 90, 103
German Methodism, 13, 15, 87
Germany, 11, 12, 44, 55, 58, 59, 80, 103
Gerstner, John H., 196, 200, 210
Goldstien, Samuel, 17
Goltz, H. de, 63, 66
Gonthier, J. G., 64
Gordon, Adoniram J., 27, 78, 85
grammatical-historical, 105-106, 108, 110,
113, 118, 126, 132-133, 138, 192, 239,
248
Grant, Frederick W., 34, 115, 179, 183, 186,
188-189, 252, 261
Gray, James M., 26, 85, 99
Great Tribulation, 38, 55, 69, 74, 126, 150,
165, 177-178, 181-182, 189, 213, 236,
238-239, 242
Grimm, C. F., 16
Grimm, Emma, 16, 17
Guers, Émile, 6-7, 15, 18, 21-23, 35, 57, 61-
73, 83, 87, 89, 101, 123, 133, 247-248,
254, 261, 263

H

Haldane, Robert, 63
Haman, 58, 60
Harris, Elmore, 26
Hebrew, 15, 17, 18, 19, 20, 31, 53, 75-76
Hebrew Christian Mission, 18, 23
hermeneutics, 4, 7, 104-105, 139, 142, 215,
219, 232, 234, 256-258, 260, 263
Herzl, Theodor, 75-76, 78
Hezekiah, 159
Hitler, 12, 52, 54, 58, 59, 62, 80
Hoboken, New Jersey, 17, 23
Holocaust, 6, 12, 43, 54, 57, 73, 84
Holy Spirit, 19, 44, 77, 110, 123, 129-130,
136, 140, 146, 158, 165, 170, 173-174,
178, 180, 186-187, 196, 199, 201, 203,
205, 208, 212, 243
Hope of Israel Movement, 24, 33, 86, 88,
244

I

Illuminati, 47, 48
imminency, 36, 38, 41-42, 237, 238
India, 17, 242
Inglis, James, 84

International Prophetic Conference, 34, 36,
87
Ireland, 65
Ironside, H. A., 115, 127, 251, 260
Irving, Edward, 40, 63
Irvingism, 63, 65
Isaac, 158-159, 221-222
Islam, 75
Israel, 1, 8-9, 11-12, 19-23, 25, 27, 29, 33,
35, 38, 41-42, 49-52, 60, 65-71, 74, 77-
79, 81-84, 86-88, 93, 101-103, 107, 109-
115, 117-118, 120-121, 124-127, 129,
131-135, 137-138, 140, 143, 147-148,
150-152, 154, 156, 158, 160, 163-169,
171, 175, 178-187, 189-194, 200, 205-
206, 212- 214, 218, 220- 222, 224, 226-
233, 235-236, 239-246, 248-249, 254,
256-258, 261-263

J

Jacob, 56, 107, 122, 158, 221-222, 225, 233,
236, 239, 242
Jared, 142
Java, 17
Jehoshaphat, 107-108, 140-141
Jehovah, 75, 81, 136, 140, 183-184, 224
Jehu, 107-108, 140-142,
Jesse, 158
Jesus Christ, 9, 11, 16-17, 19, 22, 30-33, 36,
38, 40, 55-56, 60, 65, 67, 69-70, 79, 82,
93-96, 99-100, 112, 114, 116, 121-123,
127-133, 135-137, 140-141, 143, 146,
150, 155, 158-159, 164, 166, 172-177,
180-181, 182, 184-186, 188-190, 196-
201, 205-208, 211-219, 223, 225-242,
244-246, 249, 253, 255, 259
Jews, 7, 13, 15, 17-19, 21, 23-24, 27-28, 30-
33, 44-56, 59, 68, 70-76, 78-79, 82-88,
91, 96, 102, 107, 109110, 114-115, 123,
125, 131-132, 134, 136, 141, 158, 161-
163, 166-169, 180, 182, 186-188, 200,
223, 226, 236, 239, 248, 253, 262-263
Jezebel, 140-141
John the Baptist, 183, 186, 190, 230
Johnson, Elliott, 106, 113, 138, 174, 187
Joseph, 159
Jude, 160

K

Kaganovich, 55
Kattowitz, 81
Kelly, William, 34, 260-261

W

Z

Scripture Index

298